Studies in American Popular History and Culture

Edited by
Jerome Nadelhaft

A Routledge Series

STUIES IN AMERICAN POPULAR HISTORY AND CULTURE

EARLY AMERICAN WOMEN DRAMATISTS: 1775–1860
Zoe Detsi-Diamanti

THE LYRICS OF CIVILITY
Kenneth G. Bielen

WRITING THE PUBLIC IN CYBERSPACE
Redefining Inclusion on the Net
Ann Travers

HOLLYWOOD'S FRONTIER CAPTIVES
Cultural Anxiety and the Captivity Plot in American Film
Barbara A. Mortimer

PUBLIC LIVES, PRIVATE VIRTUES
Images of American Revolutionary War Heroes, 1782–1832
Christopher Harris

TALES OF LIBERATION, STRATEGIES OF CONTAINMENT
Divorce and the Representation of Womanhood in American Fiction, 1880–1920
Debra Ann MacComb

READING COMICS
Language, Culture, and the Concept of the Superhero in Comic Books
Mila Bongco

THE CLUBWOMEN'S DAUGHTERS
Collectivist Impulses in Progressive-Era Girls' Fiction
Gwen Athene Tarbox

THE FACTORY GIRLS AND THE SEAMSTRESS
Imagining Gender and Class in Nineteenth Century American Fiction
Amal Amireh

WRITING JAZZ
Race, Nationalism, and Modern Culture in the 1920s
Nicholas M. Evans

AUTOMOBILITY
Social Changes in the American South, 1909–1939
Corey T. Lesseig

ACTORS AND ACTIVISTS
Politics, Performance, and Exchange among Social Worlds
David A. Schlossman

STUDIES IN THE LAND
The Northeast Corner
David C. Smith

FIRST DO NO HARM
Empathy and the Writing of Medical Journal Articles
Mary E. Knatterud

PIETY AND POWER
Gender and Religious Culture in the American Colonies, 1630–1700
Leslie Lindenauer

RACE-ING MASCULINITY
Identity in Contemporary U. S. Men's Writing
John Christopher Cunningham

CRIME AND THE NATION
Prison Reform and Popular Fiction in Philadelphia, 1786–1800
Peter Okun

FOOD IN FILM
A Culinary Performance of Communication
Jane Ferry

DECONSTRUCTING POST-WWII NEW YORK CITY
The Literature, Art, Jazz, and Architecture of an Emerging Global Capital
Robert Bennett

HOLLYWOOD AND THE RISE OF PHYSICAL CULTURE
Heather Addison

Homelessness in American Literature
Romanticism, Realism, and Testimony

John Allen

Routledge
Taylor & Francis Group
New York London

Published in 2004 by
Routledge
711 Third Avenue, New York, NY 10017, USA

Published in Great Britain by
Routledge
2 Park Square, Milton Park, Abingdon, Oxfordshire OX14 4RN

First issued in paperback 2018

Routledge is an imprint of the Taylor and Francis Group, an informa business

Library of Congress Cataloging-in-Publication Data

Allen, John.
Homelessness in American literature : romanticism, realism, and testimony / by John Allen.
p. cm.
Includes biblographical references and index.
ISBN 0-415-94589-5
1. American literature—20th century—History and criticism. 2. Homelessness in literature. 3. American literature—19th century—History and criticism. 4. Homeless persons in literature. 5. Romanticism—United States. 6. Realism in literature.. I. Title. II. Series: American popular history and culture (Routledge (Firm))
PS228.H65A45 2003
813.009'355—dc21 2003007258

ISBN 13 :978-1-138-86890-8 (pbk)
ISBN 13: 978-0-415-94589-9 (hbk)

Contents

Acknowledgments

THIS BOOK WOULD NOT HAVE BEEN POSSIBLE WITHOUT THE HELP OF MANY wonderful people. First and foremost, Andy Martin helped me along throughout the entire writing process. Thanks, Andy. Jim Sappenfield, Jim Kuist, Cam Tatham, and Peter Paik provided very productive comments on the first complete draft; Elana Crane, Paul Kosidowski, and Barbara Lindquist offered important feedback on drafts of early chapters. Allen Carey-Webb inspired me to write about the topic of homelessness in American literature. Beverly Allen nurtured (among other things) a deep appreciation for books, reading, libraries and research. Paul Allen and Karina O'Malley taught me about compassion for others. Mark Allen showed me how much fun literary studies could be. Rachel Baum loaned me books about testimony which became the basis of Chapter Five and the Conclusion. I'd like to thank all of these people as well as my friends and colleagues at the University of Wisconsin-Milwaukee and the University of Wisconsin-Waukesha who have helped and encouraged me as I wrote this. (Tom Ullmer asked me if I would put his name in one of my books, but I told him I wouldn't.)

Special thanks to Kimberly Guinta, Farideh Koohi-Kamali, Jerry Nadelhaft, and everyone at Routledge for their interest in and support of this project.

Finally and most importantly, thank you Johanna. There is no way I could have completed this or any of my significant undertakings without you (nor would I have wanted to). You provided comfort, support, patience, love. This book is dedicated to you.

Homelessness in American Literature

Introduction

Representations of Homelessness in American Literature

In his book *The Literary Rebel*, Kingsley Widmer captures the range, history, and motivation of literature dealing with homelessness:[1]

> [W]ith wandering blind Homers, peripatetic Cynics, homeless rhapsodists, drifting jongleurs, mendicant goliards, rhyming beggars, fluent picaros, itinerant preachers imitating Christ, literary students on a *wanderjahr*, restless romantic poets, footloose folk singers, exiled revolutionary memorialists, artistic mariners, professional literary hobos and aspiring hitchhiker novelists–among others!–large parts of our significant literature have found the muse on the road, if not down-and-out in the streets. (77)

Given the range and apparent universality of homelessness in literature, it is surprising to note how little critical commentary exists which examines homelessness *per se*.[2] Widmer notes the two dominant paths that authors and critics have followed in their treatments of this theme. On the one hand, the romantic hero who goes "on the road" for adventure and freedom has been the subject of numerous novels, essays, and commentaries throughout European and American literary history.[3] In the context of realism and naturalism, conversely, homelessness has been condemned as a result of social and economic failures, and those who are "down and out" are seen as victims. From Stephen Crane's *Maggie: A Girl of the Streets* to George Orwell's *Down and Out in Paris and London*, for example, homelessness is used to symbolize the abjection and degradation of their characters. While the first category elevates the homeless wanderer as a rebel, an explorer, or an adventurer, the second attempts to educate readers by observing and describing life "on the street"–spatial metaphors such as "the other half," the "submerged tenth," and the "lower class" indicate the position of the author (and reader) as "above" or as distant and separate from the observed. Generally speaking, then, homelessness in literature has been either romanticized or objectified.[4] I believe this division needs to be questioned: not in order to ascertain which is more "true," "real," or "accurate," but to see how this division influenced and bound together authors, critics, and readers who participated in the cultural and ideological discourse of homelessness in America.

Homelessness in American Literature: Romanticism, Realism, and Testimony looks at literature as a site of ideological conflict over the topic of homelessness and, in turn, intends to examine such related issues as the home, work, charity, and American identity. I contend that homelessness as a theme or trope in American literature should be examined more closely precisely because it offers a unique perspective on these issues. Moreover, while the division between romantic and realist approaches to homelessness is relevant, it also limits analysis. It has excluded texts and authors, and it elides the ambiguity and contradictions imbedded in texts about homelessness. One purpose of this study, therefore, is to describe the range of responses in literature and the often conflicted attitudes about homelessness therein.

The second purpose is more speculative, but equally important: to examine the "cultural work" of these texts. Jane Tompkins explains this goal in her book *Sensational Designs: The Cultural Work of American Fiction 1790–1860*:

> It is the notion of literary texts as doing work, expressing and shaping the social context that produced them, that I wish to substitute finally for the critical perspective that sees them as attempts to achieve a timeless, universal ideal of truth and formal coherence. (200)

Likewise, I hope to assess how representations of homelessness in American literature have "express[ed] and shap[ed] the social context that produced them."

As Widmer points out, homelessness has been a specific source of literature since the Middle Ages. Indeed, Adam and Eve could be considered homeless if one wanted to go back a bit further. In *The Satanic Verses*, Salman Rushdie reminds us of Satan's "homelessness" after being expelled from heaven, referring to the devil as a "vagabond" in an introductory quotation taken from Daniel Defoe. Martin Luther's Preface to *The Book of Vagabonds and Beggars*, written in 1528, describes the history and kinds of beggars in England and Germany, as well as advice for readers on how to properly respond to them. These examples and many others indicate a profound if not universal interest in the topic.

Perhaps homelessness is compelling because of its liminal nature. It interests us because it is a condition which is not conventional, but not so foreign as to be incomprehensible. Reading about it can be a form of vicarious adventure or may provide a glimpse of abject poverty. In both its romanticized and its objectified manifestations, homelessness represents the condition of the Other. A desire to define and circumscribe the Other, as many critics have noted, prompts members of the dominant culture to read and write texts which "speak for" marginalized groups such as homeless people. These treatments have certainly changed and evolved since the Middle Ages, but homelessness has remained a compelling and conflicted discursive construct throughout Western history.

In the United States, homelessness has played an important role in defining national character and establishing American identity. Early colonists were "homeless" when they arrived in America, and successive waves of immigrants and adventurers sought to establish homes in cities and in unsettled rural areas of the west. In his famous essay "The Significance of the Frontier in American History," Frederick Jackson Turner argued that this sense of expansionism helped define American values and identity until the "closing" of the frontier in the 1890s. In urban areas, immigrants often struggled to find decent employment and housing. Economic conditions and responses to the poor (foreign and native born)–including literary responses–contribute to classifications of the homeless in each of four relatively distinct periods of American history. I will briefly survey these periods and the attendant literary texts in order to contextualize the critical responses and my own argument later in this chapter.

First, the antebellum era of the United States saw instances of "wandering" poor, but almshouses, police lodging houses, and local government support to families kept homelessness and poverty relatively invisible. Although the presence of the poor in city streets prior to the Civil War led to public debates about what to do with them, their presence was much more formidable after the war and during the period of rapid industrialization. As Kim Hopper and Jim Baumohl state, "Colonial American poor relief was a jumble [. . .] . But however patchwork the apparatus of relief, few went begging" (6).

Literature and sociology dealt with homelessness indirectly. The "vagabond" archetype, popularized by English writers such as George Borrow, Thomas De Quincey, Robert Louis Stevenson, and others, surfaced in a somewhat different form in the work of Thoreau and Whitman (as Arthur Rickett argues in *The Vagabond in Literature*). During the 1840s, the "mysteries of the city" genre became popular, as epitomized by Ned Buntline's *The Mysteries and Miseries of New York: A Story of Real Life* (1848) and George Lippard's *The Quaker City* (1844). The expansion of cities and the presence of the poor and homeless created suspicion and speculation over the merits of city-living which would linger well into the twentieth century. The tone of *The Quaker City* reveals how the city was often seen as mysterious and threatening during the nineteenth century:

> These were the Outcasts of the Quaker City! In the day-time, vagabond man and woman and child, lay quiet and snug, in the underground recesses of Monk-Hall; in the night they stole forth from the secret passage thro' the pawnbroker's shop in the adjoining street, and prowled over the city, to beg, to rob, or perchance to murder. (405)

Supernatural elements, dark passageways, eerie sounds and the like demonstrate how the mysteries of the city genre resembles the gothic novel and creates apprehension over the city and its inhabitants which will be seen in later works. The presence of beggars and other poor people symbolizes the failure and danger of the city already in the 1840s, although homelessness does not seem to be a specific focus at this time.

The second period of American homelessness–between the Civil War and World War II–saw a rapid increase in the number of wandering poor and tramps. This increase was a result of industrialization, immigration, urbanization, and economic depressions, as well as the displacement of soldiers and slaves after the Civil War. During this period the discursive treatments of homelessness also multiplied dramatically. Literature, sociology, journalism, and even photography complicated the notion of what it meant to be poor and without a home.

Writers associated with the "Gospel of Wealth" (such as Russell Conwell and Andrew Carnegie) teamed with "scientific" charity organizations such as the Charities Organization Society to criminalize homelessness and link it to "personal deficiencies and faults of moral character" (Hoch 21). Such an assessment could be made, according to this tradition, because everyone in America had an equal opportunity for economic advancement, provided they were diligent and hard-working. Conwell, for example, spread this message throughout America in his book *Acres of Diamonds* and in a lecture of the same title which he delivered more than five thousand times. Like St. Jean de Crevecouer years earlier, Conwell portrayed America as a land of opportunity where "acres of diamonds" waited for anyone who worked hard enough. Since anyone could get rich, sympathy and charity were unwarranted. Conwell stated, "I sympathize with the poor, but the number of poor who are to be sympathized with is very small" (qtd. in Zinn 256). Schools across the country reinforced the same message by using McGuffey readers, millions of which were published in the nineteenth century. These educational texts taught the values of hard work and wealth, and suggested that poverty was a sign of moral failure.

As I will discuss in Chapter Two, homelessness was often seen as a symbol of personal irresponsibility and immorality. The poor and homeless were accountable for their own plight because they did not take advantage of the opportunities America had to offer.

Similarly, journalism contributed to a severe backlash against homeless tramps during this period. For example, an article in the *Chicago Tribune* in 1877 advocated the eradication of tramps by poisoning food donations with strychnine. Other newspapers proposed poisoning with lead, labor camps, even whippings to deal with the "tramp menace."[5] Publications from the scientific charity organizations suggested that readers band together and refuse to give handouts to beggars and tramps. Furthermore, newspapers and magazines frequently exaggerated the violence and crimes perpetrated by tramps. As a result of these movements, anti-tramping laws passed in all but four states. Vagrancy became illegal and police lodging houses for the poor were virtually eliminated. An Ohio Supreme Court Justice remarked, "The whole system [of tramping] has become so gross an abuse as to require the strong hand of the law for its suppression" (qtd. in Monkkonen 162). This comment epitomizes the attitude of many as a result of the discursive backlash against homeless tramps at the time.

Literature, in general, did not contribute directly to this backlash, and even when the "tramp menace" was portrayed most fervently in the media, the general public remained ambivalent if not sympathetic. The reading public was certainly interested in tramps, as indicated by the publication of dozens of tramp autobiographies between the Civil War and the Depression. A sarcastic comment in a 1930 edition of *The Publishers' Weekly* attests to the prominence of the genre: "any tramp can find an outlet in print for his trampish writing" (Sumner 2736). While the impact of these autobiographies is uncertain, they served to counter the image of the lazy or violent tramp as portrayed in many magazines and newspapers. Their popularity also indicates a national interest in and awareness of the issue.

Literary precursors to the tramp can be seen in the mid-nineteenth century. Walt Whitman's "Song of the Open Road" contained elements which would be seen in later work by Vachel Lindsay, Jim Tully, Jack London, W. H. Davies, even Mark Twain and Art Linkletter, and many others.[6] In most of these texts, tramping was a carefree, often sublime experience. A sense of freedom, adventure, and opportunity underlies most of the autobiographies, as I will explain in Chapter Four. "Song of the Open Road" begins:

> Afoot and light-hearted I take to the open road,
> Healthy, free, the world before me,
> The long brown path before me leading wherever I choose.
> Henceforth I ask not good-fortune, I myself am good fortune,

> Henceforth I whimper no more, postpone no more, need nothing,
> Done with indoor complaints, libraries, querulous criticisms,
> Strong and content I travel the open road. (120–121)

Later, I hope to show how the strength, health, and sense of opportunity Whitman and most of the other tramp writers portray contradict the hunger, unemployment, and homelessness that many tramps experienced. But the positive image also contradicted the notion that all tramps were lazy or violent.

Tramp autobiographies began to appear in the 1870s and are still being published today. Indiana University Press, for example, published *Done and Been: Steel Rail Chronicles of American Hobos* by Gypsy Moon, "A National Queen of the Hobos," in 1996. Most were published between 1890 and 1940, however, and shared similar traits: an intellectual or literary sensibility; an optimistic tone; a sense of freedom and adventure; a lack of criticism of the dominant culture; and, frequently, a return to domestic life or a renunciation of the tramping lifestyle. Although London and others wrote about the values of socialism, these writers did not seriously challenge the American economic and political system. In fact, the tramp autobiographies reinforce the idea that homelessness is an individual choice, rather than an economic necessity. The effect of locating responsibility in the individual rather than in society or the economic system will be traced throughout this study.

The third historical period emerges as a result of the social reforms associated with the New Deal and the economic effects of World War II–described by Paul Taylor as "'the greatest public works project ever conceived'" (qtd. in Baum 105). Between 1940 and 1980, homelessness decreased significantly because of the improved "safety net" and the low unemployment rate after the War. The decreased visibility of homelessness also coincides with the (re)affirmation of the home and the family as essential American values. As the United States emerged as a global power, attention turned toward the cultural values of stability and security, and homelessness became discursively less visible. The homeless individual is represented as a skid row "bum" who symbolizes disaffiliation and destitution. Howard Bahr, for example, wrote and edited several sociological texts on homeless men during this period, including *Disaffiliated Man: Essays and Bibliography on Skid Row, Vagrancy, and Outsiders* and *Homelessness and Disaffiliation*. Dozens of similar texts made direct connections between homelessness, alcoholism, and disaffiliation. Thus, the image of a single male alcoholic dominated the discourse of homelessness between 1940 and 1980.

By contrast, the self-imposed "homelessness" of the Beat Generation illuminates the dominant culture's valuation of the home. In the literary texts of Jack Kerouac and other Beat writers, homelessness symbolizes social dissatisfaction. Like many of the earlier tramp writers, the Beats emphasized the sense of freedom and adventure associated with being on the road. The Beat lifestyle, however, was not an economic necessity, and it more clearly represents a rejection of domesticity and permanence. Kerouac's *On the Road* epitomizes this response; other examples include John Clellon Holmes's *Go* and John Rechy's *City of Night*. Movement, restlessness, and an inability to find satisfaction underlie these texts, as characters constantly pull up stakes to find a better city or a better experience. As Kerouac writes, "We were all delighted, we all realized we were leaving confusion and nonsense behind and performing our one and noble function of the time, *move*" (133). This sense of movement parallels the earlier tramp autobiographies, but differs markedly from earlier and later periods. Whereas the Beats reveled in their rejection of the status quo, the tramp writers attempted to align themselves with the dominant culture by posing as intellectuals and sociologists, as I will demonstrate in Chapter Four.

Each of these periods contrasts with the current conception of "the homeless" as a group of unemployable, permanently displaced people, who live in large urban centers and are frequently drug dependent or mentally ill. Federal cutbacks in social services, deinstitutionalization, and decreases in earnings and in affordable housing, among other factors, contributed to a rise in homelessness since 1980. The discourse also shifted. One begins to see texts such as *The Demolition of Skid Row* by Ronald Miller which describe the process of gentrification, increased rent, and urban renewal that led to the elimination of the skid row "bum." Numerous articles about "the new homeless" displaced the discursive construction of the disaffiliated homeless individual. As Charles Hoch states,

> The homeless once again became an important social problem in the early 1980s when the worst economic recession since the 1930s hit at the same time that a newly elected president initiated unprecedented cutbacks in federally funded public assistance programs. (27)

The increased visibility of homeless people in American cities corresponds with the increased attention to homelessness as a social issue. As Susan E. Wright quips, "In the 1980s everyone discovered the homeless" (4). Indeed, texts about homelessness in journalism, film, art, literature, and throughout popular culture proliferated after 1980.

For example, in 1993, St. Martin's Press published *Travels with Lizbeth: Three Years on the Road and on the Streets* by Lars Eighner. Featured on the front page of *The New York Times Book Review* on October 10, 1993, the book combines the sense of adventure from being "on the road" with a socio-political awareness of homelessness as it is currently defined. The chapter entitled "On Dumpster Diving" (which was republished in at least two composition anthologies) reinforces the image of the homeless individual picking through garbage containers for food and other items. However, Eighner also notes the attraction of living on the road:

> As bad as things had been I cannot deny there is a romance of the road. The Golden Thumb and Dallas Matsen [fellow "super-tramps"] were part of something very appealing to me, and I suppose I will always wonder whether things would really have turned out so badly if I had given in to my desire for it. (32–33)

Eighner, like earlier tramp autobiographers, praises the wandering lifestyle but decides to "settle down." This tension between the contemporary notion of homelessness and the earlier "romance of the road" indicates the effect of discourse: without a tradition of stories by "real" homeless people, a book such as Eighner's is written and marketed as travel writing, that is, as romanticized homelessness.

Other contemporary examples also follow the pattern of either romanticizing or objectifying homelessness. *Rule of the Bone* (1995), a novel by Russell Banks, presents the story of Chappie, a teenager who becomes homeless after running away from an abusive stepfather. Chappie lives in an abandoned bus, a boarded-up summer home, and with some small time drug dealers, but he eventually moves to Jamaica after hooking up with a wise Rastafarian. While *Rule of the Bone* draws attention to the existence of homeless teens, Chappie's experiences in Jamaica are undoubtably atypical. He experiences many difficulties, but a sense of adventure also permeates the story.

At the opposite end of the spectrum, *In the Open: Diary of a Homeless Alcoholic* (1996) by Timothy E. Donahue and *My Life on the Streets: Memoirs of a Faceless Man* (1992) by "Joe Homeless" represent homelessness as a state of virtual abjection. In both books, the authors describe degradation and discrimination as a result of being homeless. Books like these may provide some realistic insights about such a lifestyle; however, like realist/naturalist texts, a distance exists between the reader and the homeless individual (which also objectifies him/her). In Chapter Five, I suggest that more attention should be given to texts in American literature which represent homeless individuals as purposeful, active members of a community, rather than as solitary, passive victims. Contemporary literature, while exhibiting several new twists, continues to either romanticize or objectify homelessness.

As previously mentioned, relatively little critical commentary exists which discusses homelessness directly, particularly when one considers the range of texts in American literature. Furthermore, the criticism which does exist tends to perpetuate the glamorization or objectification of homelessness. Literary criticism on the theme of homelessness in America can be divided into four categories: metaphorical homelessness, related themes, literary romanticism, and literary realism/naturalism.[7] As I hope to show, these categories should be questioned or examined in order to ascertain how certain treatments of this theme have been excluded or marginalized.

METAPHORICAL HOMELESSNESS

Since about 1980, homelessness in America has been more prevalent, visible, and poignant than at any time since the Depression. Consequently, it has become the subject of intense scrutiny in sociology, journalism, and even popular culture. Perhaps coincidentally, but more likely as a result of this circulation of texts, literary critics have appropriated homelessness as a metaphor to describe a variety of conditions and states of mind. Sociologists Peter Berger, Brigitte Berger, and Hansfried Kellner anticipate this trend in their 1973 book *The Homeless Mind: Modernization and Consciousness*. Describing the sense of loss and alienation as a result of religious and epistemological uncertainty, they remark: "*modern man has suffered from a deepening condition of 'homelessness.'* The correlate of the migratory character of his experience of society and of self has been what might be called a metaphysical loss of 'home'" (82). Similarly, Georg Lukács sees the novel as the artistic form best suited to this loss of center, labeling the novel an expression of "transcendental homelessness" (41). In "Homelessness and Worldliness," Bruce Robbins discusses the work of Edward W. Said and compares the literal displacement of Palestians with the "homelessness" of the modern critic. Berger, Berger, and Kellner's characterization of "modern man" closely resembles more recent accounts of the "postmodern condition." Caren Kaplan states, "'Deterritorialization' is one term for the displacement of identities, persons, and meanings that is endemic to the postmodern world system" (358). Referring to the work of Deleuze and Guattari, Kaplan describes deterritorialization as one of several related terms that critics have adopted to characterize postmodernism. In *Toto, I Have a Feeling We're Not in Kansas Anymore: Discussions of Pynchon's Novels*, Laurel Kaye Brett argues that Thomas Pynchon used the theme of homelessness to represent this postmodern, epistemological loss of center. Nomadism, displacement, diaspora, and homelessness have become increasingly prevalent in recent criticism in a variety of contexts.

In critical discussions of American literature, homelessness functions as a metaphor in other ways as well. Often, it is the artist/writer who is psychologically "homeless." David Geesham Myers, for example, asserts that Raymond Carver's short story "Put Yourself in My Shoes" is about Carver's "homelessness": "If the intellectual is an exile because he lives between cities, Ray [Carver] was an exile because he lived–and lived nowhere else than–between stories. And to live between stories is to be without a home" (464). Psychological "homelessness" is also used to describe Washington Irving in *Adrift in the Old World: The Psychological Pilgrimage of Washington Irving* by Jeffrey Rubin-Dorsky and to characterize Nathaniel Hawthorne in "Hawthorne's English Romance: The Return of a Homeless American" by Masahiro Nakamura. Critics have also used the same metaphor to symbolize the sense of alienation for women writers. In *Homelessness at Home: Oppositional Practices and Modern Women's Writing*, for example, Ronald Thomas Foster argues that women lacked a "place" and lacked recognition as writers, making them feel "homeless" in their own homes.

In addition to portraying authors as "homeless," critics also focus on the metaphorical or figurative *use* of homelessness. In "Home and Homelessness in Faulkner's Works and Life," Michel Gresset addresses both functions, calling Faulkner "the poet of homelessness." After looking at comments in Faulkner's speeches about the nature of "home" and applying them to selected novels, Gresset states, "it is likely that there is only one predicament which is repeated over and over again in Faulkner's fiction, and this predicament is homelessness" (36–37). While this conclusion may be overstated, Gresset's analysis of the differing role of homes for men and women in Faulkner's fiction is valuable. Andrew Scoblionko uses the same metaphor to describe Faulkner's characters in *Soldiers' Pay*: "Unlike their counterparts in the Yoknapatawpha novels, most of the characters in *Soldiers' Pay* are 'homeless' in one way or another. Instead of intimate familiar places they have only alienating spaces as material with which to constitute their own subjectivity" (63). Scoblionko's Lacanian analysis of *Soldiers' Pay*, like Gresset's essay, offers a new and productive way of understanding Faulkner's work. But Faulkner's characters, and the authors discussed in the previous paragraph, aren't "really" homeless. Scoblionko rightly puts "homeless" in quotation marks, indicating the metaphorical/rhetorical function of the term. While I think certain appropriations of the word push the limits of practicality (is homelessness applicable to Raymond Carver?), it is not my intention to challenge individual critics' or the general use of homelessness as a metaphor.[8] Instead, I wish to address what seems to me to be an imbalance. I believe a need exists to analyze literal homelessness in addition to metaphorical uses of the term, and in addition to related themes or traditional literary categories such as realism and naturalism.

RELATED THEMES

Critics frequently address homelessness indirectly or in passing while dealing with related themes such as alienation, exile, escape, rebellion, the city, travel, the Other, domesticity, and the home. Widmer's quotation at the beginning of this chapter, for example, subsumes all of the different forms of literal homelessness under the category of rebellion. His book, *The Literary Rebel* (1965), covers more forms of literary homelessness than perhaps any other single work. While Widmer challenges misrepresentations of the wandering poor, he focuses on the decision to wander, rather than the condition of (forced) homelessness. He states, "My basic point is simple: wandering may be many things, but most certainly includes fundamental expressions of human awareness and aspiration" (84). Although Widmer addresses the range of literary responses, the texts he discusses represent homelessness as a choice, that is, as a form of rebellion. The characters assume the form of the romantic hero, and homelessness is therefore elevated and glamorized.

ROMANTICISM

Like Widmer, several critics discuss homelessness in the context of literary romanticism. These commentators usually focus on the figure of the tramp or hobo: a solitary, male character who serves as the narrator. Whether or not they invoke romanticism directly, these critics generally focus on primary texts told in the first person, in an optimistic tone, and which recount travels and adventures rather than poverty and degradation. The condition of homelessness is glamorized and celebrated as a form of freedom or, at worst, a challenge for the romantic hero to overcome. The protagonists who are analyzed are strong, free-willed individuals who persevere and triumph over the limits of society, consistent with Donald McQuade's description of romanticism: "Generally speaking [. . .], the writers in the Romantic tradition emphasized the possible triumph of the human will" (12). Critics also cite other romantic traits such as rugged individualism, heroism, inspiration, exploration, and "taming the wild."

While critics admit the suffering caused by poverty, they often link the American hobo to the figure of the romantic vagabond or to the picaresque genre. For example, the title of William Brevda's essay, "At the Crossroads of Vagabondia, Hobohemia, and Bohemia: Harry Kemp's *Tramping on Life*," signifies the affiliation of the vagabond, the hobo, and the bohemian. Brevda describes this progression:

> Vagabondia was an essentially romantic idea that celebrated the spirit of wanderlust and the figure of the carefree traveler, especially the artistic and literary traveler, in the open air (realm of the English

> vagabond), or the open road (the more down-to-earth domain of the American vagabond). (46)

Likewise, in *Marginal Manners: The Variants of Bohemia*, Frederick J. Hoffman collects writings by Kemp, Stephen Crane, Hart Crane, Dos Passos, Steinbeck, Kerouac, Alan Ginsberg, and others. These apparently disparate writers share a sense of marginality and disaffiliation. Brevda and Hoffman illustrate the tendency in criticism and literature to represent homeless characters as counter-cultural, as falling outside the norms and expectations of society. Regardless of their background and motivation, the characters remain noble, solitary, and somewhat heroic.

Frederick Feied describes this process in his book *No Pie in the Sky: The Hobo as American Cultural Hero in the Works of Jack London, John Dos Passos, and Jack Kerouac*. Feied states, "As far back as the Middle Ages there has existed a body of literature, in song, bawdy verse and story, celebrating the life of the homeless migrant" (7). Feied distinguishes between the authors in his title and earlier tramp autobiographers who tended to exaggerate the romance of the road: Dos Passos's depiction of the Vag, most notably, cannot be considered romantic or optimistic. Feied also attempts to situate London, Dos Passos, and Kerouac in their respective cultural and social contexts in order to explain the significance of their homeless characters. But the hobo remains a "hero," and the condition of homelessness is represented as a struggle to endure, rather than a socio-economic problem to rectify.

Similarly, in his book *On the Fringe: The Dispossessed in America*, Henry Miller associates the hobo (as well as the contemporary homeless) with other marginalized "misfits": cowboys, the forty-niners, loggers, mountain men, and, later, hippies. Although Miller recognizes the struggles of the homeless, his book participates in a discourse which conflates homelessness with free-spirited adventure. Referring to sociology directly (and literary texts indirectly), Miller correctly notes that "The literature on vagrancy and hoboism is overwhelming and partisan. It is almost impossible to find an authority who is not either repelled by or enamored of vagrant life" (xiii-xiv). *On the Fringe* addresses this polemic, but Miller does not problemitize the binary.

The beat who goes "on the road" represents another manifestation of the romanticized traveler in America. Although critics do not describe the beat generation as "homeless," they do focus on the rejection of the home as a symbol of rejection of the dominant culture. In *Romance of the Road: The Literature of the American Highway*, Ronald Primeau states,

> Each road narrative is an individual text, but it becomes a part of the genre that represents a culture in dialogue about national and self iden-

> tity, social values, and opportunity. The form is particularly American and immensely popular because so many of the questions remain open to debate. (16)

Primeau notes that the road narrative as a genre "has received only hesitant and reserved attention from academic critics" (12), despite its popularity. The lack of critical commentary belies the fact that distinctions between the beat, the hobo, the vagabond, and "the homeless" frequently blur. Individual critics comment on the suffering of the poor and the homeless, but I believe the impact–the cultural work–of criticism and literature which "celebrates" the condition of homelessness (directly or indirectly) needs to be considered more fully. For example, Feied, Miller, and Primeau share an interest in the figure of the solitary tramp or hobo, generally represented as a "hero." As I suggest above in the discussion of Eighner and Banks, I believe this influence has not disappeared: homelessness continues to be romanticized in some cases, despite the inherent contradiction. This critical discourse, however inadvertently, may lend credence to the belief that the poor "choose" to be homeless. At the very least, it perpetuates the image of the solitary homeless Other, separated and isolated. In chapter Five and in the Conclusion, I suggest that discourse has marginalized texts which present contrary images.

REALISM/NATURALISM

Whereas the romantic depiction of the tramp or hobo tends to glamorize homelessness, realist and naturalist treatments condemn it. Realist and naturalist writers turned to common, low, or disturbing themes and characters in order to resist the "myths" created by earlier, romantic authors. In order to present the experiences more realistically, these writers often became participant-observers: actual witnesses of life in tenement housing, factories, public shelters, and the slums. They also sought to educate the general public about the terrible conditions in such places, and therefore recounted pessimistic tales of degradation, danger, and abjection. For their efforts, these realist and naturalist writers are sometimes accused of "speaking for the Other" by recent commentators.

Discussing writers like Stephen Crane, Jacob Riis, and Jack London, Mark Pittenger states,

> In an era of deepening urban segregation by class, ethnicity, and race, the sense that readers were being introduced to strange beings and alien worlds was enhanced by the common conceit that the American poor inhabited a domestic "Dark Continent" whose denizens were effectively a primitive and "unknown race" [. . .] . (48)

In other words, realist and naturalist writers portrayed the "down and out" as decidedly different from "normal" people, even while attempting to represent them realistically. I believe it is somewhat disingenuous to critique writers of the early twentieth century for misrepresenting the poor and homeless from our contemporary point of view; however, Pittenger's analysis, like other critiques of naturalism, reveals how a writer's subject position in relation to his/her material affects the text he or she produces. He remarks, "If down-and-outers blurred the border between 'us' and 'them' through the rituals of disguise and descent, they largely re-established it when reconstituting their experiences as texts" (46). In Chapter Three I discuss the effects of this posturing and I extend Pittenger's analysis of this type of discourse.

Critics also address other "uses" of homelessness in literary realism and naturalism. In her dissertation *Encoding Imperialism: Homelessness in American Naturalism, 1890–1918*, Janet M. Whyde agrees that naturalist writers portrayed homeless characters as foreign and Other. But Whyde sees this trend in the context of a wider historical movement in America. She argues that

> as characters in naturalist texts struggle to define themselves in the context of "homelessness," they reveal at the same time the parallel effort that marked U.S. struggles to redefine itself in the face of a changing world role as an imperial power. (2)

Whyde's study parallels my own effort to look at the association between the home and American identity by examining characters who lack homes. She concludes that "naturalists were supportive of imperialism as a general policy, but critical of a policy of exploitation" (21). Like Whyde, I believe that certain authors used homelessness as a theme or trope to produce certain responses or effects, and I assert that this perspective has been generally overlooked.

In the remainder of this chapter, I explain how this study seeks to examine these responses and effects in texts dealing with homelessness. The texts and authors I have chosen represent the range of literary responses discussed above and establish a trajectory which can be followed into current discussions of the term. Underlying these texts is an ideological struggle over American cultural values associated with work, the family, the home, and charity. Literature provides a unique focal point to examine these contested values and a means of influencing them. Consequently, the publication and distribution–or the marginalization and rejection–of certain depictions of homelessness also have effects and should be addressed. In other words, what alternatives exist in addition to romanticizing or objectifying homelessness?

ROMANTICISM, REALISM, AND TESTIMONY

This study focuses on the period from the Civil War through the Depression–the second period described above. This period, corresponding to the growth of industrialization, witnessed a wide range of responses to homelessness which parallels the current situation in the U.S. In both periods, a rise in the incidence of homelessness precipitated an increased interest in texts about the subject. Referring specifically to the period from the Civil War to the Depression, Kenneth L. Kusmer states,

> I find the history of the homeless valuable because the response of people and institutions to this group and its wide interconnections, both symbolic and real, to many important aspects of American society can help clarify the larger transforming experience of an industrializing society. (97)

Although I recognize the pitfalls of attempting to cover such a relatively long period, I agree with Kusmer that responses to homelessness in this era resonate in other times and in the context of other issues. Therefore, my approach is somewhat diachronic, but I concentrate on a period of relative discursive coherence (as I tried to indicate in the discussion of historical periods above).

Chapter One demonstrates how Harriet Beecher Stowe used homelessness as a specific rhetorical trope or device in *Uncle Tom's Cabin* to create empathy for slaves. Although critics agree that Stowe opposed slavery on moral and religious grounds, the use of homelessness as a specific strategy has not been discussed. In her *House and Home Papers* (1854), Stowe describes the home as having the "elements of love, rest, permanency, and liberty" (56). I argue that these values are repeatedly violated for slaves in *Uncle Tom's Cabin*. Stowe, therefore, reflects and contributes to the moral, ethical, and religious dimensions of the home in America by emphasizing the homelessness of slaves. In this chapter I draw on the work of critics such as Jane Tompkins, Elizabeth Ammons, and Gillian Brown who suggest that Stowe advocated the displacement of the chaotic, masculine marketplace through the substitution of a (feminine) domestic economy. However, I attempt to reassert Stowe's anti-slavery purpose and I suggest that the opposition of the public and private spheres in recent discussions of domesticity ignores the subject position of slaves. Subsequent chapters also question the public/private binary in discussions of domesticity. In other words, homelessness can be seen as an oppositional space "between" the public and private spheres. Chapter One augments Tompkins's influential analysis of the cultural work of *Uncle Tom's Cabin* by looking specifically at how Stowe used homelessness in the novel. In doing so, I hope to illustrate the potential for such an approach in later chapters.

Chapter Two examines how homelessness is tied to identity, class, and respectability in the work of Horatio Alger. Like *Uncle Tom's Cabin*, Alger's works were enormously popular, and they reveal the underlying cultural distaste for homelessness and the valuation of the home. And, like Stowe, Alger used homelessness didactically. Until recently, literary criticism about Alger was quite limited (if not inaccurate). Critics held that Alger intended merely to educate young boys about the value of honesty and hard work. This view has been challenged recently, and whereas the "Alger myth" and Alger's role within the "Gospel of Wealth" tradition has been widely discussed, the specific function of homelessness in his work has not been analyzed in depth. Michael Denning does note the conflict over the "deserving" and "undeserving" tramps during the late nineteenth century and declares that the "dime novel also became an arena of this ideological struggle over the tramp" (150). But Denning only addresses Alger's tramp characters briefly. As Carol Nackenoff reveals, Alger's *Ragged Dick* and *Tony, the Tramp* series reveal a greater complexity of cultural issues and values than the "rags-to-riches" myth might suggest. Chapter Two argues that Alger simultaneously appealed to the romantic sense of freedom associated with homelessness and to the realist interest in "the other half"–in this case, street children of New York.

Alger's interest in "life on the street" anticipates the attention given to the "lower classes" by literary naturalists such as Stephen Crane and Jacob Riis. Unlike Alger's charming street urchins, though, the characters that Crane and Riis create are products of a harsh, debilitating environment. Chapter Three addresses the objectification of homelessness in participant-observer accounts by Crane and Riis. I am wary of contemporary criticism which condemns naturalist writers for objectifying the poor, but I believe the effects of this type of discourse were profound. Like Pittenger, I question the results or effects of participant-observer treatments of homelessness and the slums, rather than the motives of the writers. Naturalism reinforced the image of the city as dangerous and oppressive, and implied that inhabitants of the slums were helpless victims, if not deficient and flawed. In other words, the city and the poor became, at least discursively, pathological. As David Wagner contends, "the public equates the streets, the slums, and the poor with social pathology and social disorganization" (119). Naturalist writers such as Riis and Crane contributed to the idea that the poor and homeless are isolated, passive victims, rather than constitutive members of a community.

A very different type of participant-observer narrator emerges in the dozens of tramp autobiographies which appeared between 1890 and 1930. Chapter Four analyzes how these writers–most notably Jack London–attempted to romanticize homelessness by describing the freedom and adventure associated with life "on the road." These tramp autobiographies exhibit similarities which represent a well-defined though unexamined sub-genre of American literature. Frequently, these authors mention the inability to resist the sense of "wanderlust" that draws them to the open road. By becoming transient they undermine the American work ethic, the stability of the family, and the need for a home. The threat posed to these values led to a vicious backlash against tramps, particularly around the turn of the century. However, many of these stories conclude with the author returning home and renouncing the need to travel and/or extolling the virtues of the home. The writers also repeatedly distance themselves from "real" tramps by describing themselves as observers of tramp culture who are drawing on the experience for their writing. Harry Kemp, for example, remarked, "I am a tramp for the sake of my art" (qtd. in Brevda, *Harry Kemp* 117). This comment typifies a desire on the part of the tramp writers to come across as well educated, intellectual investigators, rather than as genuinely needy or destitute. By posing as amateur sociologists and intellectuals, the tramp writers attempted to avoid the stigma attached to being homeless at the time. The tramp autobiographies complicate American notions of class and identity when homelessness is involved. I argue that the tramp and the intellectual turned to one another for legitimation as each emerged as a distinct class in America in the early twentieth century. In fact, the autobiographies reveal a keen understanding of "identity-politics" on the part of the tramps. In this chapter, however, I also emphasize the negative effects of romanticizing homelessness.

Chapter Five uses Meridel Le Sueur's *The Girl*–an account of homeless women during the Depression–as an example of American testimony. Le Sueur's style and subject matter contrast with other Depression-era writers such as John Steinbeck who received more popular and critical attention. I contend that "testimony" as a genre has been neglected in American literary history and that recovering examples such as *The Girl* will produce positive effects. In other words, the cultural work of testimony is productive because it avoids some of the limitations imposed by the traditional divisions of fiction/nonfiction and romanticism/realism, and because it has the potential to effect social change.

Throughout this study I hope to emphasize the relationship between literature and the "real world." Hence, I have made extensive use of Tompkins's concept of cultural work in discussing the effects of literature. Testimony, in my opinion, also provides an important and overlooked means of examining the potential uses of literary texts. While testimony has occasionally been used in the context of American literature, the term is more frequently associated with Holocaust studies or Latin American literature (as "*testimonio*"). John Beverly states,

> By testimonio, I mean a novel or novella-length narrative [. . .], told in the first person by a narrator who is also the real protagonist or witness of the events she or he recounts. The unit of narration is usually a "life" or a significant life experience (for example, the experience of being a prisoner). Since, in many cases, the narrator is someone who is either functionally illiterate or, if literate, not a professional writer, the production of a testimonio often involves the tape recording and then the transcription and editing of an oral account by an interlocutor [. . .]. (70–71)

Beverly's definition will be augmented and applied in Chapter 5, but it clearly reveals the unique role of the "author" in testimony. In earlier chapters I question the authenticity of participant-observer accounts of poverty and of "intellectual" renditions of the tramp lifestyle. Rather than debate the veracity of any specific text, however, I attempt instead to analyze the relationship between the author and the subject matter. Testimony/*testimonio* relies on a different relationship than is present in either romanticism or realism/naturalism. The "author-function" (as Foucault posits) has remained fairly constant in American literature to the exclusion of testimony. Le Sueur provides an effective example to illustrate the differences between traditional literature and testimony, as well as the potential ramifications of testimonial literature. I argue that American testimony has been marginalized or displaced, and that efforts should be made to recuperate texts like Le Sueur's. In this chapter and throughout this study I also suggest that the cultural work of literary criticism can and should be addressed more frequently, in addition to the analysis of primary texts.

The Conclusion briefly traces the trajectory of the discourse of homelessness into current discussions of the term.[9] I also look at recent efforts to use testimony in discussions of American literature. In this chapter I reiterate the value of examining the discourse of social issues and the cultural work of texts *and* criticism. Expanding the use/currency of "testimony" in American literary criticism is offered as a means to this end. Literary testimony deconstructs the notion of "us" and "them" which pervades literature, journalism, popular culture, and sociology (past and present) dealing with homelessness. "Homelessness" is a construct in America: one which has been influenced by literary texts and criticism. The "real" voices of the homeless have been excluded in favor of treatments which either romanticize or objectify the condition of homelessness. Ideally, literary testimony avoids this division and provides a more authentic mode of representation. Mary Beth Tierney-Tello notes how this can be advantageous:

> [P]reviously silenced voices [. . .] have the opportunity to make their particular and collective plights (which may include poverty, exploita-

> tion, imprisonment, or genocide) known to a wide reading public and possibly to garner that public's support and solidarity. (79)

This study attempts to create a space in American literature and literary criticism for testimonial literature which deals with homelessness. Previously, that space has been occupied for the most part by romantic treatments of the hero who goes "on the road" or naturalist accounts of abjection "in the streets." Neither approach tends to increase solidarity between readers and the homeless subjects. For this reason, I offer testimony as a means of recognizing and discussing literary texts which may have been previously excluded. Ideally, the inclusion of testimony about homelessness in the American literary canon will foster the solidarity described by Tierney-Tello above.

Chapter One

"In My Father's House Are Many Mansions"

Homelessness and Domesticity in Uncle Tom's Cabin

WHILE ON BOARD THE BOAT THAT WILL TAKE HIM TO HIS NEW "HOME" Tom takes comfort in a verse from his ever-present Bible: "In my Father's house are many mansions. I go to prepare a place for you" (229). Indeed, Tom finds his place *only* when he dies. Although he remembers his wife, children, and lifestyle in Kentucky fondly, he quickly corrects George Shelby who assumes Tom will return "home" to the Shelby estate once again:

> "I've come to buy you, and take you home," said George, with impetuous vehemence.
>
> "O, Mas'r George, ye're too late. The Lord's bought me, and is going to take me home,–and I long to go. Heaven is better than Kintuck." (589–590)

This passage epitomizes the difficulties and complexities of slaves having or going "home." George must first purchase Tom and then return him to "Uncle Tom's cabin," but can Tom consider the cabin his home since it and he are both owned by the Shelbys?

In this chapter I discuss how slaves, (and blacks in general) as Stowe recognized, could not have homes in antebellum America. Furthermore, Stowe uses this form of homelessness to create sympathy in her readers in a way that is analogous to the widely accepted strategy of maternal empathy. While some critics see the elevation of the domestic sphere as Stowe's primary goal, I attempt to reassert the anti-slavery purposes of *Uncle Tom's Cabin* by demonstrating how Stowe used homelessness as a rhetorical strategy to that end. More specifically, I argue that Stowe used homelessness to hasten the end of slavery because she considered it a sin against human beings: Her success demonstrates the potential for texts to do "cultural work"–a point of emphasis throughout this study–at a time when women were chastised for speaking out on such subjects and blacks were not seen as fully human. Critical interpretations which oppose the domestic sphere to the public sphere ignore the subject position of slaves and therefore reinforce the depersonalization that Stowe attempted to overcome.

HOMELESSNESS AS A SIN

Although much recent criticism regarding *Uncle Tom's Cabin* discusses the role of the home within the domestic economy, and further demonstrates the importance of this sphere for Stowe, the variety of homes and their symbolic role remain largely unexplored.[1] Moreover, Stowe's deliberate and extended use of homelessness as a trope in the novel has not been addressed. The homelessness of slaves complements maternal love as a means of creating empathy in readers and a corresponding distaste for slavery. Before tracing this progression in the novel I briefly situate Stowe within the anti-slavery debate of the time. This will allow me to characterize more accurately her motives for using such a rhetorical strategy.

Stowe held specific beliefs about the "evils" of slavery and the role of Americans in resisting it. In her introduction to *Uncle Tom's Cabin*, Ann Douglas describes Stowe's position within the range of anti-slavery commentators:

> Much as she loved and admired her tempestuous, vital father, she dismissed his moderate antislavery stance as inadequate [. . .]; despite her enduring differences with the extreme abolitionists Theodore Weld, the Grimké sisters, William Lloyd Garrison, and Wendell Phillips, she took her stand with them on this point: slavery was a "sin," the gravest and most far-reaching in American history. (22–23)

Stowe's belief that slavery was a sin should be emphasized for two reasons. First, it establishes that arguments about the purpose of *Uncle Tom's Cabin* should consider Stowe's religious–rather than secular–motives as paramount. As Douglas notes, "Almost no one in antebellum America wrote about slavery in secular terms" (22). Therefore, critical commentary should attempt to account for Stowe's religious background and motivation. Second, the importance of homelessness in the novel becomes more apparent because it represented a specific sin against slaves. Stowe believed homes (not merely houses) were necessary for everyone. The lack of homes for slaves was a sin that needed to be remedied. Although *Uncle Tom's Cabin* is not explicitly *about* homelessness, it demonstrates how this theme resonates throughout American literature and culture.[2] These moral, ethical, and religious dimensions will be traced throughout this study.[3]

Stowe opposed slavery on religious grounds, but even within the anti-slavery rubric several options existed. Whereas Douglas sees Garrison et al. as "extreme abolitionists," other historians contrast the Garrisonians with even more radical abolitionists. Similarly, Howard Zinn, in *A People's History of the United States*, differentiates between black and white abolitionists. According to Zinn, blacks were willing to use more extreme measures to further their cause (179). Stowe did not advocate extreme measures such as physical rebellion. Instead, she closely parallels the Garrisonian position described by Waldo Martin which emphasized "'the strategic value of moral suasion and the importance of altering public consciousness'" (qtd. in Jay 269). In order to "alter the public consciousness," she attempts to create empathy for slaves by describing the separation of slave mothers from their children and the displacement of slaves from their homes. In addition, she consistently represents slaves as literally "homeless."

Whereas strict abolitionists would criticize slavery for disrupting families and homes, Stowe maintained that some differences exist between the races. As Douglas reveals, Stowe viewed slavery as a sin. As such, it demanded every rhetorical tool at her disposal to eliminate. But, unlike strict abolitionists, Stowe did not suggest integration. She reveals her position in the "Concluding Remarks" to *Uncle Tom's Cabin*:

> Let the church of the north receive these poor sufferers in the spirit of Christ; receive them to the educating advantages of Christian republican society and schools, until they have attained to somewhat of a moral and intellectual maturity, and then assist them in their passage to those shores, where they may put in practice the lessons they have learned in America. (626)

For Stowe, homelessness (and slavery) must be eliminated because it is a sin; it is not a problem to be rectified by providing homes to African-Americans in the United States—free or enslaved.

William Andrews describes the particular significance of the home in the debate over slavery. He states,

> Each side of the slavery issue claimed the institution of the family as its guiding ideal and the protection of the domestic well-being of black slaves as one of its chief reasons for existence. For every James A. Thome who complained that "no ties of sacred home" were allowed to exist in the slave quarters, there was a C. G. Memminger to reply that under slavery "domestic relations become those which are most prized," since "each planter in fact is a Patriarch" who views the welfare of his "children and servants" as part of his sacred familial duty. (242)

Williams shows how both abolitionists and apologists used the preservation of the family and the home to support their respective sides, and how slave owners purported to uphold their "sacred duty." According to Theodore R. Hovet, the family as "home or centre" took on a "mystical significance" at the time due to this theory of correspondences. This theory, articulated primarily by Thomas Upham and Horace Bushnell, posited the interdependence of individuals in the family/home and the whole of society, and was familiar to Stowe (Hovet 502). Such a theory elevates the importance of the family as the center of (Christian) society and civilization itself.[4]

This historical information helps to establish the importance of homes and (perhaps more importantly) homelessness as a rhetorical strategy for Stowe. More specifically, Stowe uses this strategy throughout *Uncle Tom's Cabin* by constantly revealing the importance of homes and the lack thereof for slaves.

In her *House and Home Papers*, first published in 1854, Stowe describes and defines "homes" at length. For Stowe, "The word home has in it elements of love, rest, permanency, and liberty" (56). She focuses on two elements in particular: "*No home is possible without love*" (57); and "*There can be no true home without liberty*" (60). The discussion of these values removes any economic connotations from the word "home." While recent criticism describes the role of the home within the domestic sphere and in contrast to the marketplace, Stowe turns our attention to the ethical and religious dimensions of "home": "Of so great dignity and worth is this holy and sacred thing, that the power to create a HOME ought to be ranked above all creative faculties" (56). She goes on to describe a perfect home as a "New Jerusalem" and "that which is the nearest image of heaven" (78). (The Legree plantation, to take just one example from the novel, represents the "sin" of slavery and stands in sharp contrast to these descriptions.)

When one considers the importance of homes in the entire anti-slavery debate and the moral (rather than merely economic) significance Stowe places in homes, homelessness becomes a highly charged rhetorical strategy in *Uncle Tom's Cabin*. The Legree plantation may be the most obvious example, but throughout the novel Stowe reveals the importance of homes and their inaccessibility for slaves. This combination heightens the reader's empathy with slaves and encourages a resistance to slavery.

HOMES IN UNCLE TOM'S CABIN

The title of the novel–"Uncle Tom's Cabin"–immediately alerts readers to the importance of living spaces. The title also alerts us to the inherent irony of a discussion of slaves actually having or possessing homes. While the possessive apostrophe denotes ownership, Tom, as a slave, cannot own anything. The cabin belongs to Shelby. Furthermore, as Philip Fisher points out, the cabin plays a very insignificant role in the novel. Because most of the action takes place away from the cabin, "The title asserts [Tom's] homelessness" (Fisher, *Hard Facts* 119). It reminds us that Tom does not have a home and cannot acquire one.[5] Chapter IV, "An Evening in Uncle Tom's Cabin," does open with a description of the cabin (one of several chapters that begin with descriptions of homes), and it reveals the happiness associated with the gatherings there. But thereafter, references to the cabin are few and far between.

Theodore R. Hovet construes the cabin as a symbol within a larger critique of capitalism: "Tom's cabin, replaced by the slave villages of agricultural capitalism, has become a 'poetic legend' of a bygone era" (512). Stowe, however, defined homes in moral terms, not economic. Hovet's claim obviates this distinction. Furthermore, George Shelby's comments at the end of the novel present a more tangible and disturbing symbol. Shelby addresses the reader directly: "Think of your freedom, every time you see UNCLE TOM'S CABIN; and let it be a memorial to put you all in mind to follow in his steps, and be honest and faithful and Christian as he was" (617). As readers we cannot *see* the cabin, but we carry away the knowledge that Tom died "homeless." George's suggestion leaves a bitter aftertaste for a reader who notes that Tom is displaced from his "home" and eventually dies because he is a slave. The title itself creates empathy by highlighting his homelessness. As Walter Benn Michaels remarks, "Only in death did the slave's title to himself become 'sure'; only in death did Uncle Tom's cabin actually become his" (102).

From the first scene of the novel, which takes place inside Shelby's home, Stowe reveals the impermanence of slaves' homes. Shelby and Haley discuss the sale of Tom in the comforts of Shelby's "well-furnished dining parlor" (41). Shelby's mild displeasure hardly conceals the fact that they treat human beings as commodities and that Tom (and Harry) can be displaced from their homes and families capriciously. The element of "permanency" described in Stowe's essay "What is a Home?" is clearly violated for slaves.

Proponents of slavery said that they provided homes for slaves, and one could argue that Tom and his family had a home. Tom and Eliza, for example, refer to the Shelby estate as "home" on occasion. For Eliza, it was "the only home she had ever known" (104). Similarly, Tom has "home-yearnings" for his family on the Shelby estate. This prompts Gillian Brown to write: "The Kentucky home seems a standard of domestic excellence; it becomes both the memory of home Uncle Tom cherishes and an Edenic image" (21). Brown cites the garden of berries and flowers as evidence of this Edenic image, and such an interpretation confirms the more positive reading of the novel's final paragraph. George, paying tribute to Tom after his death, vows that he will never own slaves again. Therefore, the cabin on the Shelby estate has been described as a positive symbol of the life Tom lost. More frequently, the conclusion is used to support the criticism that the novel and Tom's character in particular promote subservience for blacks. But it seems more likely that George referred to the cabin as a symbol of Tom himself and the sacrifice he made by ultimately dying. Whether or not George realizes it, Tom remained homeless until his death.

Like Uncle Tom's cabin, the Shelby household cannot be considered either Tom or Eliza's *home*. First, it violates the elements of a proper "home" articulated in Stowe's *House and Home Papers*: permanence, rest, and liberty. Second, when Tom and Eliza refer to it as "home" the word encompasses the entire estate with their residences contained therein, not the house itself. Third, they cannot own property, including their own homes. Though the Shelby estate most closely represents a "home," and Tom and Eliza refer to it as such, Stowe undermines any possibility for a real home for slaves in the novel. Stowe introduces two "real" homes–the home of Senator Bird and the Quaker settlement–to contrast with the Shelby estate and Tom's cabin, and to reestablish the value and importance of a good home.

Chapter IX opens with a description of the Bird household:

> The light of the cheerful fire shone on the rug and carpet of a cosey parlor, and glittered on the sides of the tea-cups and well-brightened tea-pot, as Senator Bird was drawing off his boots, preparatory to inserting his feet in a pair of new handsome slippers [. . .] . (141)

The description, with its warm and inviting tone, contains all of the elements of a home as described in the essay "What is a Home?": love, rest, permanency, and liberty. In fact, the Senator dwells on having "a little comfort at home" (141) and "some of our good home living" (142). These reminders of the comforts of home contrast with the deliberations at the "*house* of the state" (142, italics added) over the Fugitive Slave Law, which Senator Bird supports. His position prompts Mrs. Bird to chastise him and pity the "Poor homeless, houseless creatures" (144) affected by the law. In this chapter, Stowe initially presents the luxuries of a real home, then discloses the "homeless, houseless" condition of slaves, particularly under the Fugitive Slave Law. This shift exposes the hypocrisy of legislators who supported the law, and increases the reader's empathy for slaves.

Stowe also engages the reader's sympathy in her depiction of the Quaker settlement. Like several other chapters, Chapter XIII opens with a detailed description of a home. Stowe provides an example of a true home which meets all of the elements described in her *House and Home Papers*. The example of the Quaker home resonates throughout the novel as slaves endure inadequate or even dangerous homes. The Legree plantation, for example, will contrast sharply with the opening description of the Quaker home:

> A large, roomy, neatly-painted kitchen, its yellow floor glossy and smooth, and without a particle of dust; a neat, well-blacked cooking-stove; rows of shining tin, suggestive of unmentionable good things to the appetite; glossy green wood chairs, old and firm; a small flag-bottomed rocking-chair, with a patch-work cushion in it, neatly contrived out of small pieces of different colored woolen goods, and a larger sized one, motherly and old, whose wide arms breathed hospitable invitation, seconded by the solicitation of its feather cushions,–a real comfortable, persuasive old chair, and worth, in the way of honest, homely enjoyment, a dozen of your plush or brochetelle drawing-room gentry [. . .] . (214)

The Quaker home is comfortable and livable, unlike the presumably ostentatious homes of the upper classes (as symbolized by their chairs). Here, Stowe reveals that a house need not be fancy to be a true home. The character of the inhabitants also parallels the positive depiction of their home. Following the Quaker tradition of resistance to slavery, Rachel Halliday and her family show compassion for Eliza and George and assist them as much as possible. As is the case throughout the novel, the condition of the home reflects the character of those living inside.

The Quaker settlement receives the most attention from critics as an example or model of the ideal home. Several critics have singled out the Quaker home, managed efficiently by Rachel Halliday, as the realization of the vision of a new matriarchy. According to Tompkins:

> In this vision, described in the chapter entitled "The Quaker Settlement," Christian love fulfills itself not in war, but in daily living, and the principle of sacrifice is revealed not in crucifixion, but in motherhood. [. . .] The home is the center of all meaningful activity. (141)

Similarly, Elizabeth Ammons characterizes the community as "a hint of the ideal" (155). Gillian Brown goes even further: "The spirit of mother-love creates a domesticity in the image of paradise: a world before separations, a domestic economy before markets" (25). I agree that the Quaker settlement reveals the importance of homes: the chapter begins with the warm description of the home and its inhabitants, and George remarks that "this indeed was a home" (224).

Drawing on Myra Jehlen's comments, however, I see Stowe's primary goal as different from the one suggested by Tompkins, Ammons, and Brown. Jehlen argues that, ultimately, Stowe does not subvert the patriarchal system in favor of a "new matriarchy":

> There is no ambiguity here and no regret: what Rachel Halliday blesses is the restoration of patriarchal power to the slave whose manhood is inextricably a matter of self-possession and of the possession of others, of *his* wife and child. (391–392)

While critics dispute the role of the Quaker settlement as a symbol or model of the ideal maternal home, I believe it advances the stated goal of the novel: the elimination of slavery. The Quaker settlement represents a desirable, perhaps ideal home–but not for slaves. George and Eliza cannot live there, as all of the characters recognize. The Quaker home is a model for the new matriarchy only if one ignores the subject position of slaves. Its greater purpose is to reveal what a true home could be like. Stowe informs the reader that such an arrangement is impossible for slaves in antebellum America.

If the Quaker settlement is an ideal home, the Legree plantation is an "antihome."[6] Stowe describes the condition of the house, inside and outside, in great detail:

> The place had that ragged, forlorn appearance, which is always produced by the evidence that the care of the former owner has been left to go to utter decay. [. . .] The house had been large and handsome. [. . .] But the place looked desolate and uncomfortable; some windows stopped up with boards, some with shattered panes, and shutters hanging by a single hinge,–all telling of coarse neglect and discomfort. (491, 492)

Once again, critical attention turns toward the relationship of the Legree plantation to the domestic economy. William R. Taylor describes the plantation as "'an evocative vision of the home become factory'" (qtd. in Hovet 514). Indeed, this structure, though marginally permanent, cannot be a home since it completely opposes the values of love, rest, and liberty. Legree, "the megamachine" according to Hovet (515), manages an economic site, rather than a home. Karen Halttunen, in "Gothic Imagination and Social Reform: The Haunted Houses of Lyman Beecher, Henry Ward Beecher, and Harriet Beecher Stowe," reaches a similar conclusion:

> This house is not a home, because Legree has violated the central tenet of the cult of domesticity: the separation of the home from the market. His house, in fact, does not even appear to have a kitchen, a significant

> omission in a novel that consistently treats kitchens as the key to domestic polity [. . .] . (121)

Gillian Brown also observes the lack of a kitchen in equating the evils of Legree's house with a rejection of the domestic economy. No kitchen: no mother: no home. Regardless of the commentary on economics, Legree clearly violates the moral imperatives associated with managing a house. In this chapter, Stowe creates empathy for slaves by describing the horrors of the Legree plantation; and she simultaneously comments on Legree's moral character as represented by his house. The disrepair reflects his immorality and lack of concern for other human beings. Stowe establishes the moral significance of homes as a result. Just as the Quaker home represents the positive morals of Rachel Halliday's family, Legree's plantation reveals his lack of morals.

Stowe also associates housekeeping with moral character in the St. Clare/Sinclare homes. Ophelia's orderliness can be traced to her immaculate home in Vermont. However, the description of the home suggests that she too will be rigid and meticulous:

> Nothing lost, or out of order; not a picket loose in the fence, not a particle of litter in the turfy yard, with its clumps of lilac bushes growing up under the windows. Within, [. . .] wide, clean rooms, where nothing ever seems to be doing or going to be done, where everything is once and forever rigidly in place, and where all household arrangements move with the punctual exactness of the old clock in the corner. (244)

The house, like Ophelia, is rigid, orderly, and lifeless. It can be seen in contrast to the less tidy but more liveable Quaker home. Ophelia also expects other people to share her sense of order and purpose: "People who did nothing, or who did not know exactly what they were going to do, or who did not take the most direct way to accomplish what they set their hands to, were objects of her entire contempt" (247). Such contempt figures prominently in her relationship with Maria St. Clare, but her sense of decorum also restricts her from voicing her opinions. As Amy Schrager Lang reveals:

> The voluptuous clutter of Augustine's New Orleans home stands in stark contrast to the "clean-swept yard" and the "wide, clean rooms" of the Vermont farmhouse which produced Ophelia. As is always the case in *Uncle Tom's Cabin*, however, the difference in the St. Clare and Sinclare households is mirrored in the moral qualities of the occupants. (44–45)

Ophelia, "a stickler for cleanliness and order," is consumed by a desire for efficiency. She demonstrates the "limitations of conscience [. . .] unsupported by feeling" (Lang 45). She cannot see slaves as fully human and deserving of sympathy because she cannot think independently. Instead, she relies on what she ought to think: "Miss Ophelia was the absolute bond-slave of the '*ought*'" (248). Her house ought to be orderly, and she ought not question slavery.

Conversely, Augustine St. Clare, who sympathizes with his slaves, fails to act on his feelings until it is too late. His lavish, decadent home reflects his attitude and behavior. He is "gay, easy, unpunctual, unpractical, sceptical [sic]" (248). Likewise, his home is "luxurious and romantic" (253). While Ophelia does not speak out against slavery because that would not be proper conduct, Augustine is not sufficiently motivated to act because of his lax attitude. He plans to free his slaves, but he is killed before he is able to. His unpunctual and unpractical disposition ultimately allows Maria St. Clare to sell Tom to Legree. Consequently, Stowe uses homes to reflect the moral character of Ophelia and Augustine in complementary ways. Ophelia, overly concerned with order and appearance as represented by her (northern) home, does nothing to oppose slavery; Augustine, enjoying the comforts of his lavish (southern) home, fails to act despite his good intentions.

Houses in *Uncle Tom's Cabin*, therefore, play a variety of roles: as ideal homes (the Birds' home and the Quaker settlement); as "antihome" (Legree's plantation); as indicators of the moral character of the inhabitants (Ophelia's Vermont home and Augustine St. Clare's New Orleans mansion); and as temporary substitutes for a real home (the cabin and the Shelby estate). However, none of these structures fulfills the elements of a true home as outlined by Stowe. In each case, directly or indirectly, Stowe reveals the importance of homes and/or the impossibility of slaves having homes. For Stowe, homes are not merely places to live; nor are they economic sites, as many critics contend. Instead, Stowe infuses homes with moral and religious significance. This rhetorical strategy creates empathy with slaves in the readers and encourages a corresponding resistance to slavery.

HOMELESSNESS IN *UNCLE TOM'S CABIN*

The struggles of four specific characters further establish this rhetorical strategy. First, Cassy explicitly reveals the slave's dilemma: "There's no beast or bird but can find a home somewhere; even the snakes and the alligators have their places to lie down and be quiet; but there's no place for us" (562–563). Cassy cannot live in her own house. Instead, she must become a ghost–she must die in a sense–to inhabit Legree's house. She reunites with Eliza and George in Canada and they eventually "return" to Africa, but she remains homeless in America. Her struggle to find a home heightens our empathy for slaves as we witness her struggle to find a real home.

Likewise, George and Eliza Harris are constantly displaced from substitute homes. Eliza dreamed of a country and "a house which kind voices told her was a home" (222). George realizes that the Quaker settlement "indeed was a home–*home*–a word that George had never yet known a meaning for" (224). Their lack of familiarity with homes increases empathy by getting readers to realize how we take homes for granted.

George and Eliza remain homeless even after they escape: "these two had not one acre of ground,–not a roof that they could call their own,–they had spent all, to the last dollar" (550). They find a "small, neat tenement" outside Montreal, but ultimately decide to move to Africa.[7]

Like Cassy, and George and Eliza, Tom does not find a home in America. Instead he goes "home" to heaven. Stowe unites home with heaven throughout the novel, particularly in the hymns that Tom sings: "Bright angels should convey me home / to the new Jerusalem" (381); "Jerusalem, my happy home" (489); "May I but safely reach my home / My God, my heaven, my All" (557); "The year of Jubilee is come,– / Return, ye ransomed sinners, home" (617). Tom, Eva, and St. Clare all describe the new home they are going to as they approach death: heaven. In fact, whereas Ann Douglas and Karen Halttunen assume that Tom moves progressively further away from his "home" in Kentucky, toward the "hell" of Legree's plantation, the references to homes actually increase toward the end of the novel and reveal that Tom's true home is heaven.

As a writer who sought an end to slavery, Stowe used homelessness as a rhetorical strategy to create empathy and achieve that goal. However, she did not advocate integration of the races, as revealed in the quote from the "Concluding Remarks." Stowe believed that African-Americans should return to their homeland. But by demonstrating that Cassy, Eliza, George, and Tom remain homeless in the United States, she also increases our pity and empathy for slaves, and awakens a corresponding desire to eliminate slavery. The yoking of religion and homes in *Uncle Tom's Cabin* and *House and Home Papers* attests to Stowe's religious dedication and reverence for homes. If her readers share this reverence for homes, they will resist slavery for the sake of the "homeless" slaves.

HOMELESSNESS, SENTIMENTALISM, AND CULTURAL WORK

All of the preceding assumes that Stowe's contemporaries thought of slaves, and blacks in general, as *human* and therefore deserving of empathy and sympathy. In this chapter I have indicated that Stowe used homelessness to end slavery because she viewed it as a sin against human beings. Up to this point I have attempted to show how slavery violated love, rest, permanence, and liberty for slaves' "homes," and therefore could be considered a sin. Acknowledging this point required readers to see slaves as people and not as (inhuman) property. I am not the first person to suggest that slaves were not seen as fully human, nor was Stowe alone in attempting to "personalize" the plight of black slaves in America. But Stowe's rhetorical choices worked successfully to persuade many of her readers. In *Uncle Tom's Cabin*, Stowe chose to "show" how slaves lived and suffered, rather than "tell" readers that slaves deserved better treatment or equal rights. Her use of narrative had more impact, arguably, than most essays and treatises. Unlike numerous pro and con essays about slavery which used the Declaration of Independence to claim that slaves did or did not have certain inalienable "rights," *Uncle Tom's Cabin* portrayed slaves as human beings, as active agents rather than passive victims.[8] In the remainder of this chapter I assess the cultural work of *Uncle Tom's Cabin* in America. I argue that, unlike some criticism, the novel recognizes the subject position of slaves first and foremost, and for this reason, its cultural work was largely productive.

In his essay "Human Rights, Rationality, and Sentimentality," Richard Rorty notes that

> Since the days when the term "human being" was synonymous with "member of our tribe," we have always thought of human beings in terms of *paradigm* members of the species. We have contrasted *us*, the *real* humans, with rudimentary or perverted or deformed examples of humanity. (179)

Rorty opens this essay by noting how Serbs in Bosnia do not see Muslims as human, and therefore they "do not think of themselves as violating human rights" when they rape, torture, or kill Muslims (167). The problem with appeals to Serbs or slave owners to consider the rights of Muslims or slaves is that the latter groups are not seen as human in the first place. Why, then, would they be afforded equal rights?

Slaves, and blacks in general, were often cast as inhuman: as property, as animals, or, at best, as children in need of protection and guidance–the rhetoric of infantilization was a frequent tactic in the pro slavery arsenal. To take just one example, Thomas Jefferson compares blacks to animals in his *Notes on Virginia*, noting that "their existence appears to participate more of sensation than reflection. To this must be ascribed their disposition to sleep when abstracted from their diversions, and unemployed in labor. An animal whose body is at rest, and who does not reflect must be disposed to sleep of course" (182). Although this appears several decades before Stowe wrote *Uncle Tom's Cabin*, similar comparisons can be seen throughout the nineteenth century. Many Americans were reluctant to recognize blacks as "fully human" at this time. As Beatrice A. Anderson explains,

> In reading *Uncle Tom's Cabin* today, when reasonable people condemn prejudice in any form, we tend to forget that the entire system of slavery was based on prejudicial thinking and that Stowe was fighting to convince her audience not only that black men and women should be granted freedom but that they were in fact *human beings*. (106)

This strategy—representing black slaves first as human beings—was necessary before any attempt could be made to persuade readers that slaves deserved empathy or sympathy. David Leverenz captures the essence of Stowe's strategy of maternal empathy, which I have been comparing to her use of homelessness in the novel. He says, "At the most obvious rhetorical level, *Uncle Tom's Cabin* insists that what white men do to black people can be changed if men can be brought to feel what any mother feels" (190). Indeed, few people would dispute the centrality of maternal empathy in *Uncle Tom's Cabin*. Rather than preach about the natural rights of slaves, Stowe hoped to hasten the end of slavery by creating empathy in her readers. When the reader imagines the suffering of a mother who has lost her child to slavery he/she should realize that slaves are human beings and deserve to be free.

Jane Tompkins, Elizabeth Ammons, and Gillian Brown argue that Stowe advocates the displacement of the chaotic, masculine marketplace through the substitution of feminine values and a domestic economy. Although maternal empathy is a powerful strategy for Stowe, some critics (Brown, Tompkins) characterize it as her primary objective. This position presents difficulties which will be addressed later. Furthermore, this group of responses neglects the slave as a subject in the novel. Neither the domestic sphere nor the "outside world" is appropriate for slaves in *Uncle Tom's Cabin* since they *belong* to both. They cannot own property, and thus cannot own houses or homes. They *are* property, and thus become commodities in the capitalistic marketplace. George and Eliza "escape" slavery, but return to their "real" home–Africa; Tom, as previously mentioned, goes home only through death.

Two different spheres arise from this critical strategy: a domestic sphere, the site of orderly, feminine, maternal values, represented by the home; and the chaotic, unreliable, masculine arena of the marketplace. Most critical interpretations of *Uncle Tom's Cabin* recognize and accept this division.[9] Critics part company, however, over the role of the home and the extent to which Stowe advocated the dominance of a domestic/maternal economy.[10]

While the "sublime rhetoric of maternal love" (Jay 267) in *Uncle Tom's Cabin* has been widely discussed and accepted, some critics insist that the elimination of slavery is only part of "Stowe's larger goal, the advent of mother-rule" (Brown 37). This hierarchical arrangement presents two problems. First, Stowe's own comments and the history of the novel suggest that, first and foremost, she wanted to end slavery. A letter from her sister-in-law occasioned the writing of the novel with the express goal of "'[making] this whole nation feel what an accursed thing slavery is'" (qtd. in Douglas 8). The "Concluding Remarks" to *Uncle Tom's Cabin* and *A Key to Uncle Tom's Cabin* discuss slavery exclusively and reiterate the same goal. No one would deny that Stowe sought to end slavery, nor that maternal empathy plays a role in that goal, but the means and the ends remain distinct.

The second difficulty arises when discussions of the domestic economy ignore slaves as subjects in the novel. When one asserts the ascendency of the domestic sphere, the slave is relegated to a powerless position. Regardless of whether one privileges the domestic sphere (the "new matriarchy") or the (patriarchal) marketplace, slaves could not participate–as agents or subjects–in either. Stowe reveals that slaves, because they could not have homes, could not benefit from a domestic economy. Whereas mothers can manage the kitchen (and thereby the country), slaves cannot participate in the domestic economy because they are servants and, therefore, implements within that system. Stowe did not advocate complete equality for African-Americans. Nonetheless, critical interpretations may marginalize blacks by disregarding their subject position in the novel. In other words, the cultural work of *Uncle Tom's Cabin* may be more productive than criticism which asserts the prominence of the domestic sphere. The novel, unlike this mode of criticism, presents black slaves as active (albeit submissive) agents; it does not assume that they have a place in the domestic sphere or the public sphere. In fact, Stowe proves that black slaves have no place of their own. Getting her audience to oppose the sin of slavery required Stowe to represent them as human beings. Stowe therefore adheres to Rorty's suggestion that "everything turns on who counts as a fellow human being, as a rational agent in the only relevant sense–the sense in which rational agency is synonymous with membership in *our* moral community" ("Human Rights" 177).

Black slaves did not belong to either the (feminine) domestic sphere or the (masculine) public sphere, as Stowe repeatedly demonstrates. Criticism which asserts the primacy of the former over the latter, regardless of the accuracy of that assertion, ignores this point and accepts the either/or binary (either the domestic sphere *or* the public sphere). Philip Fisher, drawing on Derrida and Freud, remarks that "Our everyday use of *either/or* makes possible an essential technique within logic that depends on the Law of the Excluded Middle" ("Democratic Social Space" 101–102). In the critical discussions of *Uncle Tom's Cabin* to which I am referring, black slaves occupy the Excluded Middle; in the novel, they are human beings and agents. I believe that the novel's cultural work was productive specifically because Stowe acknowledged that black slaves should be treated as constitutive rather than "outside." Ignoring the subject position of slaves unfortunately thwarts this goal. As I suggest throughout this study, the cultural work of criticism can and should be analyzed in addition to the cultural work of primary texts. In this case, some of the commentary on *Uncle Tom's Cabin* may be less productive than the novel because Stowe recognizes the irrelevance of the public/private binary for slaves, while some critics reify it.

For black slaves, the public *is* the private sphere. Like homelessness, slavery is a condition which disrupts the binary. It may be more productive to think of slavery and homelessness as spaces "between" the public and the private. Few texts–primary or secondary–recognize this possibility.

More specifically, the cultural work of *Uncle Tom's Cabin*, as well as sentimental literature generally, is productive because it portrays black slaves as constitutive, as "one of us" rather than as "them."[11] This is also the power of testimonial literature, as I argue in Chapter Five and in the Conclusion.[12] As Fisher remarks, "Sentimentality, by its experimental extension of humanity to prisoners, slaves, or children, exactly reverses the process of slavery itself, which has at its core the withdrawal of human status from a part of society" ("Democratic Social Space" 90).[13] Stowe used homelessness to demonstrate that slavery was a sin against human beings, not an economic inevitability. In the following chapters I attempt to trace how literature has affected efforts to "withdraw human status" from homeless people in America in other periods and contexts.

Chapter Two

"Street Arabs" and the "Tramp Menace"

The Function of Homeless Characters in the Work of Horatio Alger

Like *Uncle Tom's Cabin*, novels by Horatio Alger, Jr. were enormously popular. Although accurate records do not exist, estimated sales of Alger's books between 1870 and 1930 range as high as 400 million copies.[1] While critical and popular attention has risen and fallen in subsequent years, Alger remains one of the most influential (and misunderstood) authors in American history.[2] In her book *The Fictional Republic: Horatio Alger and American Political Discourse*, Carol Nackenoff describes the popularity and familiarity of Horatio Alger in American culture. She states:

> Alger heroes are part of our language of discourse about social mobility and economic opportunity, about determinism, self-reliance, and success. They are symbols for individual initiative, permeability of economic and social hierarchies, opportunities, and honest dealing. "Horatio Alger" is shorthand for someone who has risen through the ranks–the self-made man, against the odds. (3–4)

Traditionally, Alger's popularity has been attributed to his unabashed affirmation of capitalism and the values of the dominant culture, as well as the optimism represented by his characters' fulfillment of the "American dream" in their rise from rags to riches. Recently, however, critics have questioned the narrow view of Alger as a purely didactic, formulaic writer who uncritically advocated *laissez faire* capitalism. The Alger myth and Alger's role within the "Gospel of Wealth" have been examined more closely, raising questions about the history and accuracy of both "facts." Critics have also begun to explore Alger's representations of poverty, tramps, and the industrialized city, in addition to his more formulaic rags-to-riches plots.[3] His treatment of homelessness as a specific theme or trope, however, has not been examined, and provides a valuable means of assessing his popularity and his philosophy.

I have chosen to discuss the work of Horatio Alger because it was so popular and, arguably, so influential. Moreover, Alger has been misunderstood and misrepresented by readers, critics, and commentators until recently, and the effect of this misinformation has produced it own "cultural work" which deserves examination. I argue that Alger simultaneously appealed to the (romantic) sense of freedom and adventure associated with homelessness as well as to the (realist) impulse to discover "the other half"–in this case, street children of New York. As a result, he helped to entrench the division and categorization of the "deserving" and "undeserving" poor. This division has had negative consequences throughout American history for a variety of reasons which will be addressed at the end of the chapter.

This chapter is divided into fours sections. First, I assess the critical responses to Alger, both past and present. More specifically, I trace the public and critical reception of Alger–from popular writer, to forgotten figure, to cultural icon (as represented by references to the "Alger myth"). These shifts, as others have noted, developed with very little reference to the actual texts and as a result of misinformation being spread regarding Alger. Second, I discuss Alger's depictions of homeless boys ("Street Arabs"). Third, I examine the representations of homeless men ("The Tramp Menace"). In both cases I describe how Alger represented these characters: their physical appearance, behavior, and ethics. I also analyze the social/cultural/economic conditions which may have made these characters "familiar" to a contemporary audience. In others words, how did these characters "reflect" Alger's time and culture? And I suggest that Alger "shaped" his culture by choosing to highlight or omit certain traits in these characters. In the final section I speculate on the overall effects of (1) Alger's corpus and (2) the critical commentary and misinformation regarding the "Alger myth." I argue that both elements produced negative results by entrenching the division between the deserving and undeserving poor; that is, their cultural work was detrimental, despite Alger's intentions.

In general, critical commentary about Horatio Alger can be placed in one of three categories: textual, biographical, or cultural.[4] Textual criticism, appearing in publications such as *Newsboy* (the official publication of the Horatio Alger Society) and *Dime Novel Roundup: A Magazine Devoted to the Collecting, Preservation, and Study of Old Time Dime and Nickel Novels*, examines Alger's sources for particular novels, different editions of his works, pseudonyms he used, publication history, and other factual issues related to his work. Alger is perhaps the most frequently mentioned author in discussions of the dime novel, and various editions of his books are often sought by collectors. This interest in Alger indicates how thoroughly entrenched he is in American literary and cultural history.

Biographical and cultural criticism tend to overlap in the case of Alger. Significant work has been done to correct biographical misinformation, and critics have also shown how this misinformation has had an impact on American culture throughout this century. Very little traditional literary criticism has been produced, since the critical consensus holds that Alger was a poor writer and his books relied on simplistic, repetitive plots. Instead, critics have turned to Alger as an icon or symbol of the self-made man in America. This study, as with a good deal of the received critical commentary, focuses on the effect, impact, or significance of Alger in American culture (rather than his literary prowess). I am interested in the ways the "Alger myth" was created and what effect that myth has had on American beliefs related to charity, greed, capitalism, and, specifically, homelessness.

THE ALGER MYTH

Although his books sold millions of copies, his legacy continues primarily as a result of the "Alger myth." The belief that Alger actually lived the rags-to-riches lifestyle described in his books helped to perpetuate this myth, despite the fact that between 1928 and 1985 most biographical information about Alger was inaccurate. Because of a deliberate hoax initiated in 1928 by Herbert R. Mayes, inaccurate biographical information was repeated and disseminated until Gary Scharnhorst (with Jack Bales) published *The Lost Life of Horatio Alger, Jr.* in 1985.[5] Since then, Scharnhorst, Nackenoff, and other critics have revealed how misunderstood Alger and his work have been throughout this century. As Scharnhorst states, "With few facts but a surfeit of *chutzpah*, Mayes depicted Alger as a philandering neuronic obsessed with personal success, and he would fool reviewers, historians, and would-be biographers with the tale for over forty years" (xi). Mayes's book, *Alger: A Biography Without a Hero*, though written as a parody, received generally positive reviews and became the source of biographical information for numerous other sources, most notably the *Dictionary of American Biography* in 1928. Subsequent reference books, biographies, and encyclopedias relied on this misinformation and perpetuated several inaccuracies. Scharnhorst claims that "To this day [1985], entries about Alger in every major reference work, every encyclopedia from the *Britannica* up and down, contain 'facts' first concocted by Mayes which through reiteration have obtained the force and luster of truth" (xii).

Mayes wrote *Alger: A Biography Without a Hero* as "'a take-off on the debunking biographies that were quite popular in the 20's'" (Mayes, qtd. in Scharnhorst x-xi). Calling the book a "fairy tale" and a "spoof," Mayes later admitted to making most of it up, even fabricating portions of a diary Alger supposedly wrote. Although Malcolm Cowley and others suspected that Mayes had produced an inaccurate account, Mayes defended his book until the 1970s. He eventually revealed that the book was a "'complete fabrication, with virtually no scintilla of basis in fact. Any word of truth in it got in unwittingly. I made it up out of nothing. Most of the few facts I uncovered were intentionally distorted'" (qtd. in Scharnhorst xii).

Not only did Mayes fabricate details of Alger's life, he also made generalizations about Alger's plots and characters. By the time Mayes's biography appeared in 1928, Alger was no longer being read or published for the most part. Therefore, Mayes's false claim that "'All of Horatio Alger's heroes started poor and ended up well-to-do'" (qtd. in Scharnhorst xiii) was believable and influential. Recent critics have emphasized and reemphasized that Alger wrote about "rags to respectability"–rather than "rags to riches" as the myth purports.[6] This distinction is important. Alger has been stereotyped like few other authors. To this day, many believe that Alger's "heroes" got rich by looking out only for themselves and dedicating themselves to hard work, frugality, and *laissez faire* capitalism. Lies about Alger and the content of his books, initiated by Mayes and reiterated (intentionally and unintentionally) over the years by other critics, still linger, and the "Alger myth" remains quite viable.[7]

In Chapter One I suggested that the cultural work of criticism should be examined more closely, in addition to the influence of primary texts (as Tompkins argues). Clearly, the "Alger myth" has influenced American culture. In his essay "Horatio Alger, Jr.; or, Adrift in the Myth of Rags to Riches," Richard Bowerman traces the evolution of this myth in America. Bowerman shows how the biographical misinformation about Alger influenced the belief that his texts portrayed characters who were, likewise, obsessed with success. By relying on false information and only a cursory examination of Alger's own texts, critics helped to create the Alger myth which in turn served to justify values of the dominant class. In the case of Horatio Alger, then, the cultural work of critical commentary has been, arguably, detrimental.

Bowerman reveals that part of the problem can be traced to poor scholarship:

> Critics have shared a tendency to generalize, to state hypotheses without adequate tests–the general procedure has been to state that Alger wrote one story one hundred plus times and thus it is only necessary to examine a few of them. (106)

Alger certainly relied on similar plots, stock characters, and formulaic episodes. In many stories, a poor boy–frequently an orphan who has been separated from legitimate wealth by a dishonest adult–obtains basic employment, then performs an act of heroism which results in a wealthy benefactor taking notice and rewarding the boy with housing, clothes, an education, and a better job. The boy is honest, frugal, hard-working, and circumspect. There is inevitably a happy ending: The hero works his way up to a respectable position and receives his rightful inheritance.

Because several books involve rich benefactors who provide for the hero, critics have argued that Alger glossed over or ignored genuine barriers to success in America. Critics suggest that Alger's heroes do not *earn* the fortunes they receive; they are simply in the right place at the right time. For example, the title character in *Ragged Dick or Street Life in New York* saves a rich man's son from drowning and the man hires Dick as a clerk. The *deus ex machina* element is criticized for being stylistically simplistic and for perpetuating the notion that anyone can succeed in America. The truly poor, the truly destitute–immigrants who spoke little English, poor women with children, the disabled–could not expect to earn a decent living nor would they receive anything from a rich benefactor. Critics have taken Alger to task for creating unrealistic expectations in his audience and ignoring the reality of poverty in America.

In fact, Alger has been and still is identified as one of the primary proponents of the "Gospel of Wealth." Nackenoff argues that

> The *prevailing* image of Alger's stories is that they celebrate the rise of capitalism and the proliferation of economic opportunities and riches. Typical is the claim that "Horatio Alger can be held largely responsible for instilling into American boys of a former generation purely materialistic ideals." (5–6)

Nackenoff quotes Ellen Wilson, who (in 1956), like many others, became a victim of Mayes's hoax and the repetition of several inaccuracies. Similarly, in the 1983 article "Vision of Poverty and the Poor in the Novels of Horatio Alger," Yves Lemeunier contends that Alger's success is due "to his uncanny ability to reflect all the components of American conservative social thinking: the various brands of Calvinism, the gospel of work, the gospel of wealth, social Darwinism, even social pragmatism" (121). Lemeunier further states that "the sole theme" of Alger's works is "social promotion or vertical mobility" (121). Like earlier critics, Lemeunier constructs an argument which is built on misunderstandings of Alger, and on selective references to a limited number of texts–in this case, seven novels. Although social mobility plays a role in Alger's work, his affinity for social Darwinism and his contribution to the gospel of wealth have been exaggerated by critics like Lemeunier who have depended on inaccurate information and perpetuated the Alger myth.[8]

Some of Alger's heroes do become wealthy, but the majority establish themselves in fairly middle-class occupations. Several stories conclude with mention of the hero's desire to marry and settle down in a good home. Few heroes wind up in what would be considered the "upper class." More importantly, Alger's texts repeatedly reveal his distaste for greed, selfishness, and class consciousness. While the "Alger myth" means different things to different people, the general belief that he attempted to whitewash socio-economic barriers to success erodes when one examines the texts themselves.

In one of his earliest publications, Alger challenges the very myth that he is supposed to have created. *Nothing to do: a tilt at our best society*, published in 1857, laid out (in 45 brief pages of verse) many of the values Alger would reiterate in his later books. In the poem, Alger does mention his belief in social mobility ("'Tis refreshing to know that without pedigree / A man may still climb to the top of the tree" [7–8]). Until recently, critics asserted that this theme dominates Alger's work. However, Alger promotes compassion for and solidarity with the less fortunate. He questions class divisions and class consciousness, and he admonishes those who "are content to be drones, / And stand idly by while your fellows bear stones" (42). Nearly all of his later books reinforce this theme. Though the poetry lacks sophistication, the message is clear:

> So changes the world, and the men that are in it,
> That those whom we hail as our equals, one minute,
> We pass by the next with a very cold stare,
> And gruffly inquire who the dickens they are. (13)

Since the poem chastises those who take wealth for granted and ignore the poor around them, it clearly undermines the myth that Alger helped legitimize the latent selfishness of *laissez faire* capitalism.

Characters in several books reinforce Alger's belief in charity and compassion. First, he depicts the rich benefactors positively. They manage their wealth wisely, demonstrate compassion and kindness, and receive admiration from other characters. In *Tony, the Hero*, Tony–the hero–prevents George Spencer from being robbed. Spencer, in turn, puts Tony up in a hotel, buys him new clothes, and provides him with a tutor for his education. Tony eventually discovers that he is heir to an estate worth $2000 per month, but Spencer's charity helps Tony succeed and prosper. Similarly, Henry Jennings meets Carl Crawford after a tramp chases Carl in order to steal his money in *Driven from Home or Carl Crawford's Experience*. Jennings takes Carl home, instructs his housekeeper to care for him, and gives Carl a job in his furniture factory. Carl works his way up to a management position at the factory and eventually becomes Jennings's heir. In

Jed, the Poorhouse Boy, Schuyler Roper, "a generous, open-hearted young man, liberal to a fault, and ready to do anything for one he takes to" (*Struggling Upward* 526), epitomizes the rich benefactor. He is a "favorite in society" (526) and provides everything for Jed. In cases like these, Alger portrays generosity and altruism favorably. The characters are admired and respected by others. They are not greedy, self-centered, or materialistic. Despite the Alger myth of individual success, he consistently creates characters who are not self-centered, but charitable. Critics seem to have overlooked characters such as these in order to emphasize Alger's supposed reliance on heros who were only interested in gaining wealth.

Conversely, Alger portrays wealthy but greedy characters in a negative light. The accumulation of wealth does not equate with success, respect, or approval, although it is commonly thought to be the guiding principle of Alger's works. Several dishonest characters are well-off, such as Squire Dixon in *Jed*. Squire Dixon is paid by the city to manage the poorhouses, but he takes kickbacks from the managers he hires, who, in turn, provide only the barest necessities to the poor in order to maximize their own profits. Likewise, Squire Davenport tries to foreclose on the home of Ben Barclay and his mother in *The Store Boy or The Fortunes of Ben Barclay* in order to keep $1000 that Ben's father had given to Davenport to invest. Alger acknowledges that the wealthy are not always honest: "Squire Davenport was a throughly respectable man in the estimation of the community. That such a man was capable of defrauding a poor widow, counting on her ignorance, would have plunged all his friends and acquaintances into the profoundest amazement" (*Strive and Succeed* 30). Although the Alger myth suggests that his characters achieve wealth at all costs, he actually criticizes the rich for being dishonest, greedy, or miserly.

Books such as *Tony, the Hero* and *Charlie Codman's Cruise: A Story for Boys* contain stereotypical miser characters. These characters hoard their wealth, live miserable lives, and appear physically repulsive or lifeless. Avarice even causes premature aging:

> Old Peter Manson was not more than fifty-five, but he looked from fifteen to twenty years older. If his body had been properly cared for, it would have been different; but, one by one, its functions had been blunted and destroyed, and it had become old and out of repair. (*Charlie* 7–8)

Alger shows his audience that excessive concern for wealth leads to one's destruction. The misers are weak, sickly, and lethargic. They neglect their clothes and their homes, and even fail to eat properly, since they worry about spending too much money for food. Their clothes are old, tattered, and insufficiently warm; their homes are dirty, messy, and unheated. Alger displays the inhumanity of characters whose excessive concern for acquiring and hoarding money causes them to suffer miserably. Their greed even blinds them to their wretched condition. In all of these cases, Alger suggests that wealth does not ensure success, happiness, or respectability. The Alger myth of individual success tends to contradict the many texts in which Alger criticized irresponsible wealth.

Furthermore, Alger's boy-heroes resolve to use their money constructively. In *Slow and Sure; Or, From the Street to the Shop*, Paul, "a smart, enterprising boy" (9), becomes a street merchant, selling odds and ends in the city. His mother and brother discuss his talent for business and conclude that he will become rich one day. His mother remarks, "I hope he will, for I think he will make a good use of his money" (9). She implies that he will not waste his money, but also that he will be benevolent and generous. Similarly, at the conclusion of *Adrift in the City*, Oliver Conrad, separated from his mother and her wealth by a dishonest stepfather, is reunited with her and resolves to share his wealth with others: "Oliver has decided to become a lawyer. If he carries out his purpose, he will always be ready to champion the cause of the poor and the oppressed" (284). This statement indicates Alger's outlook on charity. He favored and encouraged compassion, despite critical comments and assertions to the contrary.

If Alger's books promote compassion and generosity, and condemn greed and selfishness, how and why did the notion develop that his books instilled individualism and unquestioning allegiance to capitalism? According to Bowerman, three factors contributed to the belief that Alger promoted *laissez faire* capitalism: the rise of the novel, Mayes's false biography, and "historians' need for a popular spokesman of Social Darwinism" at the time (83). Bowerman explains how Alger was "rewritten" to promote a particular agenda and how his name became synonymous with the American Dream of success. First, the novel form was attacked for undermining the morals of children of the time. As a result, Alger kept his novels morally proper in order to be published and accepted. Critics later tended to blur his morality–no swearing, no drinking, no gambling–with a conservative economic view. Second, the Mayes biography fed the belief that Alger–like his heroes–was driven to succeed and that his novels all had this same theme. Third, critics used Alger to symbolize the selfishness of the Gilded Age. Thus, the Alger myth purports that he aligned himself with Spencer and Darwin by promoting individualism and economic mobility. For Spencer and Darwin, selfish motives were desirable because they represent the laws of nature. Despite Alger's altruistic characters, critics asserted that Alger also affirmed the positive value of selfishness.[9]

Bowerman reveals that this belief arose during the Depression, when the Gilded Age became a target for social critics and historians. He states that the "Gilded Age was represented as an age of crass materialism, an age when the American culture tended toward the vulgar and ostentatious" (105). Historians blamed Alger for epitomizing and encouraging this reprehensible behavior. According to Bowerman,

> Without having seriously studied his works by reason of his role as a purveyor of popular literary trash, the historians, bitter about the failure of progressivism and the depression, and concerned with the future of democracy in an increasingly totalitarian world, attacked Alger's ideas in his books, which they in reality had not read. (106)

While Bowerman seems to generalize about historians and their ability to perform adequate scholarship, three observations made by Scharnhorst support his argument. First, commentators did not address the "rags-to-riches" element in Alger's work until well after his death. Social mobility and vulgar materialism did not register as criticisms for Alger's contemporaries.[10] Second, Alger's popularity plummeted after 1920, which supports Bowerman's claim that later historians did not read Alger when they accused him of promoting social Darwinism. Since his books were no longer published, their availability to readers after the 1920s is questionable. Third, publishers' reprints of Alger's novels emphasized the "rags-to-riches" plots and de-emphasized Alger's pro-charity stance. Scharnhorst states, "Alger's work was editorially reinvented to appeal to a new generation of readers" (151). According to Scharnhorst,

> Cheap editions of Alger's novels were issued by approximately forty publishers between his death in 1899 and 1920. However, many of the earliest novels which conclude as the hero grasps the bottom rung on the ladder of respectability were rarely reprinted, and others were silently abridged, often by deleting as many as seven of the original chapters in which the hero performs virtuous deeds for which he is later rewarded. (151)

Such rewriting "garbled the moral message of the original versions" (151). In these reprints and in the Alger myth, the accumulation of wealth and the compulsion for upward mobility eclipse his attempt to promote charity and compassion.

For a variety of specific reasons, then, Alger became associated with materialism, individualism, unencumbered capitalism, the American Dream of success, and the myth of the self-made man. The Alger Awards recognize the achievements of those who have experienced social/financial success each year, and one often hears of a person being referred to as a Horatio Alger story. Many people still believe that his books depicted characters who enjoyed a passage from rags to riches. While most of his heroes wind up financially secure, they do not become "rich." They do not join the ranks of the upper or the privileged classes. However, the cultural work of the Alger myth cannot be disputed. Alger serves as notice that barriers to success in America simply do not exist for those with enough determination and dedication. Despite the inaccuracy of their claims, critics of the Gilded Age seized on a distinctive, durable, and malleable cultural figure to highlight the flaws in *laissez faire* capitalism.

Nackenoff instructively reminds us that we should not attempt to define Alger as either for or against capitalism, as many critics have attempted to do. She states,

> Locating Alger amid the tensions and anxieties produced by the rapid industrialization of America, we see that the narrative is neither simply pro- nor anticapitalist. Alger was a creature *of* the emergence of nineteenth century American capitalism. He could not possibly stand outside it. (266)

This seems to be appropriate advice for critics who rewrote Alger to conform to their own agenda. It also offers a meaningful way to view and analyze Alger in the context of late nineteenth century American history and culture. Alger reflects many of the shifts of this period and as a result may be more valuable as a prism through which one might view the ideological conflicts of his time, rather than as a spokesman of his time. Whereas the Alger myth contributed to the false belief that everyone in America has an equal chance for success (particular after the 1930s), his texts reveal inconsistencies and uncertainties about social and economic issues, such as charity, work, the home, and homelessness.

The reception of his texts further reveals that America did not have a single, unified vison of these contested values. Several libraries also banned Alger's books between the 1870s and 1920s, despite their popularity, which proves that Americans were conflicted over his apparent message, theme, or purpose. Ministers, parents, and the press railed against "sensationalism" in dime novels by Alger and others at the time. These groups influenced librarians with the argument that dime novels would negatively influence young, impressionable readers. The *Boston Herald*, for example, suggested that boys who were looking for "'fighting, killing, and thrilling adventures'" would "'go for 'Oliver Optic' and Horatio Alger's books'" (qtd. in Scharnhorst 118). Alger remained quite popular until about 1920, but this effort to ban his work certainly contributed to his obscurity shortly thereafter. Therefore, Alger's transformation–from popular author, to forgotten figure, to cultural icon–says less about the quality of his writing or his inherent message than it does about the historical periods that ushered in those shifts.

More specifically, the responses to Alger reflect the contemporary conflicts over social and ideological issues such as poverty and homelessness. On the one hand, contemporary audiences wanted to learn more about what was happening in the slums. They were interested in "how the other half lives." On the other hand, literary and moral expectations still deterred authors from describing the truly destitute. As explained in the Introduction, various "scientific" charity organizations and religious leaders convinced many Americans that homelessness was a sin or a fault of moral character. A marginal author would not want to risk alienating readers or publishers with potentially offensive material. In this context, Alger combined romantic and realist elements in his depictions of homeless characters.

"STREET ARABS"

Numerous theories have been developed which account for Alger's popularity around the turn of the century. As explained above, many commentators (falsely) asserted that Alger's moral and economic conservativism ensured his success because he embraced the values of the dominant culture. Others argue the opposite: that Alger subverted or parodied the dominant culture and that his audience wittingly or unwittingly consumed Alger's texts for their subversiveness.[11] Another popular interpretation holds that Alger represented an older, outdated social order during a period of cultural transformation, and that this nostalgia for an earlier, more idealistic time appealed to many readers.[12] Many critics find the question of his popularity particularly baffling because he is regarded as such an unquestionably bad writer.[13] Conversely, Bowerman argues that the qualities used to indict Alger's writing skills did indeed appeal to the young boys who were his primary audience.

Jane Tompkins seems to agree with Bowerman. She argues that being subversive, unique, or out-of-step does not lead to popularity. Rather,

> The text that becomes exceptional in the sense of reaching an exceptionally large audience does so not because of its departure from the ordinary and conventional, but through its embrace of what is most widely shared. (Tompkins xvi)

As Tompkins argues, the popularity of a literary work is determined by the qualities it shares with its audience, rather than how different or unique it is. Alger's popularity is at least partially a result of his integration of competing but "ordinary and conventional" ideologies. Social, economic, and literary shifts in the late nineteenth century allowed Alger to combine romantic and realist elements in his work in a way which appealed to contemporary readers and publishers.

As the American economy became more industrial and less agrarian, and more people began to concentrate in larger cities, attitudes about work and the home also shifted. Economic depressions throughout the latter half of the nineteenth century also made poverty and homelessness more visible, particularly in large cities like New York. The importance of charity and the role of charitable organizations became more complicated as cities now became responsible for an increasing number of "foreigners"–both immigrants and people from rural areas looking for work in the city. As the poor and homeless became more visible (or less easily hidden), sociologists, journalists, and novelists examined the living conditions, lifestyles, and "character" of the poor in more detail. This interest manifested itself in numerous accounts of the poor as a separate class, such as "the submerged tenth," the "dangerous classes," and "the other half." These accounts helped to perpetuate the historical division of "us" and "them." Differences between the classes were emphasized, intentionally and unintentionally, as the poor became a separate class to study, categorize, or pity.

Alger seized on the popularity or familiarity of this trend in his depictions of homeless boys in New York, popularly called "street Arabs": poor children who sometimes worked as bootblacks, newsboys, baggage carriers, etc., and lived in tenements, lodging houses, or on the street. Although Alger demonstrated sincere compassion and concern for these boys, it is likely that the contemporary discourse encouraged him to develop plots which included street youths. Titles of several books indicate his awareness of this subject: *Ragged Dick; or, Street Life in New York With the Bootblacks* (1868); *Tattered Tom; or, The Story of a Street Arab* (1871); *Julius; or, The Street Boy out West* (1874); *Jed, the Poorhouse Boy* (1899).

Several sources raised awareness of the Street Arab subculture and the presence of homeless boys in New York at the time. *Street Arabs and Gutter Snipes: The Pathetic and Humorous Side of Young Vagabond Life in the Great Cities, with Records of Work for Their Reclamation* by George C. Needham appeared in 1887. This work warned readers to be wary of street children who may attempt to pickpocket or deceive a tourist or unsuspecting adult. Another source which Alger was definitely aware of was *The Dangerous Classes of New York, and Twenty Years' Work Among Them* by Charles Loring Brace, published in 1872. Like Needham, Brace warns readers of the dangers of the city, including the threat from children, but he also suggests that homeless children be removed from their harsh and damaging urban environment. Brace founded the Children's Aid Society and helped establish the Newsboys' Lodging House in 1853 and 1854, respectively, to provide for homeless children. Relocating children to the country, placing them in caring families, and instilling religious values offsets the negative effects of a large city like New York, such as crime, poverty, prostitution, and overcrowding, according to Brace.

In the Preface to *Julius or The Street Boy Out West*, Alger acknowledges Brace's book by name and recommends it to his readers: "I take pleasure in recommending it to all who feel an interest in street life and its representatives, as equally instructive and entertaining" (*Strive and Succeed*). Alger frequently mentions his desire to instruct or inform wider society about the existence of homeless children, their poor living conditions, and the jobs they performed for minimal pay. For example, in *The Young Outlaw; or, Adrift in the Streets*, he says, "The writer is glad to believe that [his stories] have done something to draw attention to a neglected class of children, whom it is important to elevate and redeem" (viii). Similarly, he attacks the padrone system in *Phil, the Fiddler; Or, The Young Street Musician*. Alger seeks to alert his audience to the plight of young Italian street musicians who worked long hours for little pay and who were frequently abused by their padrones. He exclaims,

> If the story of "Phil, the Fiddler," in revealing for the first time to the American public the hardships and ill-treatment of these wandering musicians, shall excite an active sympathy in their behalf, the author will feel abundantly repaid for his labors. (*Struggling Upward* 282).

In this way, Alger paralleled contemporary efforts in sociology and journalism to make known the harsh conditions in the slums, the existence of homeless children, and the widening gap between the rich and the poor.[14]

Alger sought to represent his young homeless characters accurately. In order to do so he gathered information for his stories on the streets of New York. Beginning in 1866, Alger took an active interest in observing and befriending the "street Arabs." He frequently visited the Newsboys' Lodging House, the YMCA, and other lodging houses where they could be found, sometimes giving them money or candy to ingratiate himself. Alger later began to invite these children to his own room in a boarding house, and street children eventually congregated there. His sister remarked that "'Nothing delighted him more than to get a lot of boys between the ages of 12 and 16 years in the room with him, and while they were cutting up and playing about he would sit down and write letters or a paragraph of a story'" (qtd. in Scharnhorst 77). These boys' stories formed the basis of Alger's own books about the "street Arabs" and he actively observed them in order to add realistic details about their lives.

A certain level of realism was important to Alger. Describing Sam Barker in *The Young Outlaw; or, Adrift in the Streets*, Alger writes, "He looked like a *genuine* representative of the 'street Arab,' with no thought for to-morrow and its needs, and contented if he could only make sure of a square meal to-day" (9–10, italics added). Following the lead of journalists and sociologists, Alger attempted to add realism by referring to actual buildings and streets in New York, mimicking the speech of the street Arabs, and showing them without adequate clothes and food or a permanent home. In fact, Alger quoted from an early review in the *New York Evening Post* of *Ragged Dick* in an autobiographical sketch which ostensibly established his credibility on the subject. The review said that his "'sketches of the little Arabs of our streets are very life-like and effective'" (qtd. in Scharnhorst 88). As I hope to show, and as subsequent reviewers intimate, the accuracy of this assessment is doubtful.[15]

Despite realist elements, Alger's books also romanticized the life of street children. First, Alger's heroes behaved very morally. They did not smoke, drink, or gamble; nor did Alger depict any sexual or violent behavior. His heroes did not back down from a fight, but a fight was usually prevented when the hero displayed physical superiority or confidence and his opponent backed down. Similarly, his boys are attracted to and attractive to girls, but innocently and infrequently. Ben Barclay in *The Store Boy* is "too young to be a lover" (*Strive and Succeed* 79). This accurately summarizes the status of romantic relationships in Alger's works.

While his intentions are good, Alger's optimistic and flattering descriptions of homeless boys undermine his realism. All of his boy-heroes are good looking, for example. In *The Young Outlaw*, Sam Barker's "features were not unpleasing, and, had he been clean and neatly dressed, he would undoubtedly have been considered good-looking" (10). Alger strains to reconcile the optimism for his heroes with the supposedly dreadful conditions they endure. In *Slow and Sure; Or, from the Street to the Shop*, we meet Julius: "His clothes were soiled and ragged, but his face was clean. Water was cheap, and he was unfashionably neat for the quarter in which he lived" (80). Here, Alger seems to be aware of his dilemma. He wants to represent the street Arabs realistically, but not too realistically as to be depressing or tragic. Indeed, (in addition to their good looks) his heroes exhibit the qualities of those found in romantic literature: they are solitary protagonists who endure difficult adventures and who experience success or victory in the end.

Alger includes several romantic elements in these works dealing with homeless boys. First, the experience of degradation and poverty becomes a positive value. Enduring hardship builds character in several instances. For example, at the end of *Herbert Carter's Legacy*, Alger describes the positive outcome of poverty:

> For our young friend Herbert we may confidently indulge in cheerful anticipations. He has undergone the discipline of poverty and privation, and prosperity is not likely to spoil him. He has done his duty under difficult circumstances, and now he reaps the reward. (264)

Likewise, the theme of *Walter Sherwood's Probation* is that the rich don't appreciate what they have until it is taken away. Walter lives up to his potential only after he is forced to work hard and subsist on his own. The story concludes, "For whatever success he may achieve he will be inclined to give credit to his year of probation" (248). While these characters do not experience homelessness like the street Arabs, they are forced to leave their homes and survive on their own. Alger romanticizes poverty and homelessness by portraying it as a hurdle or challenge to overcome. In the end, the romantic hero endures and learns a valuable lesson.

Alger's heroes also experience the type of romantic homelessness described in the Introduction. In these cases, the lack of a home allows freedom and adventure; the hero has no responsibilities and can occupy his time however he pleases. In *Phil, The Fiddler*, Alger attacked the evils of the padrone system, but also mentions Phil's evident freedom: "To a certain extent Phil was his own master; that is, he was at liberty to wander where he liked, provided he did not neglect his business, and returned to the lodging-house at night with the required sum of money" (*Struggling Upward* 287). Other boys have difficulty earning enough money to satisfy the padrone, but the central character in this and other works always enjoys success.

Freedom and the lack of responsibility appeal to other characters, such as Ragged Dick and Julius. Both heroes start off homeless but resolve to find homes and "grow up respectable." However, they miss their old lifestyles once they acquire jobs and homes. In *Julius or the Street Boy Out West*, Julius admits his attraction to the "vagrant life":

> Notwithstanding the comfort which he now enjoyed there were moments when a longing for his old, independent, vagrant life, swept over him. He thought of Broadway, and City Hall Park, of Tony Pastor's, and the old Bowery, of the busy hum and excitement of the streets of the great city; and a feeling something like homesickness was aroused within him. (*Strive and Succeed* 74)

Ragged Dick, likewise, sacrifices his regular trips to the theaters in the Bowery in an effort to be thrifty and upstanding. The Bowery represents an area frequented by dishonorable people and the theater becomes an unnecessary luxury when Dick decides to be respectable. Dick genuinely enjoyed these excursions and he notes the sacrifice that his new lifestyle creates. His circumspect life of studying and working contrasts with the freedom and adventure he experienced while living on the street.

Dick also exhibits "streetwise" behavior that is portrayed as a positive value of his homeless lifestyle. Like Julius, who is "preternaturally sharp" (*Strive and Succeed* 30), Dick is clever and wise, directly or indirectly because of his life on the street. Karen Halttunen notes that Dick possesses the skills of a confidence man. He plays three confidence games in the book and even admits to tricking unsuspecting country boys or gentlemen who were new to the city. Halttunen acknowledges that Dick says, "'I ain't knocked round the city streets all my life for nothin'" (Halttunen, *Confidence Men* 201). This experience allows Dick to prevent pickpockets and other con men from stealing from him and other innocent victims because he recognizes when a con is taking place–an ability that someone from the country or the upper classes would not possess.[16] Living on the streets creates certain advantages and opportunities for some of Alger's heroes. In these cases, his street Arabs become romantic heroes.

This combination of romantic and realist elements is a logical product of Alger's literary and cultural times. Social critics denounced novels for promoting immoral or improper behavior, so Alger could not expect to publish books for boys if he did not present wholesome, and therefore unrealistic, stories. Having already attempted unsuccessfully to publish for an adult audience, Alger experienced his greatest success writing for boys. He could not jeopardize this career by describing the behavior of actual street children, such as drinking, swearing, smoking, gambling, stealing, and begging. When these activities do occur, they are not committed by the boy-heroes, and the immorality of the behavior is obvious.

"THE TRAMP MENACE"

In the Introduction, I indicated that the figure of the tramp became more visible after the Civil War. Economic depressions, the railroad system, industrialization, immigration, and the Civil War itself contributed to an increase in the number of wandering poor, some who actively sought employment and others who "tramped" from town to town with no specific plan or agenda.[17] Set in the 1870s and 1880s, *The Vacation of the Kelwyns* by William Dean Howells describes the tension and fear associated with the "tramp menace" at the time:

> There was that summer a great alarm of tramps. The times were bad, as they must be every now and then, in an economy as little regulated as the weather, and men without work were prowling the country everywhere. They were mostly long past the hope of work, or the wish for it, but they still wanted to eat. They found shelter for themselves in barns and hay-stacks, and any rags sufficed in summer; but a handout was good for only a few hours at a time, and the newspapers teemed with stories of the insolence and even violence which repaid the charity done the vagabonds. (34)

Howell's description captures the sense of fear, disarray, and distrust directed at the poor and homeless at the time. These feelings were created by numerous articles and essays about the "Tramp Menace" in America.

The discourse surrounding the figure of the tramp became most prominent–and vitriolic–from the 1870s to the 1890s, precisely the period in which Alger wrote. This discourse–characterized as a "backlash" against tramps by several sources–indicates the power of texts to do cultural work. Whereas most Americans were ambivalent or even concerned about the poor or homeless, "scientific" charity organizations led the effort to define unemployment and homelessness as moral traits. Because the tramp threatened traditional values associated with work, the home, and charity, he became a target for social scientists, religious leaders, politicians, and then journalists. Kenneth L. Kusmer elucidates this apparent threat:

> Attitudes toward work and idleness, toward the emerging technological/bureaucratic order, and toward the ideas of charity and benevolence were all connected in a way with the figure of the tramp, who represented not only the outsider and rebel, but the image of failure in a society long dominated by the success ethic. (98)

For some, the visibility of the poor and homeless exposed the gap between the rich and the poor; for others, the tramp threatened traditional regard for a stable job, a permanent home, and the nuclear family. The threat to these values evoked the most caustic responses.

Migratory workers were needed as laborers throughout America; they served a very specific and necessary function in an evolving economy.[18] The presence and visibility of these tramps also increased for identifiable reasons, but the discourse shifted attention to their moral deficiencies and faults of character.[19] In 1877, for example, the dean of the Yale Law School regarded the tramp as "'a lazy, incorrigible, cowardly, utterly depraved savage'" (qtd. in Denning 150). The *New Englander and Yale Review* published an article in 1878 calling tramps hostile, cruel, and atrocious. The author warns that they must be "throttled" before they threaten legitimate civilization. As previously mentioned, articles published in major newspapers and magazines advocated labor colonies, whipping, and poisoning to deal with tramps. The violent and criminal behavior of tramps was also exaggerated to justify the backlash against them. These and other examples prove that the "Tramp Menace" was a real and meaningful threat to Americans, at least in the discourse of the time.

Of course, many Americans felt otherwise, and numerous pro-charity articles were also published in newspapers and magazines. Public sentiment was clearly divided over both the physical and moral threat posed by tramps, as some declared a "war on tramps" and others called for compassion and understanding. As Michael Denning states, "The dime novel also became an arena of this ideological struggle over the tramp" (150). Although he does not discuss Alger at length, Denning notes that, in fact, Alger was one of the earliest authors to depict tramp characters in fiction. Therefore, he may have contributed directly to the tone and direction of debates over the tramp.

Although it is difficult to gauge the effect of any text or author on public opinion, Alger's books must have been somewhat influential given his readership and the lack of background his readers would have had on the subject. In other words, tramps were controversial; the discourse was evolving at the time Alger wrote; his books were very popular. Therefore, one can reasonably assume his texts did cultural work in influencing public perceptions of the tramp. If readers encountered a tramp for the first time in the pages of one of Alger's books, what could they have expected to behold?

First, Alger's tramps are physically unattractive. They are ugly, dirty, and unconcerned with hygiene or appearance. Their clothes are tattered and old. *The Store Boy or The Fortunes of Ben Barclay* opens with Ben encountering a tramp:

> He was a stout-built, dark-complexioned man, with a beard of a week's growth, wearing an old and dirty suit, which would have reduced any tailor to despair if taken to him for cleaning and repairs. A loose hat, with a torn crown, surmounted a singularly ill-favored visage. (*Strive and Succeed* 1)

Just as his boy-heroes are consistently attractive, the tramps in his books are always loathsome. In *Tony, the Hero*, Alger emphasizes the differences between Rudolph, a tramp, and Tony, his companion: "A man and a boy were ascending a steep step in a country town in Eastern New York. The man was tall and dark-complexioned, with a sinister look which of itself excited distrust. [. . .] His companion was a boy of fourteen. Between the two there was not the slightest resemblance" (7). Ben even calls attention to their physical differences: "You're dark and I am light" (9). In their values, behavior, and appearance, Alger's tramps differ markedly from his homeless boys.

Alger further implies that his tramp characters are foreign-born, a common but misinformed stereotype of tramps at the time.[20] Tony is light, but Rudolph is dark. He is "dark-complexioned" and gives the impression of "gipsy blood" (7). The tramp character in *The Store Boy or the Fortunes of Ben Barclay* is also "dark complexioned" (*Strive and Succeed* 1). Such a description emphasizes the difference between the deserving, "light" homeless boy and the undeserving, "dark" homeless tramp. In two other cases, the tramps do not look dark, but we learn that they were never "real" tramps: they had been separated from legitimate income just like many of Alger's heroes.

Character is also *visible* for Alger's tramp characters. Rudolph, in *Tony, the Hero*, as previously mentioned, has a "sinister look which of itself excited distrust" (7). In *The Young Bank Messenger*, Ernest Ray encounters two men in a store. One of the men "looked rough, but honest and reliable" (5). The other "may best be described as a tramp, a man who looked averse to labor of any kind, a man without a settled business or home, who picked up a living as he could, caring less for food than for drink, and whose mottled face indicated frequent potations of whiskey" (5). In *Driven from Home or Carl Crawford's Experience*, Carl is accosted by "an ill-looking tramp": "Carl started and looked into the face of the tramp. It seemed to him that he had never seen a man more ill-favored, or villainous-looking" (75). Just as good character can be seen in the face and appearance of Alger's heroes, one can recognize the detestable, depraved essence of the tramps just by looking at them.

Not only do Alger's tramps look bad, they behave dishonestly and immorally. Tramps invariably try to drink, smoke, steal, and gamble in Alger's works: behavior which his boy-heroes avoid at all costs. In *The Store Boy or the Fortunes of Ben Barclay*, a tramp teases Ben Barclay for going to Sunday school and for not smoking or having matches. In *The Young Bank Messenger*, Tom, the tramp, constantly tries to get money to buy whiskey. When a main character encounters a tramp, the tramp invariably tries to rob or steal from him. The tramps lie, cheat, and connive. Tom avoids work and begs for money: "if there was anything to which Tom was bitterly opposed it was work of any kind" (41). In short, Alger's tramps exhibit every possible negative stereotype. While they display immoral and unethical behavior at every step, Alger contrasts them with his young heroes who demonstrate proper values. In *Tony, the Hero*, Rudolph forces Tony to help him steal from a farmer, but Tony resists and runs away. Rudolph claims to be Tony's father, but somehow Tony knows that they are not related. He also knows instinctively what is right and wrong. He confronts Rudolph and demands an education and a different lifestyle:

> "You don't want to be like me. Is that it?" asked Rudolph, angrily.
> "No, I don't want to be like you," answered Tony, boldly. "I want to have a home, and a business, and to live like other people." (10)

Tony represents "us," the readers who would have known better than to avoid work and live a vagrant lifestyle. Rudolph is one of "them," the bad guys who drink, smoke, gamble, and avoid work. Alger creates two categories of tramps: the dishonest homeless adults who do not deserve compassion because they are immoral, lazy, and dishonest and the innocent homeless boys who are deserving of the numerous forms of charity that come their way.

Of course, Alger's bad guys are fictional constructs, and he needed protagonists and antagonists to tell a story which would appeal to his readers and publishers. However, texts do cultural work, and the culture in which Alger wrote would have been particularly susceptible to texts which represented tramps negatively. Alger reflects the ideological conflicts over the tramp and related issues such as work, charity, and the home. And, unfortunately, choices he made in the construction of his characters could have been more useful or rehabilitative.

ALGER'S LEGACY

It may seem disingenuous to critique the cultural work of Alger's texts after questioning other critics who took him to task. I have argued that critics who chastised Alger for promoting the American Dream of success and for ignoring genuine barriers to social or economic mobility did so as a result of their historical context and with little regard for the accuracy of their claims. In other words, the Alger myth rests on misinformation about Alger and the actual content of his books. Criticism of Alger for creating this myth in the Gilded Age depended on faulty information, and indeed Alger promoted charity and compassion much more than he is ever given credit for. Despite his intentions, I believe his texts did cultural work which is detrimental to the poor and homeless for reasons which have not yet been articulated and which differ substantially from traditional criticisms of the Alger myth. Alger did not crusade for greed, materialism, individualism, and *laissez faire* capitalism, as others have argued, but he contributed to a discourse which stereotyped and categorized the poor and homeless. This discourse–literature, social science, journalism–deserves examination since it obviously affected not only beliefs and attitudes, but behavior as well.

In his essay "A Poor Apart: The Distancing of Homeless Men in New York's History," Kim Hopper maintains, "The denunciation of the tramp is thus one of those cultural moments in which a distance is enacted because something near and feared (or remembered and prized?) must be disavowed" (117). Although Alger advocated compassion and charity for the poor, he shared the opinion of scientific charity organizations that only the deserving poor should receive help. Distance is created between those who give and those who do not deserve to receive. The tramp was disavowed in the late nineteenth century for undermining traditional values associated with work and the home. Just as Tony knows that it is proper to work and have a home, Alger insists that it is wrong, improper, and even immoral to be homeless and unemployed. Thus, Alger contributes to the historical division between the "deserving" and "undeserving" poor, a division which has been debated and criticized throughout American history.

As I suggest above, character is visible for Alger's characters. Good character is perceptible in the innocent street Arabs, as evidenced by the examples of Julius, Sam Barker, Ragged Dick, and many others. Conversely, one can see that a tramp is disreputable, "villainous," and "ill-favored." In *Slow and Sure; Or, From the Street to the Shop*, Julius notes the appearance of his mysterious guardian, Jack Morgan: "He was certainly a disreputable-looking ruffian, and his character did not belie his looks" (84). In *Tony, the Hero*, Rudolph dons new clothes, but his true nature cannot be hidden:

> He regarded his reflection in a long mirror with considerable satisfaction. He felt that he would now be taken for a respectable citizen, and that in discharging his old dress he had removed all vestiges of the tramp. In this, however, he was not wholly right. His face and general expression he could not change. A careful observer could read in them something of the life he had led. (153–154)

Similarly, Tom, the tramp in *The Young Bank Messenger*, goes to a woman's house to beg for food and money, but she sees that he lacks character:

> "My good lady," said Tom, putting on a pitiful expression, "I am a very unfortunate man."
> "Are you?" said the woman, scanning him critically. "You look like a tramp."
> "I do, madam, yet I was once a thriving merchant."
> "You don't look like it." (33)

The woman tellingly responds to his claim that he is "unfortunate" by saying he looks like a tramp. The contemporary discourse portrayed the tramp as lazy, unwilling to work, dishonest, and conniving. Americans were taught not to trust tramps, although many people remained generous at the time.

Character can be visible for Alger because one is naturally good or bad. In other words, Alger resisted social and environmental determinism. One's character is determined from birth, not by upbringing or environment. His street Arabs flourish in what would actually be harsh and debilitating conditions. Several examples indicate that Alger resisted the notion that the slums or tenements could adversely affect a child's development. The title character of *Jed, the Poorhouse Boy* has an "attractive" face, and "an observer skilled in physiognomy would have read in it signs of a strong character, a warm and grateful disposition, and a resolute will" (*Struggling*

Upward 401). He resides in a poorhouse, but naturally possesses these positive traits. In *Tony, the Hero*, Tony, fourteen years old and raised by a tramp, instinctively resists smoking, drinking, and stealing. Alger even struggles with this apparent lack of verisimilitude as Tony looks in on a weak miser counting two bags of gold:

> If Tony was honest, it was an instinctive feeling. It could not have been expected of one reared as he had been. But, singular as it may seem, beyond a vague longing, he felt no temptation to deprive old Ben of his money. (55)

Tony's "guardian" constantly teases him for being too virtuous, while searching for opportunities to steal from and deceive others. Finally, in *Slow and Sure; Or, From the Street to the Shop*, Julius defies the odds by becoming honest and hardworking, despite being an orphan raised by a guardian who was always in trouble or in jail. Again, Alger seems to realize the discrepancy:

> The chances seemed to be in favor of Julius growing up such another as his guardian. Had he been differently constituted he would have been worse than he was. But his natural instincts were healthful, and when he had been left entirely to himself he had lived by honest industry, devoting himself to some of the street occupations which were alone open to him. (81)

These attempts to define character as a visible trait and to minimize the environmental effects of poverty and homelessness on children parallel efforts by "scientific" charity organizations and social scientists to ascertain verifiable differences between the deserving and undeserving poor. The charity organizations wanted clear demarcations between these groups to ensure that unworthy tramps and beggars would not receive aid. This was not seen as cruel or dishonorable because it was intended to "save" the tramps from their own immoral behavior. If they knew they could not get free food and shelter, they would be forced to find a job and a home. Since unemployment and homelessness were tantamount to sinning, denying charity was actually in the tramps' best interest, according to these groups.

In *Out of Place: Homeless Mobilizations, Subcities, and Contested Landscapes*, Talmadge Wright indirectly explains why Alger's boy-heroes had to be naturally good:

> The normal/abnormal distinction was converted into the good/bad dualism through the medicalization of difference, creating the rationale behind establishing nineteenth century poorhouses for the destitute, where inmates were expected to work to correct the moral deficiencies

> that had led them to such poverty in the first place, to reverse their degenerate status. (69)

For Alger and others in the late nineteenth century, tramps were immoral and, therefore, they posed a threat to traditional values related to work, the home, and the family. If this immorality was visible, the deserving and undeserving poor could be fairly separated and both groups could be "saved." Unfortunately, such neat divisions rarely exist in the real world. Jeffrey Louis Decker shows that "moral character," far from being a neutral, color-blind principle, is "coded as white, male, and middle-class" at the time Alger wrote (xxiii). Although people deserved charity, only certain people were deserving.

The discourse of homelessness at the time Alger wrote was evolving rapidly, just as Americans' attitudes about work, charity, the home, and poverty were changing as a result of social, cultural, and economic shifts. Although Alger promoted compassion and charity, only his boy-heroes deserved compassion. As Nackenoff argues,

> The boy who moves in search of work is making his way, seeking brighter opportunities. The adult who tramps is highly suspect. Both tramp and hero were economically marginalized, mobile figures. It was vital that the two not be confused. Should the young, whatever their station, fail to obtain the community's consideration and assistance, both hero and Republic lose. (73)

Alger's use of romantic elements and realist elements not only emphasizes the historical division discussed at length in the Introduction, it also contributed to an emerging discourse in the late nineteenth century which defined the deserving and undeserving poor, and in turn perpetuated divisions between good and bad, normal and abnormal, "us" and "them." When one considers the power of discourse to inspire whippings and poisonings, it seems reasonable to challenge the literary and cultural conventions attending that discourse.

Chapter Three

The Other Half and How It Lives

Jacob Riis and Stephen Crane's Vision of Poverty and Homelessness

In his story "A Self-Made Man," Stephen Crane satirizes and assails the American myth of the self-made man popularized by writers such as Horatio Alger. Though Alger did not wholeheartedly believe in the "rags-to-riches" opportunities some of his texts intimate, Crane's version lambasts the notion that poor, honest boys can succeed in America with a little "luck and pluck." Alger allows his boy-heros to experience good fortune as a result of their perseverence, hard work, and honesty, while Crane practically mocks Alger and his readers for their naiveté. The charming street urchins in Alger's work are replaced by a conniving street tough. Although Alger is more of a realist than he is given credit for, and Crane less of a naturalist than he is criticized for, "A Self-Made Man" represents a significant challenge to the belief that poor children (or "street Arabs") could rise above their circumstances to become either rich or respectable.[1]

"A Self-Made Man," originally published in *Cornhill Magazine* in 1899, follows the structure of several Alger stories in which a poor boy–depicted as honest, upstanding, and hard-working–encounters an older gentleman; the boy does a favor for the man, and as a reward the man becomes the boy's benefactor. However, Crane inverts several details in his story.[2] The subtitle, "An Example of Success That Any One Can Follow," alerts the reader to the possibility that Crane is satirizing Alger, since Alger and other proponents of the "Gospel of Wealth" were spreading a similar message at the same time.[3] The main character, Tom, does experience success, but through duplicity and pure luck. The story is clearly not "An Example of Success That Any One Can Follow."

Tom randomly encounters the old man, reads a letter for him which reveals that his son withheld money (since the old man can't read), poses as his lawyer, and intimidates the man's son into giving back the money.

The old man is overjoyed, vows to desert his son, and finds a job for Tom. Tom, of course, experiences success in the end. Crane writes:

> So it came to pass that Tom grew to be Thomas G. Somebody. He achieved that position in life from which he could hold out for good wines when he went to poor restaurants. [. . .] At the present day he is so great that he lunches frugally at high prices. [. . .] Newspapers apply to him now, and he writes long signed articles to struggling young men, in which he gives the best possible advice as to how to become wealthy. (*Sketches* 204)

This conclusion parallels several Alger stories in which the hero achieves success (and a title of some sort) in the concluding chapter. The mention of the advice columns seems to refer to writers associated with the "Gospel of Wealth," though clearly to parody them. Crane, influenced by a variety of factors, believed that environment played a crucial role in determining the lives of the poor and lower classes, unlike the proponents of the Gospel of Wealth, who generally asserted that anyone could succeed through hard work and honesty. By presenting Tom as a dishonest, opportunistic example of the "self-made man," Crane satirizes and rejects this myth and the "American dream" of success for all people.

This debunking of the myth of the self-made man corrects some of the earlier, unrealistic beliefs about America as a land of opportunity. The realists, naturalists, muckrakers, and reformists in the late nineteenth century countered the false or uniformed beliefs of many who thought there were no legitimate barriers to social or economic success in America. These achievements should not be minimized; however, as recent critics have argued, this movement produced its share of detrimental cultural work as well. In this chapter I extend the analysis of critics such as Alan Trachtenberg, Mark Pittenger, and Keith Gandal who have questioned, contextualized, and criticized the work of writers such as Jacob Riis and Stephen Crane who went "down and out" to study and describe the "other half."

Jacob Riis's landmark work *How the Other Half Lives: Studies Among the Tenements of New York* epitomizes the late nineteenth century impulse to expose the hidden conditions in the slums and tenements of the United States. The "other half" (like the "lower class," like the "submerged tenth," like the "social abyss"–terms that appeared in sociology of the time and throughout the twentieth century as well) denotes a division of identifiable and, more importantly, qualitative categories (which are, of course, socially constructed rather than actual). The lower class is below and inferior to the upper class in such an arrangement, which presents difficulties that I address throughout this chapter. Moreover, Riis's original title, which he presented as a lecture and which he copyrighted, was "The Other Half:

How *It* Lives and Dies in New York" (italics added). The use of the pronoun "it" indicates the depersonalization of the poor as an object of study. In this chapter I argue that naturalists (or "down-and-outers"[4]) such as Jacob Riis and Stephen Crane objectified the condition of homelessness and, as a result, produced cultural work which was detrimental. In order to foreground my analysis of Crane and Riis, I first discuss some of the historical and cultural contexts which contributed to the effects mentioned above, and then examine some of the manifestations of these historical/cultural shifts during the late nineteenth century.

I am grouping contextual issues into three categories: Otherness, urbanization, and science. I suggest that these social/cultural/historical influences manifested themselves–in naturalism generally, and in Crane and Riis specifically–in four ways: in the desire to reform society; in the conception of the slum as spectacle or entertainment; through a point of view which distanced the observer from the lower classes; and through increased discursive divisions between the upper and lower classes.

HISTORICAL AND CULTURAL CONTEXTS: OTHERNESS, URBANIZATION, AND SCIENCE

Giles Gunn, among others, has discussed the category of Otherness as a theme or preoccupation of American literature. In his book *The Interpretation of Otherness: Literature, Religion, and the American Imagination*, he describes the urge to understand and represent the Other in Whitman, Emerson, Melville, Dreiser, and Fitzgerald, as well as our "inability to see, much less feel, other people as real human beings" (177). He goes on to define the central problem associated with representations of Otherness:

> Anyone who deviates from the official norm, whatever that is, anyone who fails to bear a likeness to the Standard Product, is simply not viewed as fully human, and then becomes at best invisible, at worst a threat to the national security. (177)

Perhaps Gunn overstates the problem somewhat, but it is not unreasonable to suggest that the poor and homeless have been treated as "invisible" at various times in American history. Nor is it unreasonable to say that they have been characterized as a "threat to the national security" when one notes the various forms of backlash against tramps in the 1870s and 1880s discussed in Chapter Two under the rubric of the "tramp menace."[5]

Naturalists like Riis and Crane insisted that poverty, homelessness, and poor living conditions could not remain invisible. They brought needed attention to problems that many people ignored or dismissed. However, difference and otherness underlie much of the discourse surrounding the slums produced by Riis, Crane, and others in the late nineteenth century. Immigration and race were pronounced issues that were often tied directly to social and financial success in this discourse. Attempts to explain the failures of slum dwellers and the different responses to poverty and overcrowding by various races were common (as Riis does at length in *How the Other Half Lives*). Thus, the positive intentions of writers like Riis and Crane to expose the problems in the slums did not prevent them from treating the people who lived there as foreign or "other."[6] The interest in "the other half" at this time can be seen as an extension of the historical attraction to the Other in a variety of specific ways.

A second contextual consideration, discussed briefly in Chapter Two but which also plays a direct role here, is increased urbanization in America. Urbanization includes a host of satellite issues including unemployment, immigration, overcrowding, crime, and poverty which received increasingly more frequent and dire commentary in the late nineteenth century. With the "closing" of the American frontier, an increase in industrialization and the corresponding decrease in the agrarian economy, as well as increased immigration, large urban centers began to supplant smaller towns as the norm for American cities. This shift was met with apprehension in many cases.

The "mysteries of the city" genre symbolizes the fascination with as well as the fear of the city as a place of crime, overcrowding, and debauchery–in essence the antithesis of rural areas. This genre became popular in the 1840s, but treatments of the city as mysterious occur throughout the late nineteenth century. According to Alan Trachtenberg,

> In the nineteenth century the big city appeared often in the guise of mystery. [. . .] We find the image on all levels–in guide books and newspapers, in popular Gothicized "mysteries," in serious poetry and fiction: the city as a swarming mass of signals, dense, obscure, undecipherable. (138)

Though Trachtenberg and others have likened realism and naturalism to the novels of George Lippard, George Foster, and Ned Buntline–as representative of the mysteries of the city genre–few critics explore the quasi-gothic elements in works such as *Maggie* and *How the Other Half Lives*. In other words, critics note the gothic traits in Buntline, Foster, and Lippard's work, and admit the influence of the mysteries of the city genre on naturalist writers like Riis and Crane, but stop short of associating naturalism with the gothic novel.

This connection and influence is particularly significant because it represents the ability of naturalists like Riis and Crane to dramatize the lives of people living in the slums and tenements for discursive purposes. While the gothic novel and the mysteries of the city genre are regarded as precursors to naturalism, the dark, evocative, vaguely supernatural elements in naturalism remain more prominent than many critics recognize. In *New York in Slices by an Experienced Carver* (1849), George G. Foster attempted to

> lay bare the fearful mysteries of darkness in the metropolis–the festivities of prostitution, the orgies of pauperism, the haunts of theft and murder, the scenes of drunkenness and beastly debauch and all the sad realities that go to make up the lower stratum–the underground story of life in New York. (qtd. in Ward 17)

Prostitution, pauperism, theft, drunkenness, and other sensational topics pervade texts like *Maggie* and *How the Other Half Lives*. Mysterious sounds, winding corridors, and dark, closed spaces occur in naturalist works and in the mysteries of the city genre (and, of course, in gothic novels). The earlier texts were more lurid, but naturalist texts still portray the hidden, undiscovered sections of the city and the inhabitants therein as mysterious and foreign (literally and figuratively).[7] This characterization increases the division between the upper and lower classes, and it legitimizes the belief that the inhabitants of the slums are distinctly different from other people.

A related contingency of the increased attention to urbanization at the time was a greater awareness of the gap between the upper and lower classes. This polarization between the haves and have-nots can be seen in depictions of poor street children juxtaposed with affluent but unaffected pedestrians (See Figure 1), and in illustrations of shanty-towns in the shadow of luxury high-rises or set against familiar metropolitan scenes (See Figure 2), which appear in newspapers and magazines of the 1880s and 1890s. In his study of American cities, *Poverty, Ethnicity, and the American City, 1840–1925: Changing Conceptions of the Slum and the Ghetto*, David Ward states, "Urban society [between 1875 and 1900] was portrayed as a contrast of extremes of wealth and poverty, or of 'sunshine and shadow' [. . .], but popular indictments emphasized moral and personal relationships rather than structural and social conditions" (48). This increased awareness of the polarization of classes is evident in the work of Riis and Crane. Both authors note the extreme differences between affluent society and the living conditions of the poor. Crane's paired essays "An Experiment in Misery" and "An Experiment in Luxury," for example, capture the contemporary concern about the rich/poor gap.

All of these factors contributed to an interest in the "other half." As a practical matter, the proliferation of major newspapers and magazines provided an audience and forum for writers like Crane and Riis, who both

Fig. 1: "The Hearth-Stone of the Poor—Steam Heat Not Wasted." Illustration by Sol Etinge, Jr. (*Harper's Weekly*, Feb. 12, 1876). (Courtesy of *HarpWeek*.)

took advantage of this new trend. In *The Virtues of the Vicious: Jacob Riis, Stephen Crane, and the Spectacle of the Slum*, Keith Gandal explains, "Made possible by specific technological advances, including photography, and also by the urbanization and immigration that created a huge city audience, the daily [newspaper] developed new forms of reporting to attract a large share of the reading market" (16).[8] Trachtenberg adds, "The big city daily, especially as it developed in the 1890s, has its *raison d'être* chiefly in the mystification of urban space, a mystification it claims to dispel as 'news' yet simultaneously abets as 'sensationalism'" (141). This tension between news and sensationalism can be seen in a variety of texts associated with naturalism and muckraking journalism around the turn of the century.[9] Urbanization, immigration, unemployment, poverty, and the polarization of classes created an audience which wanted to make sense of these issues. The dailies obliged this audience, but the sense of wonder and mystery surrounding the city–particularly the slums and tenements–was reflected back and amplified by sensational accounts of the "social abyss."

The final contextual consideration is the increased interest in and legitimization of science in the late nineteenth century. The influence of Spencer and Darwin on naturalist writers has been widely discussed, for example.[10] No longer convinced of humanity's privileged or advanced place in the world, naturalists represented the deleterious effects of environment and an indifferent universe.[11] The impulse to demonstrate the negative effects of poverty and overcrowding on the poor should be lauded, but the objective, scientific study of the poor also codifies them as objects of study.

Similarly, Americans in the nineteenth century experienced a cultural shift from "traditional religious faith and moral belief to skepticism and uncertainty" (Pizer 17). This skepticism can be seen in the questioning of earlier, Victorian beliefs and values, and in the premium placed on data, observation, and direct experience (rather than, say, inspiration or reflection). In his essay "Framing the Poor: The Irresistibility of How the Other Half Lives," David Leviatin states,

> Accuracy and objectivity were the articles of a new faith, a faith based on the perceived virtues of mechanical reproduction and scientific management. Realism, like science, was seen as a means of isolating and controlling a host of powerful new forces considered alien, wild, and dangerous. (22)

Thus, the rise of the participant-observer accounts of working and living conditions in American cities followed the preference for direct, objective, unmediated experience. Ethnographic accounts and special interest stories became more prevalent, and people from all walks of life could, theoretically, become credible writers.

Fig. 2: "The Squatters of New York—Scene Near Central Park." Engraved from a drawing by D. E. Wyand (*Harper's Weekly*, June 26, 1869). (Courtesy of *HarpWeek*.)

Crane and Riis were two of the earliest, most famous, and most influential writers to enter the "social abyss" as participant-observers. According to Gandal, Riis used his camera as a "passport" to gain entry into the homes of the poor; he became so familiar to people living in the tenements that they referred to him as "Doctor." For Crane, "The poor became his neighbors, and at least in one case, recorded in his 'Experiment in Misery' (1894), Crane did undercover work: he dressed up as a bum, spent a night in a flophouse, and ate at cheap dives" (Gandal 14). Gandal adds, "Both of these writers overstepped the old limits of slum observation" (14).

Finally, the scientific/technological advances in newspaper production and photography contributed directly to the ability of Riis and Crane to disseminate their work and influenced their message and point of view.[12] The actual development of photographic technology corresponds to the desire for objectivity and scientific "truth." Leviatin remarks,

> Photography's great appeal was related in large part to its association with science, specifically chemistry and optics. Interest in the substance (the theory and practice) and the trappings (the mechanical devices) of scientific inquiry was widespread. Americans were fascinated by the objective quest for truth, eager to record all aspects of their social reality. (22)

Of course, photography, like "objective" writing, only represents one version of the truth. The late nineteenth century interest in science and objectivity led to investigative journalism and participant-observer accounts which displaced earlier, perhaps simplistic, conceptions of poverty and homelessness. However, these accounts produced other, less valuable results as well. I wish to briefly discuss four manifestations of the increased interest in Otherness, urbanization, and science in the late nineteenth century before focusing on the specific representations of poverty and homelessness in the work of Crane and Riis.

MANIFESTATIONS OF OTHERNESS, URBANIZATION, AND SCIENCE

Social advances–in the form of better ventilation in tenement housing, increased attention to health care, and public discussion of the conditions in the slums–must be recognized as an irrefutably positive outcome of the increased attention given to "the other half." Despite the charges of sensationalism leveled against muckrakers and naturalists, they brought much needed attention to problems and conditions in the city which were previously hidden or minimized. Clearly, the efforts of reformers to represent the lives and living conditions of the poor–despite the criticism of "speaking for" the poor–are better than the alternative of ignoring the problem or, worse, hiding it. The explicit, direct depictions of poverty needed to supersede romanticized or censored accounts. This chapter and the work of other critics take naturalists like Crane and Riis to task for objectifying the poor and homeless. But as a step in the right direction, these efforts served a legitimate purpose.

Moreover, the motives of writers like Crane and Riis are not being questioned in this context. As I have been suggesting, discourse in general, and literature specifically, tends to either romanticize or objectify the condition of homelessness. In the remainder of this chapter I show how Crane and Riis contributed to this objectification. Regardless of their positive intentions, I believe they contribute to a discourse which has produced detrimental cultural work. More specifically, the discourse which objectifies poverty and homelessness treats these conditions as spectacle or entertainment, maintains a detached and hierarchical relationship to its object of study, and increases divisions between "us" and "them."[13]

First, the interest in Otherness, urbanization, and science contributed to an understanding of the slum as a site of entertainment or spectacle which also surfaces in naturalism. Carrie Tiardo Bramen and Keith Gandal have traced this phenomenon and have examined the occurrences of walking tours of the tenement districts and "slumming parties" in the late nineteenth century. Bramen argues that the walking tours (actual and literary) offered a means of understanding or coming to terms with the rapid changes in the city at the time. She says,

> The late Victorian *flâneur* recognized poverty and swarthy immigrants as familiar sights of modernity partly on the basis of the textual cues of intra-urban walking tours. By making the alienation of the rag picker less alienating for the viewer, these tours transformed the shock of modernity into a mild surprise. [. . .] The tours provided a pedagogy of spectatorship, instructing the reader how to transform the congested and impoverished districts of the metropolis into a sense of "rough and rugged pleasure." (456)

Bramen goes on to show how Riis used the tour as a form within *How the Other Half Lives*. She notes, with Trachtenberg, how sections of the book read as if Riis is showing someone through town,[14] and she demonstrates how the lower class sections of New York functioned as a spectacle for Riis by referring to his comment that Chinatown was not interesting because it was not filthy enough. According to Riis, "Chinatown as a spectacle is disappointing. Next-door neighbor to the Bend, it has little of its outdoor stir and life, none of its gayly-colored rags or *picturesque* filth and poverty" (Riis 120, italics added).[15] It is a short step from here to the objectification of the poor and homeless themselves. In his writing and in the framing of his photographs, Riis emphasized the differences between the classes by sensationalizing poverty and the poor themselves. Riis marketed extreme and stereotypical representations of the poor to a curious middle/upper class audience who would not have been exposed to other, more positive images.

Similarly, Gandal refers to the "unprecedented fad for 'slumming parties'" in New York during the 1890s (15). He traces in considerable detail how the slums became a spectacle in-and-of themselves during this period, rather than a source of compassion or pity. He affirms, "Riis and Crane were providing middle-class readers with a new way of approaching the slums: as spectacle for its own sake" (62). The representation of the poor and homeless within the slums as objects of entertainment, it must be noted, produced lasting, unfavorable consequences.[16]

One manifestation of the interest in Otherness, urbanization, and science in the late nineteenth century, then, is the treatment of the slums as spectacle or entertainment. These influences also manifested themselves in the detached, dominant point of view adopted by writers such as Riis and Crane. For Trachtenberg, "[Crane's] narrative point of view remains cool and aloof [. . .]; his spatial penetrations end at the edge of sympathetic identification" (154). Like the tramp autobiographers I will discuss in Chapter Four, Crane and Riis remain separate from the object of their study, despite the stated intention of entering the slums in order to represent them as accurately as possible. Both groups of authors maintain their own identity as members of the upper classes; their excursions are temporary and purposeful. Describing *Maggie*, Henry Golemba observes, "Whether one adopts the vantage point of reformer or novelist, photographer or reader, the point of view is privileged; reality is observed from on high" (238).

Not only is the point of view detached, but it is dominant or superior in many cases.[17] Mark Pittenger contends that

> down-and-outers had power–the power to define difference, and to specify who and what others were. In exercising that power, they reaffirmed their own positions as representatives of a higher civilization and a superior culture. In the pages they wrote, laundry workers, road-builders, waitresses, and the drifting, homeless unemployed became the objects of their discerning, discriminating, middle-class gaze. (45–46)

Although positive results of social reform were gained from these efforts, and the poor did not necessarily feel victimized by this process, I address several examples of the type of power Pittenger describes in the context of Riis and Crane below.

Finally, the interest in Otherness and urbanization, coupled with scientific principles of social management, resulted in divisions between "us" and "them," namely, between the upper and lower classes, as well as between the deserving and undeserving poor. My previous point has to do with the indirect effect of distancing the poor and homeless from the participant-observer writing about them. Here, I maintain that certain people were directly objectified by the discourse which attempted to represent them fairly and accurately. While writers such as Riis and Crane may have had the best interests of the poor in mind when they sought them out as material to write about, they consistently portrayed the poor as different, noteworthy, and unusual. The poor could be an object of investigation–particularly because of the desire for direct, scientific data–but they were not seen nor represented as constitutive or "normal" members of society. They were an object/subject/topic to be studied and discussed by the established classes.

Pittenger explains that

> it was often those counting themselves as friends of the poor who provided the raw materials for the idea that these were a separate people, sometimes effectively a separate race or species. The very poor seemed mentally, physically, and morally different from middle-class Americans, and were becoming more so all the time under the impact of a self-reinforcing combination of environment and heredity. (39)

He adds, "If down-and-outers blurred the border between 'us' and 'them' through the rituals of disguise and descent, they largely re-established it when reconstituting their experiences as texts" (47). Perhaps I am being simplistic, but the separation of "us" from "them" offers a valuable, meaningful, reasonable criterion for evaluating the cultural work of a text. In the Conclusion I return to this touchstone of analysis.[18] The objectification of the poor and homeless by naturalist writers such as Crane and Riis–as well as in the wider discourse of homelessness in sociology, photography, and history–produces detrimental cultural work because it legitimizes the difference between categories of people.[19]

EXPERIMENTS IN MISERY: CRANE'S REPRESENTATION OF POVERTY AND HOMELESSNESS

In "An Experiment in Misery," Crane depicts two men considering a tramp and speculating over how he feels. The older man says that it would be impossible to understand his condition "unless you are in that condition yourself. It is idle to speculate about it from this distance" (*Sketches* 34). The younger man agrees, and resolves to try it. He borrows old clothes from an artist friend, "And then the youth went forth to try to eat as the tramp may eat, and sleep as the wanderers sleep" (34).[20] The story, based on Crane's own effort to experience the lifestyle of the tramp for a brief period, represents the interest in homeless tramps at the time and the desire to understand or capture their experience. (The youth says of the tramp: "I suppose he is homeless, friendless, and has, at the most, only a few cents in his pocket. And if this is so, I wonder how he feels" [33]). The title ("an experiment") and the method of direct observation reflect the scientific aim to collect data, but they also reveal that Crane, like his narrator, entered the slums temporarily. As Alan Trachtenberg says, "The youth is transformed only provisionally, however; he is not converted, not reclassified as a tramp" (153). Down-and-outers, to borrow Pittenger's term, maintained a distance between themselves and the poor and homeless they observed.

Had Crane and other investigators remained completely detached, social reform in the slums and tenement districts would have been impossible. Realistic, uncensored, graphic details serve to convince readers of the reality of the situation, and, perhaps, the need for reform. In a variety of other ways, however, Crane objectifies the poor and homeless, and he increases the division between "them" and "us"–his audience. In these ways, his texts shaped the attitudes of his readers and produced cultural work which was detrimental.

First, the narrative point of view undermines the desire to create solidarity in many cases. In "An Experiment in Misery," the narrator is well-intentioned; he wants to understand the lives of the tramps in the lodging house. However, the point of view makes the reader feel fearful or threatened:

> Shortly after the beginning of this journey the young man felt his liver turn white, for from the dark and secret places of the building there suddenly came to his nostrils strange and unspeakable odors that assailed him like malignant diseases with wings. They seemed to be from human bodies closely packed in dens; the exhalations from a hundred pairs of reeking lips; the fumes from a thousand bygone debauches; the expression of a thousand present miseries. (*Sketches* 37)

The threat of disease, the offensive odors, the "dark and secret" location, and the implication of debauchery and misery occur in several of Crane's works about the slums. His narrator seeks an understanding of what a tramp feels, but fear and apprehension are created. The point of view does not represent the thoughts or aspirations of the men; it captures the narrator's shock and horror and relays those feelings to the audience. Crane clearly ignores the actual point of view of the tramps in the room, and represents only the sensibilities and responses of a middle class observer.

Similarly, the narrative point of view of *Maggie: A Girl of the Streets* perpetuates divisions between the book's audience and the poor. June Howard, in *Form and History in American Literary Naturalism*, asserts,

> Stephen Crane's *Maggie* [. . .] juxtaposes unreasoning characters and a highly sophisticated narrator; the incongruity of Homeric language in a description of urchins fighting in the street provokes the reader to think, but also widens the chasm between the ignorance and brutality of the slum dwellers and the literary sensibilities of the narrator and reader. (105)

Crane's desire to produce a sophisticated, intellectual text clashes with the subject matter and how it is treated. In the context of cultural work, Crane reflects and shapes his society. He cannot be faulted for knowing the literary market and catering to it, but he also contributed to a discourse which treated the poor as different and unusual.[21] The elevated style of the narrator may have met the literary expectations of editors and readers, but it contradicts the representation of the mundane, even banal, characters. The unintended effect is discord and a greater awareness of the differences between the two types of people.

In addition to the narrative point of view, a second authorial device which creates distance is the manipulation of the dialect of the lower class. Whereas Alan R. Slotkin claims that the youth in "An Experiment in Misery" adopts the dialect of the poor and thereby demonstrates an increased familiarity with them,[22] I find the supposedly realistic dialogue off-putting. Perhaps if we read aloud the effect would be more realistic, but I find the dialect of the poor to be stereotypical and difficult to comprehend at times. It also makes the poor characters seem more profoundly different or strange. Discussing *Maggie*, June Howard argues,

> Not only content and vocabulary but orthography itself locates these characters as irredeemably Other; their speech is an exotic dialect, virtually a foreign language in comparison with the "standard English" that is the medium of communication, the common ground of narrator and reader. (106)

Therefore, while the reader and narrator/writer may be similarly oriented, the reader is increasingly aware of how different he or she is from the poor who speak in a strange and confusing manner.

To take just one example, in Chapter XIII, Maggie's mother speaks directly about how Maggie has become immoral; then, Jimmie reflects on her comments from an omniscient point of view:

> "An' wid all deh bringin' up she had, how could she?" moaningly she asked of her son. "Wid all deh talkin' wid her I did an' deh t'ings I tol' her to remember? When a girl is bringed up deh way I bringed up Maggie, how kin she go teh deh devil?"

> Jimmie was transfixed by these questions. He could not conceive how under the circumstances his mother's daughter and his sister could have been so wicked. (75)

The incorrect grammar ("bringed") and mispronunciations contrast sharply with the wisdom of Jimmie's thoughts as described in the elevated style of the narrator. This type of disharmony occurs throughout the novel and in Crane's sketches about the poor and homeless. With Howard, I contend that this serves to increase the sense of Otherness felt by the audience toward the poor.

A third form of objectification is the representation of the poor and homeless as passive/inactive and as victims. One of the principle tenets of naturalism, according to most literary historians, is a belief in, or at least recognition of, the forces of environment. Influenced by Spencer and Darwin, naturalists portray their characters as generally helpless victims of environment and an indifferent universe–this simple and common definition of naturalism has been echoed throughout the commentary on naturalists such as Crane. His inscription on the first edition of *Maggie* supports such an understanding. Crane wrote, "'It is inevitable that you be greatly shocked by this book but continue, please with all possible courage to the end. For it tries to show that environment is a tremendous thing in the world and frequently shapes lives regardless'" (qtd. in editor's introduction to *Maggie* 3). If one's life is determined by environment, then the poor are automatically coded as victims, rather than contributing members of society.

Critics have at times overstated Crane's belief in determinism. Patrick K. Dooley discusses this trend in *The Pluralistic Philosophy of Stephen Crane*. Dooley offers a more nuanced understanding of Crane's philosophy:

> Regarding social position and justice, Crane sees only a coincidental connection between the forces that govern city life and elemental human needs, although he does find that the unconcern, animosity, and intransigence of city life throttle individual hopes. He suggests that although the artificial environment of the city is, like nature, indifferent to aspirations, nature's rhythms and laws have a neutrality amenable to human effort. (57)

Determinism and environment are not absolute, in other words. Dooley's reading of Crane supplants earlier, more simplistic explanations of Crane's determinism (which sometimes struggled with the fact that Maggie "blossomed in a mud puddle"). Nevertheless, Dooley does not suggest that Crane's treatment of the poor and homeless is necessarily fair or constructive. Effort *can* overcome environment, but rarely does. One does not encounter a poor or homeless person in Crane's work who succeeds or thrives (in any conventional sense) in the slums.[23] In many cases they are, in fact, inactive.

In "An Experiment in Misery," Crane entitles a section "Men Lay Like the Dead." Crane represents the men as passive and abject: "For the most part they were statuesque, carven, dead" (*Sketches* 38). Like Riis's penchant for photographs of homeless men and street boys sleeping on the floor, Crane sees the poor as abject victims. Put simply, abjection is a form of objectification. Trachtenberg concurs. Discussing "An Experiment in Misery" and "An Experiment in Luxury," he reasons that "The two 'experiments' conclude that the rich are banal but live well and that the homeless poor are victims whose inner acquiescence is form of cowardice" (153).

Fourth, Crane objectifies the poor and homeless by representing them as animalistic, primitive, violent, and deformed. In other words, they are distinctly Other.

Violence pervades *Maggie*, and, by extension, the tenements of New York overall. Crane attempts to show how violence is a learned response to one's environment. Chapter I opens with Jimmie fighting other boys "for the honor of Rum Alley" (36). The boys fight violently, until Jimmie's father intervenes. Ironically, Jimmie's father threatens him with violence for fighting: "Here, you Jim, git up, now, while I belt yer life out, you damned disorderly brat" (39). Children witness their parents fighting, and violence becomes the common, accepted response to nearly every conflict. Crane wants his readers to realize that something is wrong: that children should not be exposed to such violence.[24] However, the reader is left with the impression that the poor are inherently violent.

Violence, as a form of difference or Otherness, occurs frequently, as do images of the poor as animalistic, primitive, and deformed. Donald Pizer traces the images of battle and prison in *Maggie*, representing two ways that the poor are treated as different and dangerous. He argues that the Johnsons are guided primarily by instinct, not higher reasoning. Pizer notes, "Once introduced, this image of the Bowery as an amoral, animal world is maintained throughout *Maggie*" (126). In Chapter XI: Jimmie "snarled like a wild animal" (70); "The glare of a panther came into Pete's eyes" (70); The combatants "bristled like three roosters" (70); "The bravery of bull-dogs sat upon the faces of the men" (71); and Jimmie ducked "with the quickness of a cat" (71). While this imagery may have appealed to the literary sensibilities of Crane's editors, an association is made between the inhabitants of the Bowery and animals.

Crane's narrator also mocks the primitive, unrefined tastes of those who sought entertainment in the cheap theaters and clubs that Maggie and Pete attend. The poor also seem to be driven by instinct, as Pizer mentions. At times, Crane directly describes these characters as deformed and defective. In "An Experiment in Misery," the narrator observes homeless men in the lodging house who "showed bumps and deficiencies of all kinds" (40). He continues, "There were others who exhibited many deformities. Shoulders were slanting, bumped, pulled this way and pulled that way" (40). Overall, Crane depicted the slums as a mysterious space populated by primitive, animalistic, deformed beings who differed substantially from his middle-class audience.

At times, Crane hints at the humanity of the poor and homeless. "The Men in the Storm" shows that some of the homeless men waiting in line at a five cent lodging house have a sense of humor. But this is treated as a revelation or inconsistency because "one does not expect to find the quality of humor in a heap of old clothes under a snowdrift" (*Sketches* 94–95). Crane depersonalizes the homeless men in this case by legitimizing the belief that the poor are not or should not be happy or jovial, and in the characterization of them as inanimate objects ("a heap of old clothes").

In the same essay, Crane perpetuates the historical distinction between the deserving and undeserving poor. Therefore, not all of the poor were defective. Rather,

> Many were strong, healthy, clear-skinned fellows with that stamp of countenance which is not frequently seen upon seekers after charity. There were men of undoubted patience, industry and temperance, who in time of ill-fortune, do not habitually turn to rail at the state of society, snarling at the arrogance of the rich and bemoaning the cowardice of the poor [. . .] . (93)

The strong, healthy, clear-skinned, deserving poor are contrasted with the deformed, primitive, complaining, undeserving poor. David Ward explains how this type of discourse influenced attitudes toward the poor in general:

> Presumed to be devoid of any local or familial attachments, vagrants were regarded as outcasts who had abandoned the values of society at large and ought, therefore, to be ineligible for assistance. Although they were only a small minority of the total residents of the slums, the pathological social conditions associated with itinerant able-bodied but unemployed adult males were often assumed to be typical of the slums in general. (54)

Ward acknowledges the ability of late nineteenth century Americans to categorize the homeless poor and see their condition as pathological. Crane reflected his culture in his awareness of the categories of the deserving and undeserving poor, and he influenced it by contributing to a discourse which reified this distinction.

To complete my examination of the cultural work of Crane's texts, I believe it may be instructive to contrast his work with another writer who did not sensationalize or objectify the poor and homeless to the extent that Crane did. I have suggested that discourse has objectified poverty and homelessness, and, in turn, affected public perceptions of the inhabitants of the slums. Because the slums became a site of entertainment or spectacle, the discourse required unusual, startling, thrilling, mysterious details, which certain writers gladly provided. The poor and homeless needed to be depicted as different in order for the text to be interesting, marketable, and publishable. Crane reflects the contemporary cultural values of the dominant culture, but other writers saw the poor as much less foreign, mysterious, and Other.

William T. Elsing published an essay entitled "Life in New York Tenement-Houses" in 1892. Although it addresses the same topics Crane addresses, Elsing's text presents a much different, less sensational account of the tenement districts. First, compare Elsing's remark that "I have been a frequent guest in the homes of the humble" (133) to the disguise and posturing Crane employs in his investigation of the poor. The participant-observer occupied a position of adventure or excitement. Something vaguely dangerous or forbidden accompanies the effort to trick the poor into believing that the writer is actually one of them. Keith Gandal even compares the slums to wars and the West as sites of adventure in the 1890s.[25] Elsing, however, positions himself as a "guest" rather than an adventurer, spy, or invader.

Elsing knowingly remarks,

> I have noticed that nearly all those who work among the poor of our great cities fall into the natural habit of drawing too dark a picture of the real state of things. The outside world has always been more inclined to listen to weird, startling, and thrilling statements than to the more ordinary and commonplace facts. (133)

Discourse can be viewed as the "natural habit" of texts to follow precedent set by other texts. Since literary texts have either romanticized or objectified the condition of homelessness, texts like Elsing's may not "fit" expectations of form, content, or orientation and therefore may have fallen outside the discourse (or the literary canon). Elsing even admits that he could have presented a sensational but misleading account which would have been consistent with the contemporary discourse which treated the poor as spectacle.

Elsing provides a model of how a text can address the subject matter of poverty and homelessness without subscribing to the belief that the poor are substantially different from or inferior to anyone else. His realistic account, unfortunately, did not have the advantage of being interesting to an audience which was confronting the mysteries of the city and the effects of urbanization. A balanced account of the tenement districts simply was not compelling. Elsing says that

> There are homes where the interior is bare and dirty, the furniture broken and scanty, the table greasy, the bedlinen yellow, the air foul and heavy, the children pale, frowsy, and sticky, so that you squirm when the baby wants to kiss you; but there is also another and brighter side. There are at the same time thousands of cheerful, happy homes in the tenement-houses. (135–136)

The unpleasant details Elsing alludes to in this passage are representative of a host of similarly appalling details in a text such as *Maggie*. In the work of Crane, and Riis, very few "cheerful, happy homes" are present. Because a "normal" home was not interesting or newsworthy enough, the discourse presented a vision of the slums and tenements which was mysterious, different, and Other.

HOW THE OTHER HALF LOOKS: JACOB RIIS'S REPRESENTATION OF HOMELESSNESS AND POVERTY

Like Crane, Jacob Riis had positive intentions, and both writers contributed to an increased understanding of the living conditions in the slums. David Ward discusses the use of illustrations in the work of social reformers. He states that "Jacob Riis, who pioneered the use of photography in his efforts to reach the conscience of his readers, was the most influential practitioner of this style of advocacy. [. . .] The problem of the slums received wide publicity, and the photographic realism of Jacob Riis did much [to] arouse public consciousness [. . .]" (71). However, Ward also notes how Riis "manipulated his frames to emphasize the negative aspects of slum life. The effects of flash photography on the faces and settings of his subjects exaggerated the sense of helplessness he so evocatively captured" (71). In other words, Riis, like Crane, sought to represent the slums and the poor themselves as different and shocking.[26]

First, the method Riis used to photograph his subjects suggests that he saw them merely as *objects* to be represented. Riis wished to take candid photos in order to preserve the realism of the scene. Therefore, he would attempt to catch his subjects unaware, often at night. However, the lack of available light posed limitations. Flash powder became available in 1887, and Riis immediately acquired the new technology in order to photograph the slums and slum-dwellers in areas of low light. Two men accompanied Riis on "raiding parties" on a few occasions before Riis became more familiar with the technology and the men became disinterested.

He describes the typical reaction to these "raiding parties" in *The New York Sun* in 1888:

> What [the inhabitants of the tenements] saw was a ghostly tripod, three or four figures in the gloom, some weird and uncanny movements, the blinding flash, and they heard the patter of retreating footsteps and the mysterious visitors were gone before they could collect their scattered thoughts and try to find out what it was all about. (qtd. in Peters 53)

This troubling strategy establishes Riis's ability to objectify the poor as objects to be studied and "captured" on film. Pictures of startled people in *How the Other Half Lives* prove that they were not completely aware of what was going on (See Figure 3).

In addition to objectifying them, Riis hardly conceals his contempt for the poor inhabitants of the slums at times. Early in *How the Other Half Lives*, he exclaims, "If it shall appear that the sufferings and the sins of the 'other half,' and the evil they breed, are but a just punishment upon the community that gave it no other choice, it will be because that is the truth" (60). Although this passage seems to locate responsibility in wider society rather than in the poor themselves, Riis goes on to refer to the "nurseries of pauperism and crime that fill *our* jails and police courts" (60, italics added); the "scum of forty thousand human wrecks" (60); the beggars who "prey upon *our* charities" (60, italics added); and the "standing army of ten thousand tramps with all that that implies" (60). In other words, Riis views the tramps as a menace or threat, as did other contributors to the "backlash" against tramps in the late nineteenth century. If this implication is not clear enough, in Chapter VI, "The Bend," he adds, "Here, too, shunning the light, skulks the unclean beast of dishonest idleness. 'The Bend' is the home of the tramp as well as the rag-picker" (96).

Homeless tramps receive bitter condemnation from Riis. Given the popularity of *How the Other Half Lives* in lecture and in printed form, Riis's contribution to a discourse which depersonalized and stereotyped the homeless is likely significant. The cultural work performed by his representations of homelessness is troubling. Riis refers to the tramp as lazy and as alcoholic: "For next to idleness the tramp loves rum; next to rum stale beer, its equivalent of the gutter. And the first and last go best together" (110). Additionally, "Once started on the career of a tramp, the man keeps to it because it is the laziest. Tramps and toughs profess the same doctrine, that the world owes them a living" (111). These beliefs were popular at the time and led to "solutions" to the tramp menace such as whippings, labor colonies, and poisoning. In this context, the cultural work of representations of homelessness can be severe.

Like the contrast between Crane and Elsing above, alternative responses to homelessness and poverty were present, but less familiar to a wide audience. David Ward and Lisa N. Peters refer to the photography of Lewis Hine as an example of more realistic, less sensational images than Riis's. Abjection, inaction, and isolation are the hallmarks of Riis's representations of the poor and homeless. Hine, conversely, attempted to capture the "cheerful, happy" sides of the poor, much like Elsing did. According to Ward,

> The photographic record of the slums [. . .] revealed a more complex interpretation of the immigrants' world [than just poverty and crime]; Lewis Hine, in particular, captured the intimacy and vitality of street life [. . .] . A medium that had documented the environmental deficiencies of the slums expanded its vision to celebrate the ways in which the poor *used* their environment. (115, italics added)

Hine's subjects used their environment; they were not victims of it. For example, Hine includes a photo of a group of children in the tenement district playing baseball (See Figure 4). This image (and many, many other photographs that Hine took of *working* men and women) contrasts with Riis's tendency to represent the poor as solitary, inactive, and depressed. In photos such as "Street Arabs in Sleeping Quarters," we see street boys, faces hidden, sleeping in a dark corner of an alley (See Figures 5 and 6). Although other photos do not depend on the representation of reclining figures, Riis photographed several men sleeping on the floor in police lodging houses or other cheap lodging houses (See Figure 7). This decision is unlike Hine's decision to show poor people actively participating in their environment.

In her essay "Images of the Homeless in American Art, 1860–1910," Lisa N. Peters demonstrates how Riis's work was much more graphic, realistic, and uncensored than paintings of the poor and homeless at the time, but she also indicates how Riis sensationalized his images. Like Ward, she compares the styles of Hine and Riis. She explains,

> [Hine] chose not to surprise his subjects with the sudden flashes used by Riis, instead selecting his shots carefully and considering pictorial as well as expressive aspects of his views. At times he even gathered groups of immigrants who were not necessarily related, arranging them in family-like clusters to shape his images. (61)

These family arrangements (See Figure 8) contrast with Riis's picture of a solitary Chinese man in Chinatown in *How the Other Half Lives*, and with a general tendency to portray solitary individuals (See Figure 9).

At times, it seems that Riis went out of his way to construct stereotypical images of the poor and homeless. Riis describes the composition of "The Tramp," for example, in Chapter VII, "A Raid on the Stale-beer Dives" (See Figure 10). He writes,

> On one of my visits to "the Bend" I came across a particularly ragged and disreputable tramp, who sat smoking his pipe on the rung of a ladder with such evident philosophic contentment in the busy labor of a score of rag-pickers all about him, that I bade him sit for a picture, offering him ten cents for the job. (111)

That character can be visible during this period is evident in Riis's remark that the tramp looked "disreputable." This (false) belief contributed to the accepted categorization of deserving and undeserving poor. More importantly, perhaps, Riis admits that several rag-pickers were active in the immediate area, but he chooses to stage and photograph a solitary, inactive homeless tramp. To fit his belief in the idleness of tramps and their bad habits, Riis pays the man to be photographed, sitting complacently, with a pipe in his mouth. The preeminent photograph of rag-pickers–who were actively doing work and who could have been photographed at the same time–which appears in *How the Other Half Lives* is of a woman rag-picker holding her baby in a poorly furnished home (See Figure 11). Riis chose to photograph the solitary, inactive tramp amid the active community of rag-pickers, as well as a solitary, inactive woman in her modest home who would have been actively working at other times. These choices in subject matter (unlike Hine's photo of the baseball game) code the poor as isolated, lazy, depressed, and unnecessary to wider society.

In his photos and his writing, Riis tries to bring a greater understanding of the poor to his audience. However, his rhetorical/compositional choices led to the objectification and stereotyping of the poor and homeless. For Riis and Crane, their positives intentions were undermined by the construction of their texts. Speaking generally about texts by down-and-outers, Mark Pittenger states,

> That these texts so regularly subverted themselves on questions of human unity and difference suggests that their authórs harbored a contradictory consciousness typical of an era in which environmental explanations of poverty were supplanting, but had not vanquished, moral and hereditarian ones. (53)

Pittenger suggests that naturalists or down-and-outers reflected their culture by demonstrating the contradictions felt by many of the time. The interest in Otherness, urbanization, and science produced a confusing array of ideas, beliefs, and texts about the poor, the slums, the effects of environment, and the obligation of the upper classes to help the lower classes. Logically, yet unfortunately, writers like Crane and Riis responded to the interest in poverty and homelessness as a form of entertainment or spectacle. Meeting this demand, they contributed to a wider discourse in literature, photography, sociology, journalism, and history which tends to objectify the condition of homelessness, when it does not romanticize it, as I explain in the following chapter.

Fig. 3. "Five Cents a Spot" (ca. 1890). Museum of the City of New York. The Jacob A. Riis Collection, #155.

Fig. 4. “Playground in Tenement Alley” (ca. 1909). Photograph by Lewis W. Hine. Courtesy of George Eastman House.

Fig. 5. “Street Arabs, Barelegged; Mulberry Street” (ca. 1890). Museum of the City of New York. The Jacob A. Riis Collection, #122.

Fig. 6. “Street Arabs at Night” (ca. 1890). Museum of the City of New York. The Jacob A. Riis Collection, #123.

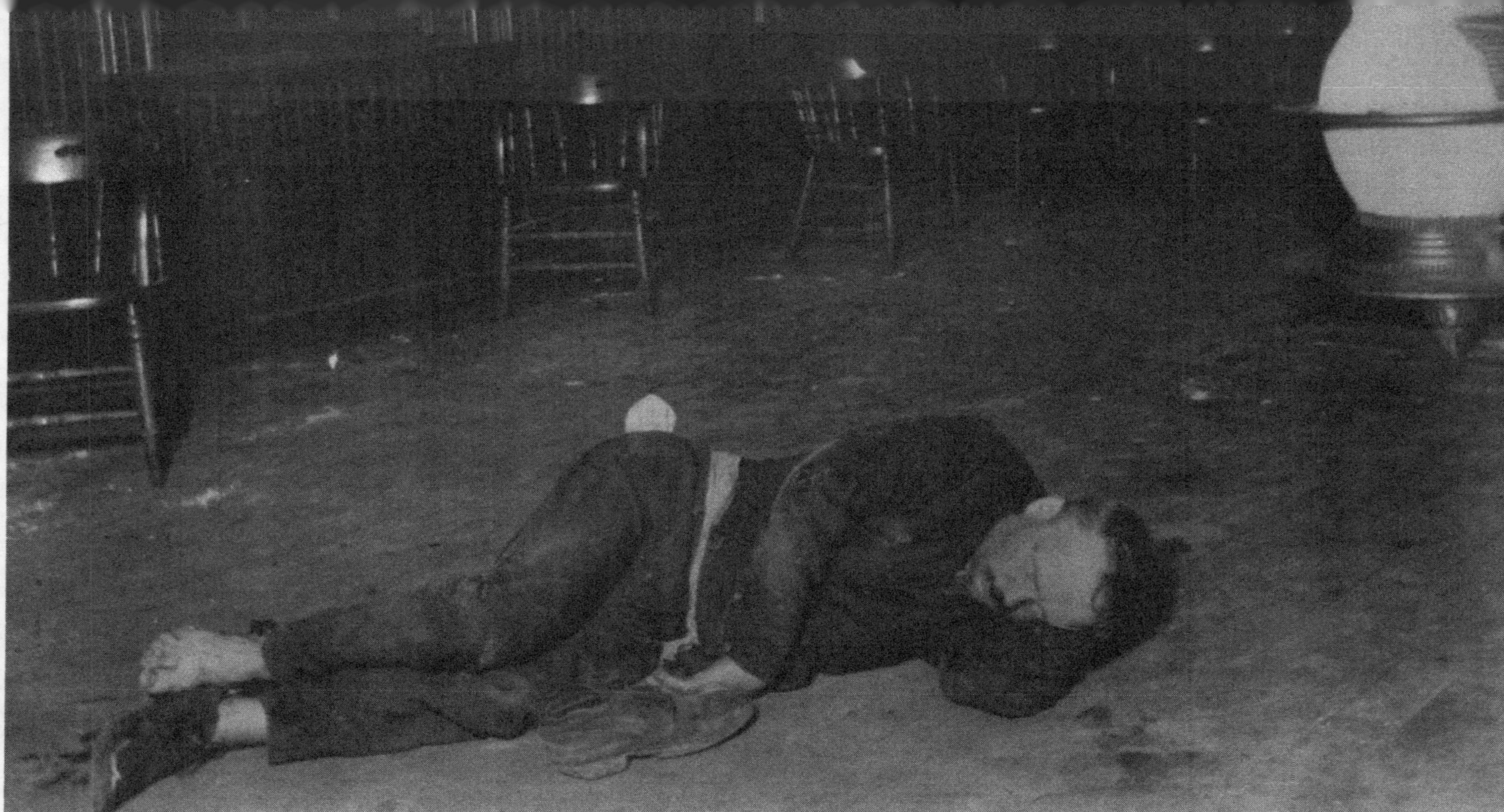

Fig. 7. "Police Station Lodger: The Single Typhus Lodger in Elizabeth Street. He Lay by the Stove in the Policemen's Room, No One Dreaming What Ailed Him" (ca. 1890). Museum of the City of New York. The Jacob A. Riis Collection, #243.

Fig. 8. "Looking for Lost Luggage, Ellis Island, 1905." Photograph by Lewis W. Hine. Courtesy of George Eastman House.

Fig. 9. "Chinatown. The Official Organ of the Colony" (ca. 1890). Museum of the City of New York. The Jacob A. Riis Collection, #260.

Fig. 10. "Tramp in Mulberry Street Yard" (ca. 1890). Museum of the City of New York. The Jacob A. Riis Collection, #90.

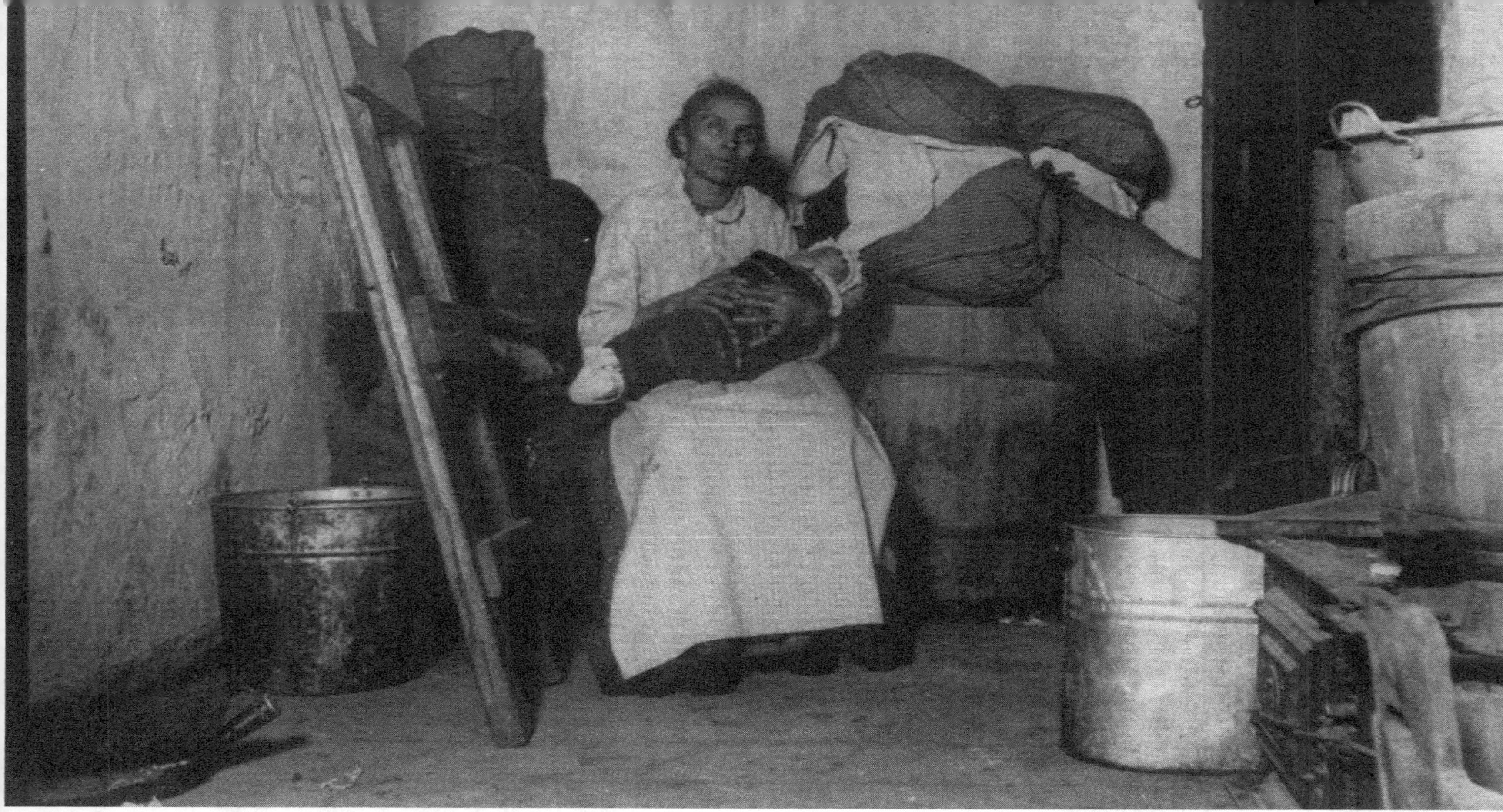

Fig. 11: "In the Home of an Italian Rag-Picker; An Italian Mother and Her Baby, Jersey Street" (ca. 1898). Museum of the City of New York. The Jacob A. Riis Collection, 157.

Chapter Four

Romance of *The Road*

Jack London and the Publication of Tramp Autobiographies in America

BETWEEN 1890 AND 1940 APPROXIMATELY FORTY AUTOBIOGRAPHIES of tramps (or "hobos") were published in the United States and England.[1] These autobiographies exhibit remarkable similarities. Given the number of these works and the relative coherence as a subgenre of American literature, it is surprising that little scholarship has focused on these texts. Sociological treatments of the tramp appear throughout the twentieth century; however, with the exception of Jack London, relatively little critical attention has been paid to tramp/hobo writers.[2]

The shared traits in these autobiographies–a sense of optimism and adventure, an awareness of being "literary," a lack of criticism of the dominant culture–parallel the traits exhibited in what Christopher P. Wilson calls the "popular naturalists" of the Progressive era. Wilson argues that authors such as London, Upton Sinclair, David Graham Phillips, and Lincoln Steffens became popular as a result of their interdependent relationship with a new publishing industry which "diluted" their material to an extent. Like the popular naturalists Wilson describes, the tramp writers "diluted" their work by sanitizing and romanticizing the tramp experience. In this chapter, I argue that tramp autobiographies, such as *The Road* by Jack London, romanticized the condition of homelessness; as a result, the cultural work they did was detrimental.

One way that tramp autobiographies romanticized homelessness was by representing the author as an intellectual, usually an observer of other tramps and the tramp lifestyle. Wilson notes, with Christopher Lasch, that the writer/intellectual became a viable occupation and role in the early twentieth century as a result of the new literary market and publishing industry. London, for example, a former tramp, rose from a lower class background to become one of the most popular and established writers of the time. His autobiographical account of his tramp experiences, *The*

Road, appeared in 1907, in the middle of the Progressive era and at a time when several other tramp autobiographies reached the market. In fact, the majority of these texts appeared between 1900 and 1930. Therefore, the popularity of the tramp coincides with the emergence of the intellectual during the Progressive era.[3]

This interdependence can be seen in the efforts of the tramps to make their writing seem "literary"; at the same time, professional writers and intellectuals went into the slums and on the road for inspiration and material. Such "crossing over" between classes blurs the apparent distinction between tramps and intellectuals. A subculture of intellectual tramps and hobos (centered in Chicago) also contributed to this blurring.[4] This form of "identity politics" offered a sense of security, confidence, and belonging for some. Unfortunately, it may also have led to stereotypes and false beliefs about the causes and consequences of homelessness.

TRAMPS IN THE PROGRESSIVE ERA

Several factors contributed to the interest in tramps and their autobiographies during the Progressive era. The sheer increase in the tramp population is perhaps one of the most obvious reasons. As I have indicated in earlier chapters, the existence of the wandering poor in America was less prevalent and much less visible prior to the Civil War. Poorhouses and almshouses existed as early as the 1700s, but families generally cared for the poor with the help of limited state assistance. The Civil War displaced families and individuals, causing an increase in homelessness, and a series of economic depressions between 1873 and 1893 also greatly increased the homeless population. More specifically, however, the rapid growth of industrial capitalism in the United States caused the increase in the tramp population. As Charles Hoch argues,

> The rapid expansion of the national economy after the Civil War required a mobile work force of unsettled laborers. During the last quarter of the century hundreds of thousands of such transient workers, called *tramps*, traveled across the United States. They mined, lumbered, herded, harvested, built, and otherwise labored to provide a crucial but overlooked economic contribution to national development. (19)

Thus, the need for a mobile work force corresponded to the increase in the tramp population. Increases in immigration and urbanization also affected this movement as more and more people competed (unsuccessfully) for the relatively small number of affordable dwellings in American cities. As a result, many single males went on the road in search of employment and income. These searches often led to employment in the railroad industry. Several sociologists (Miller, Monkkonen, Wormser) reveal the interdependence of tramps and the rail industry. In fact, besides agriculture, rail provided perhaps the largest number of jobs for tramps before 1920 (Monkkonen 9). As Henry Miller remarks, "The railroads were an *industry*, and it required large numbers of casual, unskilled workers" (34). It is not surprising, then, that much of the tramp literature, such as *The Road* by Jack London, links the tramp experience with the railroad.

In addition to the sheer increase in the tramp population as a result of industrialization, four other factors may have contributed to increased awareness and interest in tramping at the beginning of the century. First, efforts to minimize and/or eliminate tramps and beggars at the end of the nineteenth century called attention to the existence of homeless wanderers at the time. This has been discussed in the context of the "tramp menace" in Chapter Two and elsewhere.

The backlash against tramps by several politicians, social scientists, and journalists was most severe before the turn of the century. Although these texts indicate a severe distrust and dislike of tramps, they do not represent the attitudes of all Americans at the time. As Kenneth L. Kusmer remarks:

> If many middle-class individuals had not been prone to aid tramps and give alms to beggars, there would have been no need for the constant admonitions against "unscientific almsgiving" that issued from the pens of editorial writers and moralists. (105)

The backlash against tramps in sociology and journalism receded during the Progressive era, although similar vehemence occurs throughout American history. This backlash resulted in a variety of anti-vagrancy laws at the end of the nineteenth century; perhaps unintentionally it also alerted many Americans to the existence of tramps.

A second movement which increased awareness of tramps was the International Workers of the World (Wobblies), an organization which symbolized the political and social activism of the Progressive era. This "union" welcomed all laborers and, although its membership rose and fell throughout the early twentieth century, it increased the visibility of unskilled workers–including tramps (Zinn 324, Miller 42). By organizing, protesting, and striking, the I.W.W. called attention to the condition and necessity of unskilled labor in the United States. The organization also arranged parades and meetings to increase awareness of their agenda, and it recruited heavily among tramps and the unemployed, wandering poor. The I.W.W. attempted to unionize all laborers regardless of background, especially migratory workers who had no formal skills or occupation. Their slogan, "One Big Union," indicates the desire to recognize and unionize all laborers: a particularly valuable goal at a time when the value of migratory workers was not realized by the general public. (However, responses to the I.W.W. were not always positive. Public sympathy evaporated after World War I; members were jailed, beaten, tarred and feathered, and shot.)

Similarly, the 1894 march on Washington D.C. of "General Coxey's army," which brought together thousands of unemployed, migratory workers, focused attention on the plight of tramps. In *The Road*, Jack London chronicles his experience in a renegade division of Coxey's army led by "General" Kelly. The seriousness of the march's organizers, such as Coxey and Kelly, contrasts sharply with London's carefree, boastful account of the event. The chapter which describes his experience, "Two Thousand Stiffs," typifies London's excited, optimistic tone regarding his life on the road. Later, I describe how London's optimism fits into the overall pattern of tramp autobiographies. At this point, however, I merely wish to show how the march increased political and cultural awareness of the tramp. As Michael Davis reveals:

> Quite apart from the eccentric views of General Coxey himself or of his various subalterns in the Grand Army of the Unemployed, the great political significance of the demonstration was its massive popularity, seen in the hundreds of thousands of populists, farmers, and fellow workers who turned out to cheer on the detachments of the army in its march on Washington. The "tramp" became the hero of the hour to the sympathetic Americans whose views had never been reflected outside of the labor press. (165)

Unfortunately, London and other tramp writers undermined the intent and impact of Coxey's army by emphasizing individualism and nonconformity.

Davis also reveals a fourth and final factor which contributed to the increased awareness of tramps. In his essay "Forced to Tramp: The Perspective of the Labor Press, 1870–1900," Davis outlines the various efforts of journalists to bring attention to the working conditions of (unskilled) laborers and to the widespread existence of tramps. Four hundred labor newspapers existed in the last quarter of the nineteenth century. These papers attempted to correct the destructive misconceptions about tramps put forth in other publications–especially those of the "scientific" charity organizations like the Charity Organization Society. As discussed in the Introduction and Chapter Two, scientific charity organizations attempted to link homelessness to personal irresponsibility and moral failure. Conversely, the labor press suggested that the tramp was an economic product and necessity of increased industrialism, rather than a threat or menace. Although the labor press and the popular press often offered contradictory messages, they informed most Americans of the existence of tramps at the beginning of the twentieth century.

The increased number of tramps, the positive *and* negative media attention, the International Workers of the World, Coxey's army: these factors created a tremendous interest in tramps at the beginning of the century. Very few first-person accounts appear before the 1890s, however.[5] Previous to the Progressive era, tramps were a source of material for various writers, but they were not authors themselves. The patronage system and the romantic notion of an "author" essentially prevented the lower class from writing for publication. The widespread publication of autobiographies by tramps required changes in attitudes and sensibilities, as well as a corresponding change in the publishing industry.

THE PUBLICATION OF TRAMP AUTOBIOGRAPHIES

Two related contingencies of the early twentieth century were a result of a rejection of earlier Victorian/romantic tendencies and a shift in literary tastes and practices. Because the market and the publishing industry could sustain writers for the first time, anyone could theoretically become a writer during the Progressive era. Previously, the writer-intellectual required either private patronage or independent wealth to survive–both of which were rare and excluded the majority of the population. At the turn of the century, however, writers sought new experiences for material and could (sometimes) make a career out of writing. Christopher Lasch argues that "Seeking experience, [American intellectuals] rejected a culture which seemed to them increasingly artificial, increasingly cut off from life" (101).

Furthermore, Lasch contends that intellectuals envied the working class because they had easier access to this direct experience of real life. This led to the (un-Victorian) "discovery" of the "uncivilized man" who "had never accepted the restraints of adulthood or consented to become a responsible member of society" (143–144). Victorian values and romantic conventions were rejected in favor of a more direct, realistic experience of life, which in turn led to an interest in those people who were already adept at such a lifestyle: outcasts, the down and out, and, I would argue, tramps. Christopher P. Wilson elucidates: "The new cultural premium on experience counseled any writer, whatever his or her origins, to see American society from the 'outside in' or the 'bottom up'" (*Labor* 113). Thus, the "cultural premium on experience" opened the door for books describing the previously unfamiliar experiences of tramps.

Moreover, the rejection of the romantic notion of the "inspired artist" allowed formerly marginalized writers to tell their own stories.[6] Literature was no longer reserved for upper class authors inspired by their muses:

> Writers from the lowest layers of the national life could arise and testify to experiences previously beyond the ken of accepted literary discourse; conversely, formerly isolated writers could investigate and expose the ills of American society. (Wilson 3)

As Wilson shows in *The Labor of Words: Literary Professionalism in the Progressive Era*, the democratic intentions of the Progressive era were not fully realized. However, the growing acceptance of marginalized writers and the interest in direct experience allowed for the publication of dozens of tramp autobiographies which may not have been possible in any other period.

Writing in 1930, John S. Sumner reveals just how willing publishers were to accept tramp/hobo autobiographies: "any hobo temporarily sober can find a publisher to place on the market with great éclat an epic of Hobodom, provided there is sufficient of the hobo atmosphere" (2736). The fact that approximately forty such autobiographies appeared before 1940 demonstrates their popularity at the time. Leon Ray Livingston successfully published his own work under the pseudonym A-No.1, as did a few other tramps, but most of the autobiographies came out of established publishing houses which were certainly aware of the literary market, thereby suggesting a significant popular appeal.

The reception of these texts was mixed. Harry Kemp's *Tramping on Life*, published in 1922, received exceptionally good reviews and sold very well (Brevda, *Harry Kemp* 129), but few others had the same success. *The Road*, accepted for publication only after London became an established writer, was not well received and went into remainders. None of the autobiographies remain popular today, and only London's fame persists–largely *in spite of* his tramp fiction (Etulain 21–27). Nevertheless, the publication of so many autobiographies during the Progressive era indicates a strong interest in writings by tramps.

TRAMP AUTOBIOGRAPHIES AS A GENRE OF AMERICAN LITERATURE

The similarities in these works also indicate an awareness on the part of the authors and publishers of what was acceptable and interesting at the time. Certain traits seem to underlie almost all of the tramp autobiographies: an emphasis on tramping as an adventure or choice rather than a necessity; an awareness on the writer's part of being an author or intellectual; an optimistic tone; and a lack of criticism of the cultural status quo. These traits illustrate the homogeneity of the tramp autobiographies as a genre and offer insights into American culture during the Progressive era. In other words, the tramp writers seem to have "diluted" and romanticized their works much like the "popular naturalists" whom Christopher Wilson describes. Wilson differentiates between naturalism and popular naturalism:

> "[N]aturalism" refers to fictional or nonfictional prose which purports to demonstrate scientifically the social and environmental determinants of human existence, usually by focusing on extreme circumstances that dramatize the force of the environment. By "popular naturalism" I mean the wing of this literary movement which, by diluting its determinism with romantic elements, achieved consistent popularity. (*Labor* 203)

Just as London, Sinclair, David Graham Phillips, and Lincoln Steffens adapted to the sensibilities of their readers and publishers, the authors of tramp autobiographies also seem to have diluted their work in order to cater to the prevailing tastes of the time. While professional writers and tramps distanced themselves from certain bourgeois, Victorian conventions, they also maintained romantic tendencies which apparently appealed to their audiences. The accounts of life on the road and on the rails needed to present the realism of the "hobo atmosphere," but avoided criticism of the dominant culture and omitted excessively bleak commentary about the living conditions of tramps. The writers minimized determinism by claiming that they became tramps by choice rather than necessity, and they romanticized their accounts with the inclusion of plenty of adventure and excitement.

Lynne M. Adrian alludes to the homogeneity of the tramp autobiographies in her introduction to *Tales of an American Hobo* by Charles Elmer Fox:

> All the hobo autobiographies tell of the author's first train ride and the hobo who initiated him (or rarely her) into the ways of the road. The autobiographies include stories of decking a fast train, holding down a particularly hard train, or riding in a tough spot on the train. They include a tale of an unusual person who has taught the author something important and the tale of someone killed from riding a train the wrong way. There are tales of the beauties of nature, run-ins with the law, and developing skill at begging for food. [. . .] (Fox xvii–xviii)

This provides a fairly accurate composite of the tramp autobiographies. Beyond these shared "scenes," however, the autobiographers also mention similar motives for tramping. Some authors hint at child abuse or difficulty at home as the reason for being on the road. For example, Barbara Starke indicates that she ran away from home to escape abuse in *Born in Captivity: The Story of a Girl's Escape* (1931). Similarly, Jim Tully, forced to work at an early age because he is an orphan, "escapes" the tedium and confinement of his job in a small town, as described in *Beggars of Life: A Hobo Autobiography* (1924). These authors quickly skip over the cause of their homelessness and go on to describe the thrill and value of life on the road.

Adventure and "wanderlust" are much more frequently cited as reasons for tramping. For example, London describes his motives in *The Road*: "I became a tramp–well, because of the life that was in me, of the wanderlust in my blood that would not let me rest" (274). Josiah Flynt, to whom London dedicated *The Road*, states in *My Life* (1908), "I was simply an ordinary boy possessed of an extraordinary bump for wandering, which, when the 'go-fever' was in me, sent me off to strange parts and peculiar adventures [. . .]" (9–10). Bertha Thompson, in *Sister of the Road: The Autobiography of Box-Car Bertha* (1937), remarks, "I am truly married to the box cars. There's something constantly itching in my soul that only the road and the box cars can satisfy. Jobs, lovers, a child–don't seem to be able to curb my wanderlust" (Reitman 275).

Comments about "wanderlust" appear frequently in the tramp autobiographies and seem to divert attention from economic or social forces that cause homelessness. In other words, "wanderlust" obscures the reality of forced tramping because of unemployment, low wages, high rent, or discrimination. As a body of work, the autobiographies minimize determinism by locating responsibility in the tramps themselves, not in the political or economic system. Many of the tramp authors did go on the road in search of adventure; however, the emphasis on wanderlust conceals social and economic factors which readers might have found threatening. Directly or indirectly, the authors may have been encouraged to avoid such intrusions on their readers. This tendency supports Wilson's conclusion that some writers downplayed determinism to appeal to the semi-Victorian tastes of their audience. Unfortunately, the wanderlust explanation would have buttressed the argument made by scientific charity organizations and others that homelessness was a result of individual moral failure. Very few sources acknowledge any legitimate flaws in the economic system, and citing individual causes for tramping obscures the reality of forced homelessness which many experienced.

A second commonality among the tramp autobiographies is a self-consciousness on the author's part of being a writer or an intellectual (which also reveals an awareness of an audience). This trait manifests itself in frequent comments which indicate that the author is observing the tramp lifestyle as a source of material to write about. It is also apparent in the numerous references to influential writers and intellectuals. Likewise, several authors explicitly mention the intellectual desire and capacity of tramps.

Jack London, in a letter to Cloudesley Johns, a friend who also spent time tramping, says, "I'm think[ing] mabbe [sic] I'll take a vacation on the road this summer just for ducks and to gather material, or rather, to fresh en up what I have long since accreted [sic]" (Labor 189). This letter, written in 1900, indicates London's interest in life on the road as a source of material. London kept a detailed diary of his tramping experience in 1894 to draw on in his writing, and he submitted stories for publication as early as 1897 that dealt with tramping (Etulain 69). He also spent six weeks in 1902 gathering material for *People of the Abyss*–a discussion of poverty and homelessness in London. His tramp experiences culminate in *The Road*. References to Milton, Browning, and Nietsche, and the epigraph from Kipling referring to those who "go observin' matters till they die" identify London as an extensive reader, as well as a writer.

William Edge, Josiah Flynt, Box Car Bertha, Barbara Starke, Vachel Lindsay, Jim Tully, W. H. Davies, Harry Kemp, and Glen Mullin (among others) also identify themselves as writer-intellectuals. Edge, an ex-college student, describes his year on the road in *The Main Stem* (1927). In it, he remarks, "The hobo reads, and often he reads very good stuff" (87). He also relates how his companions broadened his education in socialism and literature. Josiah Flynt nonchalantly weaves a discussion of his doctoral studies at Berlin University and his research at the British Museum into his account of tramping throughout Europe and the United States. Throughout *My Life*, Flynt presents himself as an observer:

> The "seeing and admiring" is the privilege of the spectator who, because he is such, may be near the crowd and not of it. So, in a sense, I stood aloof, my insatiable curiosity often prompting me simply to observe where otherwise I might have freely partaken. (323)

Flynt, like many autobiographers, distances himself from the "real" tramps by positioning himself as an observer.

Box Car Bertha lists numerous authors she has read, as well as sociologists and professors at a hobo college where she studied: "I am mentioning all these illustrious names to make it quite plain that the hoboes are not a bunch of dumb ignoramuses, and that they have an interest in and capacity for good lectures and for worthwhile intellectual food" (Reitman 75). Like Flynt, she is a detached observer. She portrays her experiences as fodder to be processed for her book. *Sister of the Road* becomes a treatise on hobo subcultures–she literally studies thieves, prostitutes, drug users, social workers, and revolutionists by joining each group in order to write about them. Tables and charts in the appendix attest to her thoroughness as a "reporter," but the book does not stray from her first person perspective–all of the information is first-hand.

Barbara Starke drops the names of several authors, and notes that reading and writing came easily to her. Vachel Lindsay and W. H. Davies identify themselves as poets with artistic sensibilities. Lindsay's *Adventures While Preaching the Gospel of Beauty* (1916) describes how he traveled through the Midwest as a migrant worker, working for farmers or bartering for food and lodging with his poetry. Lindsay preaches his Gospel, "a little one-page formula for making America lovelier" (11), because "Every State is to have its Emerson, its Whittier, its Longfellow, its Hawthorne and the rest" (174). Davies is also "sincere in his love for literature" (172) and worries that his tramping will cause him to sacrifice his reading. *The Autobiography of a Super-Tramp* (1908) describes how poetry and tramping both alleviate stagnation and discontent in Davies's life. This valuation of the poet recalls the earlier Victorian idealization of the poet/author and suggests that the tramp autobiographies retain romantic conventions.

Other writers even more directly equate tramping with literature and intellectualism. Harry Kemp, calling himself the "Poet-Tramp," carried copies of Shakespeare, Shelley, and Keats with him and remarked, "I am a tramp for the sake of my art" (qtd. in Brevda, *Harry Kemp* 117). In *Tramping on Life: An Autobiographical Narrative* (1922), Kemp explains how he joined a ship's crew in order to write about the experience. The captain notices how Kemp watches everything and takes it in "so [he] can write a poem about it" (77). Kemp adds, "Once or twice, sheriffs who were bent on arresting me because I had no visible means of support, let me go, because it awed them to find a tramp reading Shakespeare" (126). Furthermore, the original cover of the book showed Kemp stepping off a pile of novels. Similarly, Roger Payne, "a Cambridge scientist who spent twenty-five years militantly striding about America preaching simple, severe living" (Allsop 235), titled his tramp autobiography *The Hobo Philosopher* (1920). As a final example of intellectual self-awareness, the very title of Glen Mullin's *Adventures of a Scholar Tramp* (1925) juxtaposes the figure of the tramp with the scholar/intellectual. Mullin's tramping experience occurs between his graduation from college and his entrance into art school. It supplements the standard features of the tramp autobiographies, such as his first train ride, with sophisticated vocabulary and frequent references to classical texts and authors. In each case, the tramp identifies himself or herself as a type of intellectual. In fact, nearly all of the tramp autobiographies call attention to the author as a writer-intellectual.

This identification of the tramp as a writer and/or intellectual throughout the tramp autobiographies seems to serve two related purposes. First, the tramps frequently refer to established writers and they describe themselves as accomplished artists or writers in order to enhance their own credibility. Although the interest in the "other half" afforded them a degree of respect as writers, they still needed to create an ethos of intelligence and professionalism in order to be accepted and published. Second, the authors announce their status as *observers* in order to distance themselves from the truly destitute and, therefore, uneducated or unrefined. By observing other tramps, they also justify their own existence as unemployed wanderers–they avoid the stigma of being a "bum" by posing as amateur sociologists observing their subjects. Rather than offering a glimpse into "life as it is really lived," the tramp autobiographies romanticized the lifestyle of tramps and obscured the actual difficulties of such a lifestyle.

In addition to the detachment from real tramps, romanticizing is also evident in the optimistic tone of the tramp autobiographies–the third shared trait among them. *The Road* epitomizes the carefree, optimistic tone of the tramp autobiographies. In it, London is always lucky: he manages to steal the very best provisions while he is with Coxey's army; he outwits all of the brakemen who try to throw him off of the railroad cars; he cajoles people into giving him food with his fabricated stories; even in prison he joins forces with an experienced inmate and becomes one of only a few "hall-men"–those prisoners who watch over other inmates and are able to profit in innumerable ways from their position. In fact, London repeatedly boasts of his "grafts" in prison. He profits by selling paper clips, extorting tobacco, writing letters, providing matches, passing messages, and trading for a variety of items. At every step, the reader has no doubt that London will survive and succeed. Such confidence and optimism contrasts with the determinism/pessimism of traditional literary naturalism.

His inevitable success undermines the sincerity of the few comments which suggest that tramping is difficult. In describing a trip across Nevada, London alerts his readers to the suffering of tramps:

> [R]emember, gentle reader, the hobo goes through such a land, without shelter, without money, begging his way and sleeping at night without blankets. This last is something that can be realized only by experience. (262)

This comment, intended as a warning about the perils of life as a tramp, rings hollow, since the tone of *The Road* is consistently positive and optimistic.

In the last paragraph of the novel, London misses a train and gets caught in a thunderstorm, prompting him to remark, "Oh, no, life on The Road is not all beer and skittles" (314). Although he is inconvenienced, he immediately undercuts his apparently serious message by indicating that he boarded the next train out and managed to eat breakfast in Baltimore. London endures a few nights of cold and hunger, but his strength, dexterity, and intelligence inevitably allow him to prosper in every situation. His portrait of tramping reveals a carefree, optimistic, adventurous lifestyle. As

Frederick Feied states in *No Pie in the Sky: The Hobo as American Cultural Hero in the Works of Jack London, John Dos Passos, and Jack Kerouac,* "Excitement and adventure are the keynotes of London's writing in *The Road*. Even where the subject is serious, his treatment remains jocular and light-hearted" (37).

This optimism pervades many of the tramp autobiographies. W. H. Davies's account of how he lost a foot in a train accident typifies the ability to minimize adverse experiences. After falling from a train, being dragged for several yards, and "feeling a little shaken," Davies is still unsure of what transpired:

> Sitting down in an upright position, I then began to examine myself, and now found that the right foot was severed from the ankle. This discovery did not shock me so much as the thoughts which quickly followed. For, as I could feel no pain, I did not know but what my body was in several parts, and I was not satisfied until I examined every portion of it. (189–90)

Later, while waiting for a doctor, Davies bides his time by smoking his pipe, an action which "caused much sensation in the local press" (191). His calm, stoic reaction to losing a foot cannot be read as anything but heroism in the romantic sense of the word. Davies is the romantic hero who endures adversity and perseveres. The unrealistic response is so exaggerated as to be humorous. This example represents the ability of the tramp writers to romanticize their experience at its worst.

Although Davies's reaction might be attributed to shock, similar detachment occurs in other tramp autobiographies. As previously mentioned, several tramps portrayed themselves as detached observers. After having sex with forty men for her study of prostitutes, Box Car Bertha states, "I knew I would go back again and again until I had learned what I wanted to know about them and about the girls who received them" (Reitman 181). She also studies drug use, shoplifting, and begging in the same detached manner. *Sister of the Road* provides information, but the author's account obscures the danger of life on the road for women by being excessively optimistic.

Like *The Road*, many tramp autobiographies include brief warnings about the lifestyle of a wanderer. For example, Charles Elmer Fox says, "Contrary to some modern writings I have read, there was very little glamour and romance in the life of a hobo. This was a hard, dangerous, and often very lonely life" (6). Fox, like most of the tramp writers, *says* this but does not *show* it. The tramp autobiographies do not testify to a hard, dangerous life. Instead, they present optimism, adventure, and excitement. Eric H. Monkkonen, in his study of tramps, briefly suggests that such representations are fabrications which conceal the actual hardships faced by tramps (3–4). He says that the true experiences of homeless tramps were not "grist for the adventure writer's mill" (207). However, few of the autobiographies corroborate the actual danger, discrimination, or isolation. The physical and verbal abuse directed at tramps of the time rarely surfaces in these texts. In the discussion of the cultural work of tramp autobiographies to follow, I attempt to document some of the actual hardships which are missing from the autobiographies.

Many of the autobiographies, moreover, are boastful in the descriptions of almost superhuman feats and accomplishments. London revels in his ability to outwit railroad brakemen and the police. He also boasts that he skipped the "gay-cat" phase of amateur tramping and became an immediate "profesh" (professional tramp) (285). Such terminology is sprinkled throughout the autobiographies and indicates a hierarchy and competition among tramps. W. H. Davies portrays himself as a "Super Tramp" because he masters all of the typical skills of a tramp: begging, stealing, sailing, peddling, and riding trains. Many of the autobiographies indicate that the authors were able to master *all* of the skills and habits of tramps during their period on the road. Furthermore, London and Flynt question whether an "average" man could have endured their experiences (London 206, Flynt 7). These boasts of very difficult, masculine feats further romanticize the life of the tramp and conceal the reality of a migrant lifestyle.

A fourth similarity in the tramp autobiographies is a lack of criticism of capitalism or the dominant culture and, furthermore, a reaffirmation of the value of the home. The autobiographies of Box Car Bertha, Starke, Kemp, Mullin, and Edge all conclude with the authors returning home and (briefly) acknowledging the futility of their tramping experience or the value of having a home. The conclusion of Kemp's *Tramping on Life*, for example, renounces the tramping lifestyle:

> I found a camp of tramps and joined with them. We drank coffee together. . .
>
> But, somehow, the scales had fallen from my eyes. My old idealisation of the life of the tramp, somehow or other, was entirely gone–an idealisation that had, anyhow, been mainly literary, induced by the writings of Jack London, Josiah Flynt and Maxim Gorky.
>
> Now, as I listened to their filthy talk . . . their continual "Jesus-Christ'-ing" over everything they said, I grew sick of them. I got up and walked away stiffly–never again to be a tramp. (339)

Such a renunciation emphasizes the distance between the author and real tramps. The reader is also reminded that Kemp chose to go on the road, a luxury which many tramps did not have. Rather than provide an understanding of the lives of tramps, Kemp's text entrenches the difference between the author (representing the reader, that is, "us") and the foul-mouthed, lazy tramps (as the Other, or "them").

Other works, such as *You Can't Win* (1927) by Jack Black and *To Nowhere and Return: The Autobiography of a Puritan* (1940) by Joseph Hilton Smyth, renounce the tramp's own behavior as a thief or an alcoholic. The last paragraph of *The Main Stem* by William Edge provides an example of a fairly typical "happy ending":

> The sheets on my bed were clean and white. My pajamas smelled sweet; over a chair was a suit of underwear as white as snow. The bourgeois live so damn clean they don't have to spray their beds with insecticide. I threw the *Hobo News* on a chair, turned out the light, and fell asleep. (212)

Edge is somewhat critical of capitalism throughout *The Main Stem*, as this passage implies. Other writers offer brief critiques of capitalism and/or mention their support of the I.W.W. Box Car Bertha, for example, spends time as an activist for the socialist cause. These criticisms, however, are muted by the overall sense of optimism and adventure. The tramp autobiographies extol the freedom of the road; they do not condemn capitalism for forcing the authors to tramp. As Ronald Primeau states, "Stories of life on the road are often romantic quests for healing grace and apocalyptic vision followed by a return to the ordinary, with a transformed consciousness" (6). Although this "transformation" often feels tacked on, it is a common feature of the genre.[7]

Jack London represents somewhat of a special case. He was, of course, much more successful than any of the other tramp writers. This financial and social stability may have allowed him to be more openly critical of capitalism and supportive of socialism. In *People of the Abyss*, *The Iron Heel*, and essays such as "Revolution," "The Scab," and "How I Became a Socialist," London expresses his distaste for capitalism. However, as several critics have noted, London remains divided between individualism and egalitarianism, capitalism and socialism, and the upper and lower class.[8] While commentators have attributed these conflicts to London's personal background and sensibilities, the conflicts also apply to most of the tramp autobiographies.

In the beginning of *Martin Eden*, London's semi-autobiographical account of his rise as an author, Eden is uneasy in Ruth's upper class world, but he is also discontented with his lower class lifestyle. The books, the language, the trappings of the upper class appeal to him. After becoming a successful writer, however, Eden feels displaced by both classes. He tries to return to his lower class roots but finds that he "had travelled far, too far to go back. Their mode of life, which had once been his, was now distasteful to him" (887). As Joan D. Hedrick argues, London found himself in the same position: "The story of Jack London's rise to middle-class success is also the story of his failure to achieve a sense of belonging within lower class culture [. . .]" (3).

THE CULTURAL WORK OF TRAMP AUTOBIOGRAPHIES

London personifies the sense of classlessness felt by other tramps throughout American history. Identity is usually tied to income and occupation in America and is often determined by the answer to the question: "What do you do for a living?" Therefore, the class consciousness and posturing in the tramp autobiographies should not be seen as surprising or condemnable. They positioned themselves as legitimate citizens temporarily living on the fringes of society. In the remainder of this chapter, however, I question the effect or cultural work of these texts. As I have been suggesting, the tramp autobiographies romanticized the condition of homelessness. Although I am not indicting the character or motives of any of these writers, I contend that the cultural work of their texts was detrimental in four related ways.

First, romanticizing the tramp lifestyle falsely elevated the condition of homelessness and minimized the actual dangers of life on the road. This, in turn, may have encouraged others, particularly young boys, to become tramps. If Horatio Alger attempted to make his fiction seem more like fact by adding realistic details, London and others tried to make their facts sound more like fiction/literature. They emphasized adventure, freedom, their ability to overcome challenges, and their heroic qualities, as explained above. As Douglas Wixson notes in *Worker-Writer in America: Jack Conroy and the Tradition of Midwestern Literary Radicalism, 1898–1990*, "The romance of the road lay in the popular reader's mind, nourished by 'tramp' writers" (101). It is difficult to gauge the impact of this glorification of the tramp lifestyle, but the popularity of these works indicates that they reached a wide audience. Rather than claim that tramp autobiographies convinced boys to go on the road, however, I wish to delineate some of the ways that these texts minimized the harsh conditions that real tramps faced.[9]

Tramping supposedly allowed the authors to observe life and society more accurately than those on the "outside." The experience of tramping gave them a special perspective and unique skills that others would not understand without sharing the experience. In his Introduction to *Walking to Work: Tramps in America, 1790–1935*, Eric Monkkonen states,

> It is unfair to see tramps as having a privileged perspective on the rest of society, for this mode of thinking finds a value and dignity in tramp-

> ing in an ultimately patronizing way. To tell those unfairly exploited by a social and economic system that they have benefited is akin to congratulating the victim of a crime for his or her remarkable and expanding experience. (4)

The tramp autobiographies elevate the condition of homelessness by claiming that it made the authors stronger, wiser, more insightful. Unfortunately, the actual tramp who experienced economic displacement would not have shared this perspective. In fact, the tramp autobiographies obscure a host of actual dangers and hardships.

In addition to the cold, hunger, and discomfort associated with being homeless, tramps were the target of a severe and violent backlash, as discussed in Chapter Two. Food donations were sometimes poisoned, and the scientific charity organizations urged people to band together against tramps. Lynching, hard labor, and whipping were also proposed as solutions.[10] Tramps could be arrested, beaten, shot, or thrown off trains by railroad police (or "bulls"). They could be arrested for vagrancy simply because they were homeless, since anti-vagrancy laws existed in all but four states by 1898. In jail, they were sometimes mistreated by police, and they were often thrown out of town. Farmers sometimes shot at tramps for trespassing. They could be robbed, beaten, or killed by other tramps as well. Deaths and injuries associated with trains were common, as several tramps fell under or between train cars while boarding or riding them. Tramps could also suffocate from the coal smoke of the locomotive engines while riding on a train as it passed through a tunnel.[11] Some of these dangers are mentioned, but by and large the tramp autobiographies focus on the excitement and adventure of the lifestyle, rather than the actual hardships. When they are depicted, the seriousness of the danger is minimized, as the example of W. H. Davies illustrates.

Second, the focus on "wanderlust" or the individual choice to become homeless in tramp autobiographies obscures the reality of forced homelessness due to unemployment, low wages, racism, economic depressions, or class discrimination. The frequent references to wanderlust mentioned above legitimized the efforts of many to locate responsibility in the poor and homeless themselves, rather than in the political or economic system. In his essay "Tramping Workers, 1890–1920: A Subcultural View," John C. Schneider says, "For those who wanted to make of tramps a lazy and irresponsible group the wanderlust theory had much to offer, and it was only part of a substantial argument reformers made about the psychological instability of homeless men" (220). Several autobiographies define wanderlust as a form of addiction, thereby contributing to the belief that homelessness is a result of individual pathologies rather than structural causes.[12]

Third, in a variety of ways, the tramp autobiographies perpetuated the myth of the homeless individual as Other, as different from "normal" members of society. The autobiographers, for example, portrayed themselves as individualists and nonconformists. Just as "wanderlust" contributes to the historical notion of the homeless as pathological, the emphasis on individualism reinforces the view that homelessness is a form of "disaffiliation." As discussed in the Introduction, Howard Bahr entrenched the discursive view of the homeless individual as a skid row bum after the Great Depression. Bahr's books and dozens of other texts in sociology and journalism linked homelessness directly to alcoholism and "disaffiliation." The tramp autobiographies, with their emphasis on individualism and nonconformity, reinforce this (stereotypical) view.

Similarly, while tramp autobiographers positioned themselves as "legitimate" members of society, they affirmed the differences between normal society, including themselves, and the vagrants they studied for material to write about. Josiah Flynt, quoted above, represents this conscious distancing: "The 'seeing and admiring' is the privilege of the spectator who, because he is such, may be near the crowd and not of it" (323). He goes on to say that he is "aloof" (323). Rather than positioning themselves as willing members of a community, the tramp autobiographers portrayed themselves as aloof, disaffiliated, and detached from society.

Moreover, tramps in reality worked in a variety of occupations as migratory labor (such as those described in the quotation from Charles Hoch earlier in this chapter), but the published autobiographies suggest that tramps were unwilling to work. The autobiographers positioned themselves as writers, intellectuals, and amateur sociologists, not laborers. London, for example, revels in his ability to avoid work by deceiving others. Although London himself and most wandering tramps throughout the century worked at various jobs, the autobiographies rarely show them performing labor. The first chapter of *The Road*, "Confession," describes some of the lies London concocts in order to beg for food: the more realistic and heart-wrenching the story, the more likely it is that London will get a handout. He boasts, "For know that upon his ability to tell a good story depends the success of the beggar. [. . .] I have often thought that to this training of my tramp days is due much of my success as a story-writer" (193). London also indicates his unwillingness to work. When a man offers him a job, London promises to show up the next day if the man will feed him first. But London has no intention of ever doing the work.[13] By portraying themselves as unwilling to work, deceitful, and "aloof," London and other tramp autobiographers perpetuate the historical separation of homeless individuals from the rest of society.[14]

In Chapter Five, I attempt to demonstrate how homeless individuals can be depicted as constitutive members of society rather than as either individualistic, romantic heroes or destitute victims. Not only did tramp autobiographies refrain from showing their heros working, but they also generally failed to show them working *with* others. Like the I.W.W. and Coxey's army, several organizations of the poor and unemployed developed around the turn of the century. These groups attempted to gain recognition and better treatment for marginal workers. Consequently, they undermine the notion that tramps were disaffiliated, aloof, or antisocial. An informal network of tramps or hobos was developed in "hobo jungles" (camps near railyards), and through a shared vocabulary and an intricate system of signs and symbols left on trains, posts, fences, and water towers. A more formal social structure was created by the International Brotherhood Welfare Association (IBWA), an organization founded by "the Millionaire Tramp," James Eads How. The IBWA, headquartered in Cincinnati, had 20 branches in cities across the country, most notably the "Hobo College" in Chicago. The purpose of this organization was to provide education in subjects such as public speaking. It also provided safe, comfortable spaces for tramps to congregate, talk, and play games.[15] Since the individual laborer had few rights and little power, organizations of the poor also led to unionization. The Brotherhood of Locomotive Engineers, the Brotherhood of Railway Trainmen, and the Brotherhood of Railway Carmen Association represented marginal workers such as tramps who often worked for the railroad.[16]

The IBWA, the I.W.W., Coxey's army, and the various brotherhoods mentioned here attempted to recognize the importance of marginal workers and to represent tramps as legitimate members of society. Whereas the tramp autobiographies mention these organizations, the texts do not always promote them positively. In *The Road*, London repeatedly mocks the leaders as well as the foolish participants of a division of Coxey's army led by General Kelly; he describes the endeavor as a "colossal picnic" (291). He demonstrates very little interest in the political demands or philosophy of its leaders. The romantic, solitary hero, in this and other works, could not be seen depending on his fellow man. Portraying solidarity with others clashes with the independent, adventuresome individual as romantic author. In many ways, then, the tramp autobiographies subscribe to the romantic ideals of literature while ignoring or minimizing actual details of the tramp lifestyle.

Finally, literary criticism has not questioned this romantic view of homelessness. As I suggest throughout this study, literary criticism performs cultural work along with the primary texts it analyzes. In this case, criticism helps perpetuate the division between romantic and realist representations of homelessness described in the Introduction. Eric H. Monkkonen states that "Social historians, in general, have ignored tramps and tramping. Instead they have opted to analyze the late nineteenth- and early twentieth-century middle-class *observers* of tramping (235, italics added). I assert that literary critics have done essentially the same thing. The historical division of romanticism and realism has been questioned recently, but it still remains firmly entrenched in accounts of American literary history. More specifically, scholars have generally not sought out, taught, or analyzed literary representations of homelessness which do not fit easily into one of these two categories. The tendency has been to rely on and analyze established texts and writers rather than to seek out alternative accounts of homelessness. If readers are only exposed to romantic heros or destitute victims, it becomes difficult to imagine people who fall outside these definitions. As I indicate in Chapter Five, the American literary canon can continue to expand by including texts which do not subscribe to the romanticism/realism binary. Literary testimony, I argue, avoids some of the potentially detrimental effects caused by this division.

Chapter Five

"I Did Not Write These Stories"
Meridel Le Sueur and American Testimonial Literature

> I did not write these stories.
>
> I recorded them.
>
> They are the words of women who are now dead, or lost, incarcerated in prisons or asylums, who forgot their names from shock treatments or lobotomies, who went insane from racism or rape.
>
> These are not stories, but epitaphs marking the lives of women who in wars, depression or holocaust are at the bottom of the social strata, are trampled on, leave no statistic, no record, obituary or remembrance.
>
> Meridel Le Sueur, *Women on the Breadlines*

STATEMENTS SUCH AS THESE REVEAL WHY MERIDEL LE SUEUR HAS BEEN alternately forgotten and praised as a figure in American literary history. As Adrian Oktenberg remarks, "The work of Meridel Le Sueur is worse than neglected; it is part of that great body of work by women which has been 'hidden from history'" (99). It has been hidden and displaced not only as a result of her affiliation with the Communist Party, but also as a result of her style and subject matter.[1] By indicating that she "did not write these stories" but "recorded them," Le Sueur occupies a somewhat unusual (and generally unrecognized) subject position as an author.[2] The Author in American literature usually represents an autonomous, educated, intellectual creator–a "great writer"–not a collective or communal project. This autonomy is preserved even when the subject matter has been life "at the bottom of the social strata."[3]

As the introductory quotation reveals, Meridel Le Sueur chose to write about the oppressed and the forgotten in a style which was largely suppressed. As a result, she speaks for marginalized people, and women in particular, in two ways. First, she attempted to expose the inequity of a society which relegated women to the domestic sphere, tolerated physical abuse against them, and ignored the suffering of men and women in poverty. Second, she utilized a writing style which violated many of the prescribed norms of twentieth century American (patriarchal) literature.[4]

In this chapter I extend the efforts of feminist critics who have attempted to recuperate the work of writers like Le Sueur who have been marginalized or displaced in American literary history. In order to do so I introduce the concept of "testimony" (appropriated for the most part from Holocaust theory and Latin American literary criticism) into the critical discussion of Le Sueur and the wider debates over expanding the canon. I contend that because of its unique style and subject matter, testimony (or testimonial literature)–as represented by the work of Meridel Le Sueur–has been generally neglected as a form of American literature. Therefore, critics should attempt to find, recuperate, teach, and discuss examples of American testimonial literature. This effort will redress some of the adverse "cultural work" caused by the division between romantic and realist literature discussed throughout this study. As I have been suggesting, this binary generally excludes texts which do not romanticize or objectify the condition of homelessness. The discourse of homelessness and the American literary canon, therefore, should be expanded to include testimonial texts such as Le Sueur's which do not subscribe to this division.

THE CULTURAL BACKLASH AGAINST HOMELESS WOMEN

Before considering Le Sueur's work as testimony, it is important to briefly contextualize the efforts of writers like Le Sueur who wrote about the experience of homeless women.[5] In previous chapters I have discussed the violent backlash against tramps and hobos in America. If tramps and hobos have been marginalized, critcized, and victimized by the dominant culture, homeless women have been relegated to the margins of a margin and received the most bitter condemnation. First, the male tramp subculture generally treated women with disdain. At best, women were tolerated. More often than not, male tramps viewed women who went on the road as inferior or inauthentic. In 1929, *Scribner's Magazine* published an article by Cliff Maxwell, a self-appointed expert on tramping, entitled "Lady Vagabonds." In the article, Maxwell argues that women could be "vagabonds" but not "hobos" because "none of them will work hard" and "None of them were on the road for the same reason I was on it: adventure, travel, or incurable wanderlust" (289). He concludes by remarking, "Show me a 'lady hobo' and I'll show you an angular-bodied, flint eyed, masculine-minded travesty upon her sex" (292).

In addition to being ridiculed, homeless women were objectified as sexual commodities almost without question. Numerous comments in literature and sociology of the period indicate that a sexual economy existed within the tramp subculture. In a dialogue with a sociologist in *The American Mercury* in 1934, a woman repeatedly associates daily events with her sexual experience at the time. Comments such as "No, he made no advances to me"; "I gave into him a little"; "Yes, he made love to me" occur throughout the dialogue (Reckless 177–178). In the hobo autobiographies of Bertha Thompson, Barbara Starke, and Ethel Lynn, each writer indicates that sex consistently became an actual or perceived threat or commodity. Thompson, for example, states that women "can usually manage the rides, but they seldom get food free unless they repay the men who set it up for them with what every man wants from a woman" (Reitman 41). Samuel Milton Elam's article "Lady Hoboes," published in *The New Republic* in 1930, describes five women he encountered on the road. In one episode, he stands by as a female acquaintance is raped by several men in a box-car. His response suggests the prevalence of sexual violence against homeless women. He confesses, "I knew what was happenin' all right, but you can see for yourself what kind of fix I was in, with all them other guys in the car, and nary a one of 'em wantin' to be trifled with" (169). Homeless women, therefore, had to take extreme precautions while traveling. Elam and others mention that homeless women would dress as men to avoid detection. They were also afforded some degree of safety if they traveled with a husband or acquaintance. But going "on the road" is clearly not safe for women overall. The lack of danger in the tramp autobiographies discussed in Chapter Four certainly obscures the actual threats that women faced and, furthermore, reveals how women's experiences have been marginalized in literature.

While the male tramp subculture commodified and mistreated women, the dominant culture vilified homeless women for being an even greater threat to morality than men. Lynn Weiner states, "Especially before the 1930s, the female tramps who chose to defy sex role conventions symbolized a criticism of cultural mores as great as any other presented by women of that time" (171). This rejection of the normal, accepted values of the time prompted a spirited discourse which condemned these women. For example, Weiner quotes Mrs. O. L. Amigh in the 1903 *Proceedings of the National Conference of Charities* as saying,

> "From my childhood up, I have seen tramp women and girls, and they are the greatest menace to the community of any class of people who tramp. They may not be quite as numerous as men and boys, but it does not take so many of them to do a great deal of harm." (qtd. in Weiner 171)

Other commentators targeted women for encouraging immorality and violating traditional values associated with motherhood and the home. In her book *Dimity Convictions: The American Woman in the Nineteenth Century*, Barbara Welter describes the four cardinal virtues of the "cult of true womanhood": piety, purity, submissiveness, and domesticity. Although the discourse which entrenched these virtues peaked in the nineteenth century, it was still widely held that "a woman's place was in the home" throughout the first half of the twentieth century. Homeless women violated all of these virtues and were condemned as a result. The widespread belief that women had a moral, even religious duty to attend to the domestic sphere helped justify the arguments made by charity organizations that homeless women posed a serious threat to the morals of others.

HOMELESS WOMEN AND TRADITIONAL LITERARY SENSIBILITIES

Le Sueur's subject matter would have been "inappropriate" to her Depression-era audience because homeless women would have been generally seen as disgraceful and immoral. Moreover, the literary form of Le Sueur's work would have been unfamiliar and questionable. Although elements of naturalism and romanticism appear in Le Sueur's work, neither tradition accepted–nor was accepted by–Le Sueur. Consequently, her work has been difficult to situate within American literary history, and it has remained, until recently, outside the canon. As I have been suggesting, the division between romanticism and realism has excluded certain texts, like Le Sueur's, because they do not conform to literary conventions and expectations.

The romantic depiction of adventure in which the author goes "on the road" would not have been a desirable genre for Le Sueur. The lives described in various tramp autobiographies had virtually no bearing on the hunger, abuse, discrimination, unemployment, and poor health experienced by homeless women and witnessed by Le Sueur. As critics such as Paula Rabinowitz, Alice Jardine, Sidonie Smith, Bella Brodzki and Celeste Schenck have also noted, a conflation of masculinity and humanity occurs in traditional autobiography. The romantic, heroic, rebellious protagonist in this tradition partakes in adventures which are generally unavailable to women. In their introduction to *Life/Lines: Theorizing Women's Autobiography*, Brodzki and Schenck explain:

> The masculine autobiography, from the definitive spiritual autobiography of Saint Augustine to Roland Barthes's fragmented "family romance," *Roland Barthes par Roland Barthes*, assumes the conflation of masculinity and humanity, canonizing the masculine representative self of both writer and reader. (2)

Autobiographical forms in general, and tramp autobiographies in particular because of their ability to obscure the dangers faced by homeless women, fail to adequately represent the experience of women in poverty during the Depression. Although many would have disapproved of her graphic, honest portrayal of homeless women, Le Sueur could not rely on traditional literary forms such as autobiography to do the cultural work she wanted to accomplish.

While romanticism ignores the suffering of the poor, realism/naturalism describes it in detail. This represents a significant shift. However, the author generally remains "objective"; that is, he maintains a hierarchical relation to the subjects through his journalistic gaze and psychological distance from the lower classes, as discussed in Chapter Three. Texts about the "other half" or the "submerged tenth" perpetuated the division between the author (as knowing subject) and the poor (as the objects of study). Le Sueur resisted this division by writing her stories in the very words of the poor. She was critical of the determinism in literary naturalism (Schleuning 124)[6] and praised *The Jungle* only because it represented a "communal wealth of mutual skills"–in other words, she valued the collaboration of Upton Sinclair and Ella Reeve Bloor, not the subject matter (Le Sueur, *Dread Road* 62). Le Sueur favored solidarity and unity, not the individualism of the isolated author; she attempted to remove herself as an author and let the poor speak for themselves.

Like other writers who fall outside established frameworks, Le Sueur has been described in a variety of ways by critics who wish to situate her work. The subject matter of her writing and her membership in the Communist Party have led commentators to describe her work as "proletarian realism," "revolutionary writing," "working class literature," and, most frequently, part of the "radical" tradition. Her writing style has been associated with "informant documentary," "participant-observer journalism," "imaginative nonfiction," and, most frequently, "reportage." While none of these descriptions is inherently more or less accurate, I believe that discussing Le Sueur's work as "testimony" illuminates certain elements in her writing that these other terms do not. It may also offer a better perspective on the subject position Le Sueur assumed as a collaborator (rather than a solitary author). Testimony may be a more insistent term than the others and, unlike the other labels, it nullifies the subject position of the author as autonomous and detached. Le Sueur's work exhibits several elements of testimony which would have contributed to her displacement in American literary history, but which represent strengths in other areas.

LE SUEUR'S *THE GIRL* AS TESTIMONIAL LITERATURE

What is literary testimony? As described by Jean Franco,

> The testimonial is a life story usually related by a member of the subaltern classes to a transcriber who is a member of the intelligentsia. It is this genre that uses the "referential" to authenticate the collective memory of the uprooted, the homeless, and the tortured, and that most clearly registers the emergence of a new class of participants in the public sphere. The testimonial covers a spectrum between autobiography and oral history, but the word testimony has both legal and religious connotations and implies a subject as witness to and participant in public events. (70–71)

Six traits or components of testimony can be ascertained from this description. In the following, I am drawing heavily on the work of John Beverly, who has written extensively about testimony (or *testimonio*) in the context of Latin American studies.

First and foremost, testimony reveals a condition or problem which was previously unknown or censored. As Franco remarks, it represents the "emergence of a new class of participants in the public sphere." This recognition of silenced or oppressed groups is an integral component of testimony. James E. Young, in *Writing and Rewriting the Holocaust: Narrative and the Consequences of Interpretation*, traces the etymology of "testimony" to its roots in "witnessing":

> In its English past, "testimony" derives from the Latin for "witness" (*testi*), while "witness" in turn derives from both the abstract concept of becoming conscious of (or to know) something and literally seeing a thing. To testify is literally "to make witness"—an etymological reminder that as witness and testimony are made, so is knowledge. (19)

Testimony, in this sense, has been used to describe the writings of Holocaust survivors, Japanese "comfort women," and indigenous people of Central America, among others. In each case, the "author" provides knowledge of a topic or situation which was previously unknown, unavailable, or unfathomable to his or her audience. As Franco notes, the testimony is a decidedly *public* form. The author enters the public sphere after being previously denied access, and the condition which was previously hidden comes to light. Moreover, a legal connotation is present. The information being presented relates to an injustice or "crime" which is being perpetrated. Like an eyewitness in a court trial, the author of testimonial literature helps to redress a wrong and correct an injustice.

Before testimony became a genre in Holocaust and Latin American studies, Carl Sandberg remarked that Le Sueur "'is a witness with a genius for moving and highly implicative testimony'" (qtd. in Duncan 61). Sandberg, unintentionally I believe, reveals the dual connotations of witnessing and testimony. He praises Le Sueur's eye for detail and description, but also implies that she is *giving* testimony as a witness in a legal sense.

Le Sueur frequently spoke out against the economic and political systems which contributed to the plight of the poor and homeless. Her membership in the Communist Party most obviously indicated her displeasure and lack of confidence in the status quo. In *The Girl*, the character of Amelia speaks out against the injustice of the system which allows her friend, Clara, to die after being forced to receive electric shock treatments. Amelia exclaims that a memorial is needed:

> Yes a memorial for Clara, a mass meeting, let our voice be heard in the whole city–a trial, a judgment against the city fathers, a trial yes, an accusation. We accuse. Yes, we point a finger. We hold them responsible. (130)

Le Sueur, like Amelia, incriminates the economic and political system by bearing witness to the injustices taking place against the poor. While literature often reveals new and unusual topics to its readers, testimony specifically denounces an injustice of some type and attempts to bring a problem to light.

Writers such as Crane and Riis also sought to bring problems to light, but their versions of poverty and homelessness differed substantially from Le Sueur's. Crane and Riis maintained a distance from their subjects by briefly visiting and then documenting the slums as a scientist would. They saw poverty as a spectacle and they accentuated individual rather than structural causes. The poor and homeless characters they created were acquiescent and hopeless. Le Sueur, conversely, was personally involved in the lives of the people she represents; she was not motivated by her own fame or the desire to publish. Most significantly, naturalists such as Crane and Riis sensationalized problems and differences related to class and poverty, whereas Le Suer's work (and other forms of testimony) neither elevates nor exaggerates those conditions.

Testimony, then, informs the audience about something which was previously unfamiliar. Despite the many investigations of intolerable working conditions and poverty under the rubric of reportage, and the detailed literary treatments of the Depression by authors like Steinbeck, Le Sueur tackled subjects which were generally "off-limits" and therefore unrecognized. She called attention to topics which others considered inappropriate or offensive, thereby giving attention to important issues that otherwise would have been censored. For example, in *The Girl*, Le Sueur describes domestic abuse directly and matter-of-factly; in doing so she calls attention to how violence pervades society to the point of being a tolerable, "everyday" occurrence.

Few writers commented on abuse before Le Sueur. Melody Graulich states, "As woman abuse was invisible in our society, so was it absent from our literary canon" (19). One could argue that the female characters in *The Girl* are complacent about the abuse they endure. They indicate sincere love of the men in their lives, even immediately after they are struck by them. A tension or paradox exists when the women simultaneously fear and love their partners. For example, the unnamed narrator seeks out a relationship with Butch, despite his threats of violence. She says, "[. . .] he told me not to be wandering with Clara to the Marigold where we danced with strangers. He said he would knock the shit out of me. Which made me shake and tremble, but it was better than being a husk full of suffering and not knowing why" (9).

Le Sueur, rather than ignoring abuse, places it prominently within the narrative. Her female characters endure it because they have few alternatives and because they learned how to endure it from their own parents. After their father dies, the narrator's sister tells another sister she should not have resisted him: "[. . .] if papa tried to whip you, you would go dancing around waving your arms and this made him mad. You should let him whip you" (31). Without saying so directly, Le Sueur suggests that this toleration of abuse must be stopped. Rather than hiding the problem, Le Sueur alerts her readers to the prevalence and acceptance of violence among the poor.

Similarly, Le Sueur wrote about birth and pregnancy at a time when they were considered inappropriate subject matter. Constance Coiner writes,

> Because pregnancy, labor, the moment of birth, and the nurturing of a newborn are among life's most profound experiences, it is striking that they appear so rarely in literature. [. . .] When Le Sueur wrote ["Annunciation"], pregnancy was considered unacceptable as a literary subject [. . .] . ("Literature" 169, 170)

In "Annunciation," *The Girl*, and other stories, Le Sueur uses birth as a symbol of hope and optimism, but she also described pregnancy, labor, and delivery forthrightly; she did not attempt to "hide" the birth process. When the narrator of *The Girl* gives birth at the end of the book, Le Sueur juxtaposes the joy/wonder of the birth of a girl with the mundane and unpleasant facts of life. The narrator says, "I saw the women pressing in to see and I held her up for all to see and heard a kind of sound like AHHHHHHHHH of wonder and delight," but the hope is undercut by: "Amelia said, Give me a newspaper to put the afterbirth in" (131). While the birth is a happy moment, the mention of the newspaper reminds the reader of the poverty of the women involved.[7]

Le Sueur addressed several other topics which would have been considered inappropriate for her time: abortion ("Annunciation"), forced sterilization ("Sequel to Love"), prostitution ("Women on the Breadlines"), hunger and starvation ("Women are Hungry"), and the surveillance of the poor by charity organizations ("They Follow Us Girls"). In each case, her intent was not to shock or titillate (as Crane and Riis often did), but to expose the existence of a serious problem which would have been otherwise hidden from the public. Le Sueur also takes up these issues in *The Girl.*

The poor women in the book discuss abortion as an option for the narrator when she becomes pregnant, and several characters reveal that they had abortions. The narrator resists the lighthearted mood of one such discussion when her friend Belle's husband, Hoinck, describes their relationship:

> Everybody laughed a lot. I never thought any of Hoinck's stories were funny. He said, Belle here is some woman. I got me some woman. She took the rap for me once when I forged a check, and she had thirteen abortions. I give her a spoonful of turpentine with sugar and it'll loosen anything, ain't that so Belle? Everybody laughed some more. Belle seemed to like it too. I didn't think any of it was funny. (11)

Later, the narrator drinks some beer and begins to find Hoinck's stories more funny, indicating an ability to accept things which would be normally unacceptable. Just as the narrator learns to accept abortion as an everyday occurrence for those in poverty, the reader learns how common and necessary abortions are for poor women.

Le Sueur also represents prostitution directly and matter-of-factly. Clara, a close friend of the narrator, is depicted as loving, kind, and compassionate. Prostitution becomes an accepted part of her life only out of economic necessity. Le Sueur resists the stereotype of the immoral prostitute which the cultural status quo would have held. Prostitution, Le Sueur insists, is not a choice but a necessity. After Clara returns from an encounter, she mentions that he was nice. The narrator asks, "You like him?" (50). Clara replies, "No, but he's quick, not like the old men and he smells good and he's young and quick and clean. It's hard now, she said, when so many men are out of work" (50). Clara educates the narrator, and the reader, about prostitution honestly and pragmatically. While the general population would tend to view prostitutes as immoral, Le Sueur reveals that they are otherwise normal people with no other economic opportunity.[8]

Le Sueur further reveals that the supposed "relief" or "charity" organizations, which many believed would assist the poor, actually put them in greater misery and danger. The surveillance of the poor by charity organizations would have been a revelation to Le Sueur's Depression-era audience, just as it would to many readers today. After the narrator of *The Girl* becomes pregnant and goes on relief, a woman (Anna Bradley) hired by the relief agency follows her around town. This is a source of shock and consternation to the narrator:

> I believe it after Amelia says it, although I was mad as hops at Bradley for always being there with her rogued up mug and her black dress, always following and following me. She gave me the willys following me around everywhere I turn, walking along feeling right good in me, and the morning real good, thinking to buy me a bunch of carrots or a head of green cabbage, and there I see her and my blood freezes right in my body, and the sweat comes in my hands and feet because I am scared, and there she is looking right above my head. (113)

While the middle and upper classes would never tolerate such treatment, the surveillance of the lower class went unnoticed and unreported for the most part. Moreover, receiving relief is tied to this surveillance. If the narrator, or other poor women, were seen with men, they could lose their aid. The relief worker says to the narrator: "You can't get any help if there are goings on with men. You have to be mighty careful" (123). The right to freely associate and to be free of surveillance (which the upper classes take for granted) did not apply to the poor women Le Sueur represents. Few people knew of this practice, yet Le Sueur alerts readers to the injustice in the hopes that the rights of the poor would be recognized.

The relief agencies' treatment of the poor women reflects the historical ability of charity organizations–as representatives of "normal" society–to objectify the poor. In addition to disallowing women on relief to associate with men, sterilization and electric shock treatments were suggested or coerced. The rhetoric of infantilization underlies these efforts. Poor women could not be trusted to think for themselves, so the relief and charity organizations assumed responsibility for their morals and behavior. In *The Girl*, Clara is given electric shock treatment against her will, which leads to her death ("*They just took Clara to give her electric shock treatments. Nothing we could do to stop them. Nothing*" [119]). The narrator also learns that the relief agency wants her to be sterilized. After being placed in the relief maternity home, she says, "I couldn't sleep in there for thinking they would sterilize me" (116). Surveillance, shock therapy, and sterilization were practices that may have been familiar to the poor women who Le Sueur knew, but members of the dominant culture would have little exposure to these topics.

Finally, Le Sueur represented the basic deprivations faced by the poor and homeless. She describes the poor living conditions, lack of affordable housing, and hunger during the Depression. The narrator of *The Girl* remarks, "Others are hungry too. Certainly people are always very quiet about hunger" (101). While many people were aware of poverty during the Depression, and coverage of the subject was common, Le Sueur went beyond the expectations and boundaries of the time to discuss problems which were common for the poor, but generally unacknowledged in the popular press.

Although the Depression affected everyone, few people "witnessed" the suffering of poor women. The lack of employment opportunities and the social disgrace of being poor and homeless forced many women to become "invisible" to society. Le Sueur remarked, "You never saw them on the soup lines. The city had no way to deal with the hungry women. [. . .] They are outside the economy, the statistics" (*Women*, "Introduction"). Le Sueur helped to make these women visible to the public.

She even opens readers' eyes to the condition of homelessness. The narrator of *The Girl* demonstrates how one can ignore or accept homelessness. She confesses,

> You can get so you can go on thinking and living in the streets because you got no home. The streets used to be only something you walked through to get someplace else, but now they are home to me, and I walk around, and walk in stores and look at all the people, or I sit in the relief station waiting to see the caseworker, and I sit there close to other women and men, and I look, and I feed off their faces. (107)

Here, Le Sueur disrupts the reader's conception of the street as merely "something you walked through to get someplace else." The street becomes a home, and the reader must confront his or her relationship to the street and to homeless people. Le Sueur exposes the street for what it really is to the homeless–their home–and, in so doing, challenges the reader's acceptance of that fact. In these examples, Le Sueur presents problems and experiences which otherwise may have gone unnoticed by the general population–such an impulse underlies all forms of testimonial literature.

A second trait of testimony is that the narrator is a real protagonist or actual witness to the events described in the text. Again, in a legal context, testimony is admissible only if the witness actually saw the crime take place. Although the objectivity of testimonial literature has been questioned, it purports to represent "the real."[9] I believe this is important because it avoids the participant-observer posturing which is prevalent in American naturalism. Whereas Upton Sinclair, Stephen Crane, Jacob Riis, and others reported on the terrible conditions in slums, factories, and tenement housing in the late nineteenth and early twentieth century, they were reporters who went to the scene to observe and then describe the situation. They remained detached from the poor and homeless, just as the tramp autobiographers did. Conversely, the subject position of testimony assumes actual participation on some level.

Le Sueur frequently struggled to find regular housing and employment, taking a variety of jobs in her twenties and thirties and even living in a condemned bus later in her life. Many of Le Sueur's stories reflect her episodes of economic uncertainty and dislocation. Additionally, *The Girl* is based on the experiences of several women Le Sueur knew, and *Women on the Breadlines* describes the lives of women she met in relief agencies and unemployment offices. In the "Afterwords" to *The Girl* she states,

> This memorial to the great and heroic women of the depression was really written by them. As part of our desperate struggle to be alive and human we pooled our memories, experiences and in the midst of disaster told each other our stories or wrote them down. We had a writers' group of women in the Workers Alliance and we met every night to raise our miserable circumstances to the level of sagas, poetry, cry-outs. (133)

Le Sueur's writing, like other examples of testimony, rejects the participant-observer point of view which is usually present in naturalism and reportage. Neala Schleuning argues that *The Girl* is generally more accurate as a result:

> While many writers during the thirties "took to the road" to "find" the American experience of the Depression, Meridel Le Sueur, like most other people, had stayed put, and in staying with her people and her neighbors, recorded a unique, and perhaps the truest, story of her times. (qtd. in Le Sueur, "Afterwords" to *The Girl* 134)

Schleuning considers *The Girl* to be realistic because Le Sueur participated in the events and because the book remains localized. While many writers observed and wrote about the poor during the Depression, Le Sueur lived with them. Her account may be more immediate and personal as a result.[10]

Le Sueur includes details from her life in most of her writing, but her work is not strictly autobiographical. Whereas autobiography presents the writer's "life story," testimony is representative of a larger social class or group. This trait represents a third quality of testimony. According to John Beverly in *Against Literature*,

> The situation of the narrator in testimonio must be representative (in both the mimetic and the legal-political sense) of a larger social class or

> group; [. . .] The narrator in testimonio [. . .] speaks for or in the name of a community or group, approximating in this way the symbolic function of the epic hero without at the same time assuming his hierarchical and patriarchal status. (74)

Therefore, not only is testimony *about* the larger group, the individual author is frequently displaced or submerged in the text itself. The subject position tends to be "us" or "we," rather than the singular "I." The overall plight of the group—Holocaust survivors, indigenous people of Central America, prisoners, Native Americans, the poor—supersedes the experience of the individual author. The "author" stands in for the larger group.

In Le Sueur's work, the narrator is rarely Le Sueur herself. Often, the narrator remains unnamed, as is the case throughout *The Girl*. As other critics have noted, "The Girl"–the unnamed narrator–represents all poor women. In the quotation from the "Afterwords" above, Le Sueur notes how several women "pooled our memories," and that this collaboration of stories formed *The Girl*. At one point, a woman who is staying at a relief house advises, "*Don't cry. We, the common people, suffer together*" (117). Another character proclaims, "Some face has got to shine with every other face. We must know that our suffering is together . . . the same enemy after us . . . the same mother over us [. . .]" (119).

In other stories, such as "Women on the Breadlines," Le Sueur uses the plural pronoun "we" to suggest the common experience of poor women:

> I am sitting in the city free employment bureau. It's the women's section. We have been sitting here now for four hours. We sit here every day, waiting for a job. [. . .] We look at the floor. It's too terrible to see this animal terror in each other's eyes. (*Women*)

Le Sueur hoped to expose the suffering of all poor women because society remained uninformed about their plight; and she insisted that other women authored her texts as much as she did. In the "Author's Note" to *Dread Road*, Le Sueur states, "This is not a book written by one person. This is a communal creation of an image, using the collective experience of a number of people" (61). She describes *North Star Country* as "a history of the people of the Midwest, told from their dimension in their language" (xix). In the "Preface" to *Winter Prairie Woman*, she says, "This is a collective book. This means it is not a performance by one author in a room alone" (5). These comments, like the quotation from *Women on the Breadlines* at the beginning of this chapter, represent a break from traditional notions of literature and authorship. This shift ruins the notion of literature as the work of individual "great writers." It becomes apparent, then, that Le Sueur's willingness to "erase" herself as the author of her texts would have contributed to her marginalization as an author. The communal element of testimony, seen as a strength by Le Sueur and other practitioners, becomes a liability in the context of American literary history.

A fourth trait of testimony is that it "*needs* to be told" (Beverly 73)–either for the psychological or physical survival of the individual narrator or of the entire group to which he or she belongs. According to John Beverly, it involves "a problem of repression, poverty, subalternity, exploitation, or simply survival that is implicated in the act of narration itself" (73). For the individual, writing can be a means of coping with trauma, violence, or oppression. In other words, the testimonial text is a restorative, a means of survival. Writing (in this context) has been described as involuntary or compulsory in that the author feels compelled to put pen to paper in order to make sense of the trauma and/or his or her role as a survivor. As Dori Laub explains, "The survivors [of the Holocaust] did not only need to survive so that they could tell their story; they also needed to tell their story to survive. [. . .] Onc has to know one's buried truth in order to be able to live one's life" (Felman 78). Testimony also reveals the danger or plight that a marginalized group faces.[11]

When a problem is hidden, it is allowed to continue. Therefore, Le Sueur exposed problems and threats faced by poor women in an effort to save them. When her friend Clara dies after receiving shock treatments, the narrator of *The Girl* wonders, "She never hurt no one. Who killed Clara? *Who will kill us?*" (130). The narrator, like Le Sueur, recognizes that if one poor woman can be killed without anyone knowing or becoming upset, it is possible to kill other poor women. A sense of urgency and survival becomes necessary for the characters. In turn, the general public needs to be more concerned with the safety of poor people.

As previously mentioned, Le Sueur's work is difficult to situate within American literary history. This has led commentators to search for terms which can accurately describe her various styles and formats. A fifth component of testimony is its resistance to categorization as a familiar genre. Testimony can be seen instead as a transition or intersection of forms. Because traditional forms and genres could not adequately represent certain experiences, alternative forms were sought. The inability of traditional forms, genres, and styles to capture the experience of the Holocaust, for example, surfaces in the accounts of numerous survivors. Therefore, testimony contains elements of a variety of genres: autobiography, autobiographical novel, oral history, memoir, confession, diary, interview, eyewitness report, life history, novela-testimonio, and the nonfiction novel (Beverly 71). This blurring of categories has led to confusion or derision of testimony as a literary form.

Blanche H. Gelfant, among others, has noted a similar difficulty in classifying Le Sueur's *The Girl*:

> Its style is conflicted, its various discourses remaining dissonant despite Le Sueur's attempts to conflate the rhetoric of proletarian politics with the language of fertility myths, urban working-class vernaculars (male and female), hieratic incantations, and biblical prophesy. The result is a rich stylistic confusion that makes *The Girl* a complicated text to analyze, though it seems superficially simple in plot. (183–184)

Gelfant goes on to note that *The Girl* contains elements of social protest, feminist jeremiad, bildungsroman, and palimpsest. The result is confusion "in its etymological sense of melting or pouring together" (183). For Gelfant, this confusion "represents an ideal of unity [Le Sueur] attempts to realize by amalgamating discrete and incompatible discourses" (183). Other stylistic choices led to "confusion" in many of her works: the lack of closure and the lack of linear plots at times, the juxtaposition of graphic details and everyday language, the blurring of fiction and nonfiction. This stylistic experimentation, typical of testimony, continues to create difficulty for those who wish to place her work in traditional literary categories, such as romanticism or realism, fiction or nonfiction. Later in this chapter I assess the aesthetic implications of testimonial literature such as *The Girl.*

A final trait of testimony is that it places demands on the reader. This can be seen in one of two complementary ways. First, the reader participates in or experiences the injustice or suffering depicted in the text. As Beverly says, "The erasure of authorial presence in the testimonio, together with its nonfictional character, make possible a different kind of complicity–we might call it fraternal or sororal–between narrator and reader than is possible in the novel [. . .]" (77). In *Testimony: Crises of Witnessing in Literature, Psychoanalysis, and History*, Shoshana Felman and Dori Laub also suggest that testimony creates a bond between the reader and the text unlike other forms of literature. A second demand would be a call to action as a result of the perceived injustice. Testimony urges the reader to remember or recognize those who have been mistreated and to act on the knowledge which has been revealed.

In *Dread Road*, Le Sueur remarks, "I demand that you listen. Be with me on the dread journey, that dread road we must take now" (2). *Dread Road*, partially based on Le Sueur's encounter with a woman on a bus carrying her dead child, prompts the reader to confront the injustice of economic inequality and the marginalization of poor women. Le Sueur also calls upon readers to remember those who are typically forgotten and ignored. Like numerous accounts of the Holocaust which indicate the need to remember the victims, the narrator of *The Girl* says,

> Memory is all we got, I cried, we got to remember. We got to remember everything. [. . .] We got to remember to be able to fight. Got to write down the names. Make a list. Nobody can be forgotten. They

> know if we don't remember we can't point them out. They got their guilt wiped out. The last thing they take is memory. (126)

This passage represents a central function of testimony. Just as a witness cannot forget or ignore a crime–he or she must testify to ensure that justice prevails–readers must remember the "facts" in texts such as *The Girl* so that injustice and mistreatment does not continue. Discussing Le Sueur's story "Corn Village," James M. Boehnlein asserts, "The direct engagement of audience lends immediacy to her text. [. . .] [Le Sueur] expects her audience to respond to the absurdity and injustice of this life" (94).

Traditionally, the reader and the writer are conceived of as separate and isolated. We think of literature as the product of a solitary, inspired writer. The author is usually depicted as autonomous and working alone; and reading is a solitary experience. As a result, a gulf exists between the writer/artist and the reader. Testimony, conversely, strives for solidarity or interaction. Le Sueur, it seems, also wished to bridge that gulf and relinquish the power of the "so-called writer" ("Afterwords" to *The Girl* 133). She attempted to give her texts over to her collaborators and remove herself as the author. As Roberta Maierhofer argues, Le Sueur resisted individualism and advocated solidarity. She states, "Le Sueur presents individualism as an aspect of an alienated society that is dominated by competition and achievement. Her answer seems to be an almost fluid identity without boundaries between individuals" (156). In almost all of the commentary on Le Sueur and in most of her own writing, "solidarity" eventually becomes a focus. Her rejection of individualism is clearly at odds with central tenets of American culture and literature.

RESISTANCE TO TESTIMONY

As I have been suggesting, certain traits of testimony are incompatible with traditional definitions of "literature" and the "author." This has led to the marginalization or exclusion of testimony as a literary form. I believe we should attempt to recuperate examples of testimony to counteract this imbalance and to redress the effects of the division between romantic and realist literature. In order to accomplish this task, I think it is worthwhile to identify, at least tentatively, some of the reasons that testimonial literature has been excluded or marginalized.

First, as John Beverly suggests, testimony contains elements of several different forms and genres. Because it does not "fit" properly in any one of those categories, there may have been a tendency–consciously or unconsciously–to overlook testimonial literature in favor of other, more familiar forms. The problem of categorization manifests itself in several different ways. Testimony may blend elements of fiction and nonfiction, literature and history, autobiography and the novel, romanticism and realism.

Because critics and scholars accept these binaries, a form which combines or elides the distinctions will be neglected because it does not conform to conventions of form or taste. James E. Young, writing about Holocaust testimonies, explains how the separation of literature and history into distinct disciplines can serve to minimize the importance of testimony. He states:

> This distinction between the hard facts of the Holocaust and the perceived softness in their literary reconstruction has also been enforced by historians, who remain especially wary of the potential displacement of hard history by its novelistic versions. (6)

Since testimonial literature disrupts the division of fiction and nonfiction, it troubles those who depend upon a strict demarcation between the two.[12]

The literary "quality" of testimony also becomes a point of contention. Since it does not seek to conform to the criteria for what is traditionally considered "good" literature, testimony has probably been neglected in favor of novels, short stories, and other recognizably "literary" forms. The compulsory nature of testimony and the fact that it attempts to inform readers about generally "unacceptable" topics set it apart from literature which attempts to present interesting or entertaining plots, characters, and themes. As Jane Tompkins has said, "When literary texts are conceived as agents of cultural formation rather than as objects of interpretation or appraisal, what counts as a 'good' character or a logical sequence of events changes accordingly" (xvii). Although Tompkins was not addressing testimony in this quotation, her argument is important. The purpose and goals of testimony are inconsistent with many of the criteria which critics have been using to evaluate American literature throughout the twentieth century.

Second, the authors, as members of subaltern groups who have been oppressed, discriminated against, ignored, or marginalized, may lack access to educational opportunities or the publishing industry–advantages which other authors take for granted.[13] Moreover, depending on an individual's circumstances, writing a book may not be exactly a priority. Other needs, such as finding food and shelter, avoiding abuse, or staying alive, take precedence. In fact, calling attention to one's membership in a subaltern group is often risky if not inadvisable. We may lack examples of testimonial literature because the dominant classes have done such a good job of convincing subaltern groups not to "make waves."

The role or definition of the author in a testimonial work is a third reason that the form may have been historically ignored. The testimonial is not narrated by a solitary artist, inspired by his or her muse, working independently to create a great work of literature–which is what American publishers and readers have come to expect. Although this tendency is shifting, the subject position of the individual author remains important if not necessary to our contemporary concept of literature. However, testimony disrupts this expectation. In his essay "What Is an Author?" Michel Foucault suggests that we reconceptualize the author as a *function* of discourse, rather than a unified, autonomous creator of meaning. (He states, "We can easily imagine a culture where discourse would circulate without any need for an author" [148].) Such a definition applies particularly well to a genre such as testimony which seeks to erase the author as an *authority*, and to insert the group (or situation) as the focus of the text.

RAMIFICATIONS

In addition to these types of resistance–because testimony is an unfamiliar form–specific criticisms have been raised by critics who have reservations about the genre. After addressing these criticisms, I propose three ways that testimony offers an unexplored and productive paradigm for literary studies.

Le Sueur has been criticized for being anti-intellectual (Dawahare 426–427), deterministic (Ellis 173), unrealistic or utopian (Coiner, *Better Red* 121; Dawahare 425), and anti-male (Coiner, *Better Red* 118–119). She is also said to essentialize the differences between men and women (Coiner, *Better Red* 120–121; Dawahare 413; Ellis 176–178) and to reinforce binary thinking. Some of these criticisms are applied directly to the conclusion of *The Girl.* Others apply generally to testimony. For example, deconstruction holds that one should not merely invert a binary: the marginalized term then takes the position of privilege, and who is to say which term deserves such as position? Thus, Le Sueur is said to (unfairly) privilege the lower class over the upper class, the uneducated over the intellectual, the poor over the rich, and nature over urbanism. Anthony Dawahare, for example, claims, "Le Sueur creates a particularly rigid binary opposition between nature/workers and the city" (420). Moreover, Le Sueur privileges "'mass feeling' over individual consciousness as the subjective basis of community" (423). While texts which promote anti-intellectualism, anti-urbanism, and anti-individualism should be questioned, it is difficult to imagine a text which details the suffering of the poor and homeless in an honest and direct manner which would not challenge some of the values of the dominant culture. One text cannot do all things for all people, and I believe the positive cultural work of testimony offsets these theoretical problems.

Critics also accuse Le Sueur and others of "speaking for" the poor, the homeless, the lower class, or other subaltern groups. In other words, one should not attempt to represent the experience of someone else because of the danger of inaccurate or offensive representations. Blanche H. Gelfant notes that "Jacques Derrida considers the scribe–one who translates the spoken word into written language [as Le Sueur did]–a conservator of the power of the bureaucratic state, a role that as a radical writer Le Sueur would wish to reject" (200). Similarly, Jacqueline Ellis ventures to say that Le Sueur adopted a "patronizing tone" (161) and wrote about poor women from her own point of view:

> [B]y placing working-class women subjects at the center of her radical writing, Le Sueur tried to write about feminism and class politics in a way that related to her own personal history. In so doing, however, the self-expressive identities of working-class women were often confined to the spontaneous reactions of their emotions and the physical demands of their bodies. (160)

In other words, according to Ellis (and others), Le Sueur represented poor women reductively and stereotypically. From this perspective her lower class characters are seen as unimaginative and one-dimensional. Because Le Sueur enjoyed an ostensibly middle-class upbringing, she has been accused of selfishly and uncritically appropriating the experiences of poor women into her own work.[14]

Recent critical awareness of the dangers of "speaking for the Other" legitimizes such a charge. However, throughout this study I have been focusing on the effects or cultural work of texts rather than the intentions/motives (conscious or unconscious) of the authors being discussed. As I argued in Chapter Three, the positive intentions of authors like Crane and Riis could still lead to negative results. In the case of Le Sueur, she may not have captured every detail of the experience of the poor accurately (what text could?), but the positive cultural work outweighs the negative cultural work. Moreover, Le Sueur did experience many of the events she describes, and her characters are significantly more developed and "round" than those of naturalists such as Crane and Riis. We should be open to alternative accounts of poverty and homelessness which may avoid the problems Ellis describes, but the alternative–excluding texts like *The Girl*–seems illogical and harmful. One ramification of studying testimony, then, would be a need for continued examination of its limitations.

A second ramification, already addressed to an extent, is the inclusion of texts and authors who otherwise may have been excluded from the literary canon. The canon has exploded, so to speak, in recent history, and the inclusion of testimony should be a welcome change. More specifically, testimony avoids the romanticism/realism binary which has been discussed throughout this study. Rather than romanticizing or objectifying the condition of homelessness, testimony offers another avenue for the discourse on the subject. Critics have questioned the validity of categorization of American literary periods (in the context of multicultural literature, for example) because it has marginalized or excluded certain texts, traditions, and writers. These efforts to recover previously marginalized texts are applicable to testimony since it falls outside of terms like romanticism and realism/naturalism.

As Tompkins argues, what "counts" as good literature may need to shift. Joseph Napora, in his essay "The Story and the Living: Meridel Le Sueur's *The Girl*," summarizes the argument for considering cultural work as a criterion for judgment. He states,

> The question is not will we fail to recognize the worth of this novel but whether we will fail to establish that larger tradition within which this novel will find a place of worth. It will not become a classic because of any critical attention (this essay is not propaganda for it). But because of its influence on readers and writers and because of their influence on the culture that has up until recently effectively kept it hidden, it is classic. (147)

In other words, rather than force individual texts to conform to traditional notions of literary merit, the canon and the criteria for evaluation may need to evolve to accept those texts.

Third, a new aesthetic theory of testimony may be needed, since historically-accepted definitions of great writers and literature may be irrelevant. Form, tone, style, and metaphor may hold different connotations in the context of testimony. As discussed above, testimony is usually a combination or blurring of traditional forms. Elaine Hedges says that Le Sueur's reportage "combined factual reporting with narrative techniques of fiction" (1806)–genres which are historically separate. Acceptance of contrary impulses within the text may be the most identifiable trait as far as aesthetic evaluation. Critics and readers will need to accept *blurring* of fact and fiction, romanticism and realism, autobiography and literature.

Testimony such as *The Girl* also disrupts a traditional understanding of tone. I cannot identify the tone as either optimistic or pessimistic. We tend to believe that texts about poverty and homelessness must be depressing. Aesthetically, this expectation may dissuade readers from seeking out these texts. Certain readers simply do not want to read depressing literature. *The Girl* is not uplifting, nor is it defeatist. Most of the events in the book are grim and sobering, but the conclusion is hopeful since the narrator gives birth and feels powerful and happy. Consequently, one must set aside the belief that poverty–as an involuntary socio-economic condition–is invariably depressing. Although many books combine optimism and pessimism, naturalism in literature is usually pessimistic, and romanticism is usually optimistic. I would argue that this fairly broad generalization is both accurate and limiting. Like "real life," *The Girl* presents a situation which is neither positive nor negative.

This sense of contrary elements pervades the book. The writing style is elevated and sophisticated at times; in other places it is simple and direct, even intentionally repetitive. Le Sueur also juxtaposes mundane details of life with passages of heightened awareness. Individual sentences sometimes capture this juxtapositioning. After she has sex for the first time, the narrator confesses, "I came out of that foul old hotel as out of the hole of hell but also the meadows of heaven" (47). On the surface, certain details may appear contradictory, such as when Butch compliments the narrator:

> Gee you're cute. You got cute hands.
> They were blistered from so much lye in the dishwater. I tried to take them away from him and hide them. (24)

Le Sueur apparently presents a contradiction: how can the narrator's blistered hands be cute? Likewise, after Butch is killed, the narrator indicates, "I was full but I was hungry" (99). She later thinks to herself that it is an "awful and wonderful life" (102). Numerous "contradictions" like this suggest that the reader must learn to accept contrary images. Like Eastern philosophy, testimony, as represented by *The Girl*, contains contradictions which are neither true nor false, realistic nor unrealistic, optimistic nor pessimistic. Thus, Le Sueur suggests that poverty, like anything else, is not entirely positive or negative.[15] Such a method of representation may be more helpful/productive than dependency on the naturalist mode of pessimism which ultimately requires pity (and depersonalization) of the poor because they are generally represented as abject. This approach depicts the poor as passive victims rather than purposeful individuals.

As a final point of consideration, testimony attempts to connect readers and formerly marginalized groups. As I have been suggesting, the elimination of categories related to "us" (the reader) and "them" (the homeless as objects of study) should be a goal of literature when possible. Le Sueur seems to share this goal. Whereas certain critics condemn Le Sueur's "mystified collectivity" (Dawahare 425),[16] others praise her attempt to solve problems by bringing people together.[17] The narrator of *The Girl* seems to speak for Le Sueur when she says,

> Now I know the whole city and the way it is and the way those in it can be together. This you can't know, or be at home with, until you have lived it. No one can tell you. Now I am at home with my own body and the bodies of others and I will do whatever there is to do. (102)

The Girl becomes purposeful and active, thereby undermining the stereotype of the poor as passive or lazy. And the conclusion, while possibly utopian, presents people who are poor and homeless as being happy and communal. Conversely, literary naturalism tends to stereotype the poor as abject and isolated.

Therefore, Le Sueur challenges stereotypes while urging readers to feel a sense of solidarity with the lower class. Adrian Oktenberg claims,

> The Communist critic in the thirties who called the emphasis on human suffering in Le Sueur's work "defeatist" and symptomatic of a "non-revolutionary spirit" missed the point. Le Sueur was anything but defeatist in her emphasis on a vision of the future based on what she called "communal solidarity." For only when people were linked fully and consciously together across the divisions of sex, class, and generation would reconstruction be possible. (100–101)

In previous chapters I demonstrate the limitations of traditional literary forms and categories for representing the condition of homelessness. In this chapter, I propose that testimony avoids these limitations and, as a result, may be more constructive in terms of the production of cultural work. Perhaps the most fundamental form of cultural work in testimony is the breaking down of divisions between subaltern groups and readers of the privileged classes. It seems that texts such as *The Girl* attempt to bring people together, a goal which today's texts dealing with homelessness do not always share. In the Conclusion, I address recent texts which, unfortunately, follow the division between romanticism and realism which testimony avoids.

Conclusion

American Testimonial Literature and the Contemporary Discourse of Homelessness

> [The] process of coming to see other human beings as "one of us" rather than as "them" is a matter of detailed description of what unfamiliar people are like and of redescription of what we ourselves are like. This is a task not for theory but for genres such as ethnography, the journalist's report, the comic book, the docudrama, and, especially, the novel. (xvi)
>
> Richard Rorty, *Contingency, Irony, and Solidarity*

IN THE ABOVE PASSAGE, RICHARD RORTY OUTLINES TWO OF THE UNDERLYING themes of this study. First, Rorty focuses on the fundamental, broad categories of "us" and "them." While these terms may be general and open to critique, I find, with Rorty, that the division can be a pragmatic and productive point of reference.[1] The "other half" has been observed, studied, categorized, analyzed, and written about throughout American history. To an extent, then, the poor and homeless as objects of study have been differentiated from those who observe, write, and read about them. Various labels designate this division: the underclass, the lower class, the submerged tenth, and, currently, "the homeless." While the denotations of these terms differ from one another, they all specify a separate category or class of people. Some of the efforts to quantify and study the issues of poverty and homelessness are beneficial and necessary. Statistical and ethnographic study, for example, contribute to social, cultural, or political responses which may assist poor people (including allocation of government or private assistance). However, the representations of these issues often lead to stereotypes of the people involved. It is hardly a stretch to say that the poor and homeless have been objectified, stereotyped, and mistreated at various times in our history.[2] I assert, therefore, that the separation of the homeless (as Other or as "them") from society in general has occurred to some degree throughout American history. The current study has been prompted by the desire to draw attention to that division in literary studies and in the "real world."

The second way Rorty applies to this study is in the attention given to the effects of narrative. He suggests that texts, stories, narratives–discourse, in other words–can affect perceptions and treatment of those being represented. In Chapter One, I cite Rorty's discussion of sentimentalism and its positive effects for Stowe and her cause. (He also refers specifically to Tompkins's notion of texts doing cultural work as a valuable mode of inquiry.[3]) Drawing on these influences, I argue in this chapter that the contemporary discourse of homelessness often continues to treat the homeless as "them" rather than "us." More specifically, homelessness continues to be romanticized and objectified as it generally has been in American literary history. I propose that contemporary examples of literary testimony dealing with homelessness should be sought out in order to augment or challenge the discourse which relies on this division.[4]

THE CONTEMPORARY DISCOURSE OF HOMELESSNESS

Mark Pittenger's essay "A World of Difference: Constructing the 'Underclass' in Progressive America," traces the historical development of the "underclass" label from the Victorian era through the Progressive era and concludes with a reminder that such an analysis provides a trajectory to be followed throughout the twentieth century. Discussing the evolution of the term, Pittenger remarks,

> To trace this genealogy forward through the twentieth century will cast light on present-day popular, journalistic, and academic discussions and images of poverty and the poor, as they inform our own public discourse and policy debates, and as we, who also live in a world of difference, continue both to confront and to evade "this unknown class." (54–55)

I share Pittenger's belief that our era parallels the late nineteenth and early twentieth century in its interest in and construction of the underclass/the homeless as a distinct and potentially threatening class of people. Likewise, earlier representations continue to "inform" contemporary attitudes and responses. Although the current discourse of homelessness differs substantially from earlier periods, certain trends and commonalities can be discerned.

Since about 1980, the discourse of homelessness in America has shifted considerably. Between 1940 and 1980, the image of the solitary, alcoholic skid-row "bum" dominated the discursive construction of homeless people. Then, homelessness became a more pronounced and visible problem in the 1980s, as a result of unemployment, deinstitutionalization, federal cutbacks in assistance, and decreased earnings and affordable housing.[5] At the same time, "the homeless"–a term representing those people, usually in large urban centers; who appear to be mentally ill, unemployed and unemployable; permanently living on the streets or temporarily in shelters; and who frequently panhandle–became a fairly stable discursive construct. "Homelessness" also became a specific socio-political term denoting the condition and often engendering political factions.

A surfeit of texts followed this increase in the visible homeless population. This discourse tries to map and comprehend the presence of the poor and unemployed much like the turn of the century texts did. The contemporary range of genres, forms, categories, and treatments may be unparalleled, however. Nearly every mode of cultural production has appropriated, used, and represented homelessness since 1980.

In addition to innumerable newspaper and magazine articles, there have been dozens of television shows, movies, and books dealing with homelessness.[6] Popular music lyrics and performance art identify homelessness as a theme. The *Atlanta Constitution* reports that a board game based on life on the streets has been produced. Street newspapers such as Chicago's *Streetwise* have become an accepted part of the urban scene. *Redwood Curtain*, a play about a homeless veteran, opened on Broadway; troupes of homeless actors have formed in Chicago and San Francisco. The "Homeless Vehicle Project," a monstrous version of a shopping cart built for the homeless, stirred attention in New York city;[7] and three San Diego artists raised a controversy over NEA funding by handing-out $10 bills to homeless immigrants.[8] This brief sampling indicates the range and pervasiveness of the discourse of homelessness.

According to Talmadge Wright, texts in popular culture contribute to the stereotypes and classifications of the homeless. He argues,

> The popular association of homeless people with dirty clothes, offensive smells, and torn clothing is reproduced in popular media portrayals of the homeless. The power of such images is reflected in the fact that homelessness is used as a trope for being "outside" of mainstream society. (206)

In other words, the homeless are represented as different from "us." Of course, not all of these texts foster stereotypes of the homeless. Children's literature, for example, offers an interesting, complex range of perspectives.

Given the penetration of the issue in American culture, however, it is surprising to note that relatively little commentary has analyzed or questioned these texts and/or their ability to perpetuate stereotypes. Some commentators have analyzed a particular genre or a group of texts;[9] others have mentioned the need for more discourse analysis of the topic.[10] But the discursive power to produce either romanticized *or* objectified accounts of homelessness seems to be generally unacknowledged.[11] This division is present in two contemporary books which seem to follow the historical predilection for either romanticizing or objectifying homelessness. I suggest that discourse shaped these accounts by offering the two primary modes of representation and discouraging other forms (such as testimony).

HOMELESSNESS AS ADVENTURE

In October, 1993, St. Martin's Press published *Travels with Lizbeth: Three Years on the Road and on the Streets* by Lars Eighner. Eighner, who was homeless at the time, recounts his travels across the country with his dog (Lizbeth) as well as details of surviving on the street. The book was promoted heavily and *The New York Times Book Review* immediately featured the selection on its front cover. As the subtitle indicates, the book conflates romantic homelessness ("on the road") with our contemporary understanding of what it means to be homeless and living "on the streets." I believe this conflation is a logical but ultimately harmful response to the discursive traditions discussed throughout this study.

As a literary text, *Travels with Lizbeth* finds itself in the tradition of "survival" literature such as *Robinson Crusoe* and *Swiss Family Robinson.* (Eighner notes his fascination with the latter as a child on page 250). In a chapter entitled "On Dumpster Diving," for example, Eighner matter-of-factly describes the most efficient ways to survive by "scavenging," and he often notes the details he learns for survival while living on the streets. The book also knowingly participates in the travelogue genre–a tradition the publishers are keenly aware of. Finally, *Travels with Lizbeth* follows the tradition of the romantic, adventuresome hobo as represented by Jack London, W. H. Davies, and other tramps, as well as the Beat Generation.

Eighner seems not to resist the association with romanticized, adventuresome notions of homelessness. Significant portions of the book consist of his series of rides between Texas and California and the places he and Lizbeth find to sleep. Unfortunate incidents occur, but a fairly optimistic feeling pervades their journeys. He is sometimes critical of the societal and institutional responses to homelessness, but his tone is generally carefree. He details the pleasure of Dumpster diving, for example:

> Dumpster diving is outdoor work, often surprisingly pleasant. It is not entirely predictable; things of interest turn up every day and some days there are finds of great value. I am always very pleased when I can turn up exactly the thing I most wanted to find. [. . .] It is very sweet to turn

> up a few dollars in change from a Dumpster that has just been gone over by a wino. (124)

Like the tramp autobiographers, Eighner shows his expertise in living on the street, and he maintains distance from the truly destitute–the "wino" in this case. He also states, "As bad as things had been I cannot deny there is a romance of the road" (32–33). This quotation, coupled with the interesting rides and campsites they enjoy, demonstrates that *Travels with Lizbeth* participates in the tradition of the romanticized tramp. It also suggests that the literary discourse has remained influential, despite the changes in our conception of "the homeless."

The title, *Travels with Lizbeth*, and the subtitle, "Three Years on the Road and on the Streets," immediately associates the book with travel literature. The subtitle even includes the title of the most famous travelogue associated with the Beat Generation and romanticized tramping, Kerouac's *On the Road*. The title minimizes the plight of homelessness and, like the rest of the book, minimizes negative thoughts or feelings associated with the socio-economic condition.

Moreover, a picture of the author and his dog is superimposed over a map of Texas, where most of the story takes place. The map intimates that the book will be about travel and adventure. Quotations about the book which appear on the back cover strengthen the connection to travel literature and also enhance the author's ethos: "Lars Eighner is a latter-day Candide" (Sarah Bird); he is the "Thoreau of Dumpsters" (Philip Lopate); "Eighner's dry, disciplined style calls to mind the best of the English travel writers, Eric Newby" (Bird). Putting Eighner in the company of Thoreau and Candide, as well as Orwell, Hamsun, and Ackerly, establishes his credibility as a writer and distances Eighner from "the homeless." Like the tramp autobiographies discussed in Chapter Four, the text maintains a distance between the author and the truly destitute.

The comparison to Newby also solidifies the connection to travel literature and is followed by an odd attempt at flattery. Sarah Bird states, "Newby may have trekked through the Congo in his day, but he never went on a journey more extraordinary than the one Eighner made and portrays so compellingly in the absolutely first-rate *Travels with Lizbeth*" (Eighner, back cover). Associating Newby's voluntary, exotic journey to the Congo with Eighner's involuntary homelessness is potentially destructive and misleading. Homelessness becomes merely a convenient experience to draw upon for a clever adventure-tale; for most, it is a forced reality rather than a voluntary choice. This representation may contribute to the misleading belief that many of the homeless choose to stay on the streets.

Similarly *blasé* comments on the back cover may also belittle the experience of homelessness. For example, (according to Lopate) the events in

Eighner's life are "grubby misadventures"–a label more befitting "Gilligan's Island" perhaps. Eighner also "knows a lot of odd, interesting stuff." This statement, while not entirely inaccurate, is somewhat glib in the context of eating out of Dumpsters. The publishers also include a quotation by Michael Silverblatt which connects the book with canonical works such as Orwell's *Down and Out in Paris and London* that present marginalized, suffering subjects in order to appeal to that potential market of interested buyers. Similarly, Phillip Lopate exclaims, "This book will become a classic of down-and-out literature."

Drawing on the work of Jane Tompkins, I question this designation for what could be an account of social, economic, and cultural marginalization. A "classic" is meant to be honored and elevated–the antithesis of being "down and out." While the two are not entirely incompatible, Tompkins provides an alternative explanation of the classics. She argues,

> When classic texts are seen not as the ineffable products of genius but as the bearers of a set of national, social, economic, institutional, and professional interests, then their domination of the critical scene seems less the result of their indisputable excellence than the product of historical contingencies. (xii)

I am not suggesting that *Travels with Lizbeth* is uninteresting or poorly written, nor am I suggesting that Lopate's personal assessment of the book is wrong. Rather, I find Tompkins's paradigm more persuasive and productive for evaluating this particular text within the wider discourse of homelessness and the cultural work it produces. At this particular historical moment, I feel that texts which romanticize or elevate the condition of homelessness might be out of step with the experiences of most people without homes.

Statements by Jonathan Raban in his review of *Travels with Lizbeth* in *The New York Times Book Review* reveal a similar tension in having to apply criteria of the "classics" to this work. First, Raban establishes that it is "unconventional": "In *Travels with Lizbeth*, Mr. Eighner's voice and form are as strikingly unconventional as the life they conjure" (33). Eighner, in the introduction to *Travels with Lizbeth*, specifically refutes Raban's claim. He says,

> Any homeless life entails certain dangers and discomforts. I have tried not to make too much of these, for I suppose people who have always lived in comfort will imagine the worst. In fact, my homelessness involved far more mundane annoyances and petty irritations than terrors and pains. (xi)

The straightforward style in this passage, representative of the entire work, is hardly "unconventional." Moreover, Eighner admits that his life consists of the "mundane" and the "petty," rather than the "strikingly unconventional" as Raban contends.

Raban bolsters his claim by selecting examples from the text of such "strikingly unconventional" details as "uncommonly stout," "to wit," and "tarry." Raban adds,

> The world he re-creates in his book is an unfailingly strange one. Time works differently there. Weeks on end go absent without leave from Mr. Eighner's memory, while a nightmare 24 hours are spent on a miserable odyssey through the suburbs of Tucson, trying to find a store that will pay cash for a $4.40 book of postage stamps. (33)

The quote evokes Faulkner's sense of chronological complexity and timelessness, when in reality Raban is noticing that Eighner took more time to explain certain important events than he did other, less significant ones. Eighner notes,

> Every life has trivial occurrences, pointless episodes, and unresolved mysteries, but a homeless life has these and virtually nothing else. I have found it best in some parts to abandon a strictly chronological account and to treat in essay form experiences that relate to a single subject although they occurred in disparate times and places. (xi)

Raban does not account for these remarks. I was never perplexed by the chronology of the narrative. While the book is interesting, it is not stylistically unconventional or chronologically complex in the ways Raban suggests. Raban's personal preference for the complex and unconventional adheres to the contemporary contingencies of literary "value" which Tompkins alludes to.

I am not dismissing aesthetics as a criterion of evaluation in literary studies. Texts can be unconventional, complex, and interesting in a variety of ways; even those that are about homelessness can be unconventional as I discuss in the context of Le Sueur. However, within the scope of this study and in the specific context of literary representations of homelessness, cultural work offers a more productive paradigm than aesthetics. In other contexts, cultural work may not be an applicable or valuable standard. Raban's comments, it seems, indicate the power of discourse to influence the recognition of romanticized homelessness, a category that may be misappropriated when to comes to forms of actual homelessness.

Raban also refers to *Travels with Lizbeth* as "a modern autobiography of a supertramp" (1), in reference to W. H. Davies's *Autobiography of a Super-Tramp*. Although most of the tramp autobiographies discussed in

Chapter Four have been largely forgotten, their discursive influence remains. Raban, as well as the publishers of *Travels with Lizbeth*, and Eighner himself perpetuate the earlier, romantic (though mostly anachronistic) version of the homeless individual as adventurer and wanderer. As a result, I believe the cultural work of the discourse surrounding this text is detrimental. It obscures the reality of social and economic displacement and justifies the prevalent misconception that the homeless choose to live on the streets.

HOMELESSNESS AS ABJECTION

Whereas the hardships of homelessness are potentially minimized by a text such as *Travels with Lizbeth*, other texts, particularly in sociology, delineate the many ways that the condition is debilitating. Recently, some sociologists have questioned this tendency to overemphasize suffering, degradation, and abjection.[12] As I assert in Chapter Three, abjection represents a form of objectification in which homeless people are seen as passive, usually pathological victims, rather than active participants in the community. David Wagner explains how the discourse which constructed the "disaffiliated," alcoholic, skid-row "bum" receded somewhat after 1980 but remains influential. He argues,

> Although some of the negative stereotyping connected with the disaffiliation label has receded with social scientists' shift in focus to the new homeless and away from the old skid row bum, the term *disaffiliation* and others such as *isolated, vulnerable*, and *disempowered* still pervade the literature. (6)

Wagner goes on to analyze forms of action, resistance, and solidarity in a homeless community in New England. While not idealizing their efforts, Wagner offers an interesting, alternative account of homeless people who challenge the disaffiliation stereotype.

Conversely, *My Life on the Streets: Memoirs of a Faceless Man* by "Joe Homeless" portrays nearly every imaginable form of degradation and abjection. Written under the pseudonym Joe Homeless, the book is the ostensibly true account of the author's experience living on the street. The chronicle of abuse and discrimination tests the limits of verisimilitude and reinforces the image of the disaffiliated, mentally ill victim, despite the attempt to be honest and informative.

In the "Acknowledgments," the author calls for recognition of the true causes and consequences of homelessness. He exclaims,

> I would like you to keep in mind that most of the homeless are homeless not because they are drug addicts, alcoholics or mentally incompe-

> tent. They are in the street as a result of the sick economy. The politicians who fouled up the economy think it is a good idea to put the homeless where they can't be seen so no one will ask them why so many people are living in the streets and subways, begging money to survive. I ask you to help their voices be heard. (vi)

This statement resembles the goal or purpose of testimonial literature to reveal a problem experienced by a subaltern group. "Joe Homeless" is also a real protagonist in the action and a member of the affected group, as is the case for other examples of testimony. He also suggests that–like testimony–his story needs to be told for his safety and the safety of other homeless people. In the "Preface," he compares homelessness to the death marches of prisoners of war during World War II and to being crucified. Like Jesus, the homeless are "tormented and tortured every step of the way" (ix). While it meets basic elements of the definition of testimony as defined in Chapter Five, *My Life on the Streets* tends to increase rather than decrease divisions between homeless people and other members of society in at least two ways.

First, the story lacks verisimilitude. The constant abuse, humiliation, and discrimination defy logic and credibility. Nearly every chapter depicts a different hurdle or threat. His family, the police, social workers, hospital psychiatrists, priests and nuns, and his neighborhood block association seem to go out of their way to make his life miserable. The random, senseless violence directed toward him can hardly be explained as inherent distrust of the homeless. A hospital guard, for example, hits him with a billyclub for no apparent reason (183). This response and others are unrealistic because they are not sufficiently motivated. His friends are helpful and do what they can, but family members, government officials, charity organizations, and the clergy are unhelpful to the point of outright rudeness and cruelty. The block association repeatedly chases him and threatens to beat him up, supposedly to drive him out of the neighborhood. Perhaps all of these events took place exactly in the manner they are described. Regardless, the text violates the principle of verisimilitude because it does not explain the motives of those who abuse him.

In other areas, the plot wanders and the purpose of the narrative is unclear. Chapter 8, "Water, Water Everywhere," for example, arbitrarily recounts memories of a baseball game, an experience with strippers, and meeting a "godfather" apparently involved in the mafia. Here and in other chapters, the purpose of the book as well as its realism is questionable.

Second, Joe Homeless tends to come across as a victim rather than a constitutive member of society. Although he attempts to fit in, and says that discrimination prevents him from doing so, he comes across as at least marginally paranoid. Readers who doubt the stability of homeless people in general will likely come away with more firmly entrenched stereotypes. He stays in a homeless shelter, receives a welfare check, and is checked in to a mental hospital. In each case, a specific stereotype is supported. The text repeatedly affirms the differences between "us" and "the homeless" as a marginalized group. Although it corrects misconceptions that may be present in romanticized accounts, it still contributes to the objectification of the homeless. Like *Travels with Lizbeth*, I believe its cultural work is detrimental.

HOMELESSNESS AND AMERICAN TESTIMONIAL LITERATURE

Whereas *My Life on the Streets* satisfies some of the elements of testimony or testimonial literature, I feel that other examples should be sought out in order to counteract the effects of texts which romanticize or objectify the condition of homelessness. Efforts have been made to publish writings which can be considered testimony and do not portray the abjection of *My Life on the Streets*.[13] For example, *Tell Them Who I Am: The Lives of Homeless Women* by Elliot Liebow and *Songs from the Alley* by Kathleen Hirsch depict the authors' experiences working with and getting to know women living in shelters for the homeless. Anthologies of writing by homeless authors have also been published recently. These include *Homeless Not Helpless: An Anthology* edited by Barbara Paschke and David Volpendesta, *An American Mosaic: Prose and Poetry by Everyday Folk* edited by Robert Wolf, *Home Words: An Anthology of Creative Works by Homeless People in the Twin Cities* edited by Leonard Lang, and *I Have Arrived Before My Words: Autobiographical Writings of Homeless Women* edited by Deborah Pugh and Jeanie Tietjen.

Pugh and Tietjen, most notably, have collected the writings of five homeless women who participated in a writing group with the editors. The collected essays represent a positive, instructive model for texts which do not subscribe to traditional stereotypes and which represent the authors as regular people who happen to have been homeless for a portion of their lives. Each essay presents the author's own life-story and may not exemplify "the homeless" as a group. But their struggles with poverty, hunger, illness, and unstable housing are universal enough to conceive of their texts as "testimony" in the way it was defined in Chapter Five. Just as important, *I Have Arrived Before My Words: Autobiographical Writings of Homeless Women* does not subscribe to the discursive tendency to romanticize or objectify the condition of homelessness. For these reasons, I believe that the cultural work of this text is productive, and I assert that it would be valuable to seek out and publish similar examples in order to challenge stereotypes of the poor. As a final consideration, I wish to analyze the essay entitled "Creativity Has Got to Find an Expressive Channel Somehow" by "Angie" from *I Have Arrived Before My Words* as an example of contemporary testimony.

Applying the concept of testimony to this and other texts may contribute to an increased understanding of homelessness and of discourse. While recent critics have utilized testimony as a category of literature, it is used primarily in the context of Holocaust studies or Latin American studies.[14] Testimony provides a means of analysis that other terms, such as reportage, participant-observer journalism, autobiography, memoir, and realism/naturalism, do not. Recognizing this capability should ideally lead to an increased awareness of testimony as a genre of American literature and to increased attention to testimony in critical theory.[15]

"Creativity Has Got to Find an Expressive Channel Somehow" epitomizes texts which can produce positive cultural work. The essay disrupts prominent stereotypes by portraying a homeless individual as dynamic, strong, resilient, yet imperfect, and it avoids the tendency to represent homelessness as either a form of adventure or abjection. Although homelessness is usually considered a "foreign" or extraordinary condition, the essay is compelling because it is universal enough to be of general interest. Angie describes events that many people who have not been homeless may have experienced, and by doing so she creates solidarity with the reader.

The essay opens with a realistic assessment of her condition. She writes,

> I am no longer homeless, but I have been through the experience. I write this in the beginning days of 1996, and have had my own shelter since the summer of 1992. The aftershocks of having been homeless would still come back to haunt me just until the recent past. I still feel a shudder now and then. To be alone without one of life's basic requirements–shelter–is a traumatic experience. (Angie 151).

Throughout the essay the tone is honest, realistic, and restrained. Although she admits she is under stress, she does not represent herself as a victim, as Joe Homeless does.

The passage also immediately calls into question one of the most prominent stereotypes of homelessness. Many people believe that it is a permanent condition and that it is (therefore) the defining characteristic of homeless people. Sociologists, however, have established that the majority of homeless people experience the condition for finite, relatively short periods of time. The image of the street person or bag lady as representative of all homeless people has probably led to the belief that the condition is permanent. Angie describes her ongoing struggles to find permanent housing, but she is not the stereotypical "street person."

As an example of testimony, Angie's text also represents an entry into the public sphere of a group which is seldom heard from directly. In his essay "Representing the Homeless," Allen Carey-Webb quotes filmmaker Bill Brand as saying, "'[w]e're so accustomed to homeless people as voiceless victims that when they speak, we no longer believe they are homeless'" (705). Like Le Sueur or Rigoberta Menchú, who represented poor women during the Depression and indigenous Guatemalans respectively, Angie speaks directly for others who have been invisible or marginalized. More often than not, the general public is exposed to discourse which has not been produced by homeless people themselves and therefore has a greater potential to misrepresent them.

Over the course of the essay, Angie reveals that her parents were uncaring and distant, that she experienced sexual abuse, that she lost her right arm due to radiation treatment for breast cancer, that she has an eating disorder, and that she was diagnosed with depression. Despite these setbacks–which contribute to her homelessness–she remains determined and purposeful. She does not makes excuses or fault others; she does not represent herself as a victim or martyr. In other words, Angie does not objectify the condition of homelessness by representing it as a form of abjection, as many other texts have. In fact, she repeatedly remarks that she feels "blessed." She states, "Today, I am stabilized, balanced, feeling more in control of myself and what concerns me; I am looking forward to the future" (152). Unlike naturalist texts, "Creativity Has Got To Find an Expressive Channel Somehow" does not rely on pessimism or misery to engage pity for the poor and homeless.

The text differs from the traditional discourse of homelessness in other ways. Angie is not isolated, solitary, or disaffiliated, as is the case in many texts. Her family is very important to her, for example. Though her parents were distant, she admits their positive influences. She remarks, "I owe this desire to see everyday things in out-of-the-ordinary ways to my mother and father, now physically deceased" (154). Her children are a source of strength and pride. Even her participation in the book editors' writing group and the publication of the essay itself affirm her social connections. While the majority of texts depict solitary, romantic, wandering individuals or disaffiliated homeless victims, Angie is seen as an empathetic, compassionate, constitutive member of society.

Similarly, she is active and purposeful, not lazy and powerless. She actively seeks treatment for depression, repeatedly tries to secure permanent housing, and develops her skill as a writer while learning to write with her left hand after the loss of her right arm. Her writing becomes a means of coping with stress and an outlet for her creativity. The essay's title, "Creativity Has Got To Find an Expressive Channel Somehow," reflects the pride and value she holds for creativity. She states, "The creative writing has helped me to actually *be* creative again as opposed to morosely musing about the nature of creativity" (166). She is also a very spiritual person. Angie remarks, "I have an *active* prayer life, though I'm not often on my knees or in church that regularly" (152, italics added). All of these traits puncture the stereotype of the homeless as passive victims of their environment and condition, permanently constrained by their plight.

For these reasons, the cultural work of a text such as "Creativity Has Got To Find an Expressive Channel Somehow" is positive and productive. Unlike romanticized versions, Angie's text does not glamorize or elevate her situation. Unlike the representations of homelessness as a form of destitution or abjection which code the homeless as victims and/or objects of study, the essay portrays an active, purposeful, constitutive member of society. Perhaps Angie's essay and the other essays in *I Have Arrived Before My Words* are not thrilling enough or depressing enough to reach out and grab the reader's attention, thereby justifying greater distribution and/or recognition as a literary form. Or perhaps the discourse of homelessness has discouraged the production of texts like this because it does not adhere to the categories of romanticism or naturalism. In either case, I contend that texts like *I Have Arrived Before My Words* should be sought out in order to redress some of the stereotypes associated with homelessness. The discourse of homelessness should be examined more closely in order to ascertain the effects or cultural work it produces and to expand the options for different, more productive texts in the future.[16]

CONCLUSION

In his book *Difference and Pathology: Stereotypes of Sexuality, Race, and Madness*, Sander L. Gilman provides a balanced, pragmatic overview of stereotypes and Otherness. Gilman argues that stereotypes are necessary, mutable, and generally bipolar (us/them, good/bad, healthy/pathological). The introduction–"What Are Stereotypes and Why Use Texts to Study Them?"–discusses the creation of stereotypes and the role of texts in challenging and perpetuating them. *Homelessness in American Literature: Romanticism, Realism, and Testimony* attempts to put some of Gilman's observations into practice by challenging certain stereotypes associated with homelessness and by examining how literary texts and criticism have contributed to those images.

I have attempted to specify the ways in which texts/discourse contribute to misleading or generalized conceptions of the homeless. Recognizing that stereotypes exist is insufficient because everyone depends upon them to varying degrees. As Gilman says, "We can and must make the distinction between pathological stereotyping and the stereotyping all of us need to do to preserve our illusion of control over the self and the world" (18). Unfortunately, it seems that specific negative stereotypes of homeless people have evolved throughout American history. These images have led to disavowal and violence at various times because it has been possible to see homeless people as different or Other. According to Gilman, "Every social group has a set vocabulary of images for this externalized Other. These images are the product of history and of a culture that perpetuates them" (20). He adds, "Texts are an ideal source for a study of the fluidity of stereotypical concepts" (26).

On one hand, concepts of homelessness have evolved significantly in America. From the pre-industrial wandering poor, to the industrial tramp, to the skid-row bum, to "the homeless," the prevailing image of homeless individuals has shaped and reflected the social, cultural, and political attitudes of each period. This process can be seen in the literary texts examined throughout this study. On the other hand, certain traits or beliefs have remained fairly consistent in each period. Discourse has tended to either romanticize or objectify homelessness, and this has led to stereotypes of the homeless as isolated, disaffiliated, inactive, pathological, and permanently displaced.

Literary studies provides a means to analyze this discourse and the "fluidity" of stereotypes regarding the homeless. As Gilman argues, stereotypes are socially constructed, not actual. Therefore, they can be challenged and modified. Active analysis of stereotypes and discourse can potentially contribute to positive effects or cultural work by minimizing the divisions between the homeless (as "them") and the rest of society ("us"). As Richard Rorty asserts,

> Solidarity is not discovered by reflection but created. It is created by increasing our sensitivity to the particular details of the pain and humiliation of other, unfamiliar sorts of people. Such increased sensitivity makes it more difficult to marginalize people different from ourselves by thinking, "They do not feel it as we would," or "There must always be suffering, so why not let them suffer?" (*Contingency* xvi)

As readers, writers, critics, and teachers, we can create solidarity and minimize differences by being aware of the ability of discourse to affect our attitudes and responses. Whereas the discourse of homelessness has historically perpetuated divisions between "us" and "them," there are texts which allow readers to become sensitive to the pain and humiliation of others without seeing them as abject or destitute, and therefore as victims to be pitied. Literary testimony resists the marginalization of homeless people and the impulse to see "their" condition as significantly different from "our" own. For this reason, testimony represents a valuable contribution to the constantly evolving discourse of homelessness in America.

Notes

NOTES TO THE INTRODUCTION

[1] I am wary of misappropriating the term "homelessness." It may be anachronistic, if not harmful, to discuss literature and other cultural products from earlier periods in the context of a term with specific socio-political denotations in our time. For example, some advocates argue that we should not call people who have been temporarily displaced by natural disasters "homeless" because it makes the plight of actual homeless people appear less serious. Others warn against simplifying or generalizing disparate conditions and causes under the same heading. For a thorough discussion of the definition(s) of homelessness, see Hopper and Baumohl. They state: "The puzzle of American homelessness, that which makes tracing its continuities and discontinuities over time so difficult, is that it is not one thing but many, gathered up under a common heading that masks as much as it discloses" (12).

I will be using the adjective "homeless" to describe anyone without a permanent dwelling, and "homelessness" to describe that general condition. I reserve the use of "the homeless" to indicate the current conception of the collective noun: those people living primarily on the streets of urban centers, unemployed or unemployable, usually destitute, and frequently exhibiting signs of mental illness. While I recognize that "homelessness" does not function discursively as it did in the past, the word "homeless" was used as early as 1615 to describe, obviously enough, someone without a home. Stowe, moreover, uses the word in this way in *Uncle Tom's Cabin*. Therefore, it seems reasonable to (cautiously) utilize the term in this manner.

[2] While literal homelessness has been addressed frequently in sociology and literature, the subject has not received equal attention in literary criticism. Moreover, that criticism has been somewhat limited in both scope and approach. Further investigation of the theme is also warranted when one considers the historical sig-

nificance of "the home" (or lack thereof) in America: the "American dream" of home ownership; the relation of home to personal identity; the backlash and response to homelessness throughout American history; the penetration of idiomatic sayings such as "Home Sweet Home"; and the sanctity of the home in America.

[3] These treatments emphasize the author's or character's sense of rebellion or adventure, rather than his (very rarely her) condition of being "homeless."

[4] I recognize the limits of this generalization, but, as I attempt to demonstrate throughout this chapter, history has favored certain depictions of homelessness and neglected others. Later, I suggest that literary testimony falls outside this division. Other exceptions may be *Housekeeping* by Marilynne Robinson, *Ironweed* by William Kennedy, "Blackberry Winter" by Robert Penn Warren. Of course, no text either elevates or objectifies homelessness entirely, but these examples are more fundamentally ambiguous than most literary treatments of this theme.

[5] See, for example: Bjorkman, Frances Maule, "The New Anti-Vagrancy Campaign," *Review of Reviews* 37 (Feb. 1908): 206–211; Denny, C. S., "The Whipping Post for Tramps," *Century Magazine* 27 (April 1895): 794; Glenn, John, "Co-operation Against Beggary," *Charities Review* 1 (Dec. 1891): 67–72; Lewis, Orlando Faulkland, "The American Tramp," *Atlantic* 101 (June 1908): 744–753; Myers, Gustavus, "Colonizing the Tramp," *Review of Reviews* 39 (March 1908): 311–316; Rood, Henry Edward, "The Tramp Problem: A Remedy," *The Forum* 25 (March 1898): 90–94; Wayland, Francis, "The Tramp Question," *Proceedings of the Conference of Boards of Public Charities* (1877): 111–126.

[6] A partial list of tramp autobiographies: Anderson, Nels, *The American Hobo: An Autobiography* (1975); Augustin, Joseph, *The Human Vagabond* (1935); Black, Jack, *You Can't Win* (1927); Brown, John, *I Was a Tramp* (1934); Crawford, J. H., *The Autobiography of a Tramp* (1900); Davies, W. H., *The Autobiography of a Super-Tramp* (1908); Digit, *The Confessions of a Twentieth Century Hobo* (1924); Douglas, Robin, *Sixteen to Twenty-One* (1925); Edge, William, *The Main Stem* (1927); Flynt, Josiah, *My Life* (1908); Fox, Charles Elmer, *Tales of an American Hobo* (1989); Fuller, Arthur F., *An Odd Soldiery* (1910); Kemp, Harry, *Tramping on Life: An Autobiographical Narrative* (1922); Lindsay, Vachel, *Adventures While Preaching the Gospel of Beauty* (1916); Livingston, Leon Ray, *The Curse of the Tramp: A True Story of Actual Tramp Life Written by Himself* (1912); London, Jack, *The Road* (1907); Milligan, James, *I Didn't Stay Honest* (1936); Mullin, Glen H., *Adventures of a Scholar-Tramp* (1925); Peele, John, *From North Carolina to Southern California Without a Ticket and How I Did It* (1907); Reitman, Ben L., *Sister of the Road: The Autobiography of Box-Car Bertha* (1937); Schockman, Carl S., *We Turned Hobo: A Narrative of Personal Experience* (1937); Smyth, Joseph Hilton, *To Nowhere and Return: The Autobiography of a Puritan* (1940); Starke, Barbara, *Born in Captivity: The Story of a Girl's Escape* (1931); Stoneham, C. T., *From Hobo to Hunter* (1956); Tully, Jim, *Beggars of Life: A Hobo Autobiography* (1924); Worby, John, *The Other Half: The Autobiography of a Tramp* (1937).

[7] I am collapsing the distinction between realism and naturalism for the sake of simplicity and organization. Most of the texts I deal with would be considered naturalist, and the distinction does not seem to contribute to a greater understanding of texts dealing with homelessness. Moreover, there does not seem to be critical consensus on what distinguishes realism from naturalism at this time.

[8] Other metaphorical treatments of homelessness in American literature include the following: *Home and Homelessness in the American Imagination*, a dissertation by Brian Joseph Whalen which focuses primarily on Hawthorne's short stories as representations of the American (especially Puritan) search for a cultural "soul"; *Dismemberment Motifs in American Literature: The Incomplete and Homeless Body as Metaphor*, a dissertation by Phylis Campbell Dryden which compares figurative dismemberment and homelessness to the shifting, unsettled nature of metaphor itself; and "Strangers in a Strange Land: The Homelessness of Roth's Protagonists" by Estelle Gershgoren Novak, which links homelessness to Roth's sense of alienation from Jewish traditions in America.

[9] If it has not become apparent already, I am relying on Foucault's definition of "discourse" as a collection of texts–literature, journalism, film, art, comics, etc.–which circulate with one another and produce other nodes in the discourse. In this case, the discourse produces texts which tend to elevate or condemn homelessness.

NOTES TO CHAPTER ONE

[1] For critical examinations of homes in *Uncle Tom's Cabin*, see Askeland, Lori, "Remodeling the Model Home in *Uncle Tom's Cabin* and *Beloved*," *American Literature: A Journal of Literary History, Criticism, and Bibliography* 64.4 (1992): 785–805; Halttunen, Karen, "Gothic Imagination and Social Reform: The Haunted Houses of Lyman Beecher, Henry Ward Beecher, and Harriet Beecher Stowe," *New Essays on* Uncle Tom's Cabin, ed. Eric J. Sundquist (Cambridge: Cambridge UP, 1986): 107–134; Hovet, Theodore R., "Modernization and the American Fall into Slavery," *The New England Quarterly* 54.4 (Dec. 1981): 499–518; Jehlen, Myra, "The Family Militant: Domesticity Versus Slavery in *Uncle Tom's Cabin*," *Criticism* 31.4 (Fall 1989): 383–400; and Tompkins, Jane, *Sensational Designs: The Cultural Work of American Fiction 1790–1860* (New York: Oxford, 1985). Several other critics who discuss homes in the novel will be addressed in this chapter.

[2] While *Uncle Tom's Cabin* may not seem to address homelessness directly, Stowe occasionally uses the term "homeless" to describes slaves. More significantly, the importance of homes, the struggle to find homes, and the lack of appropriate homes for slaves permeate the novel. In this way, homelessness is a theme of American literature even in those works which are not explicitly "about" homelessness.

[3] Religious, ethical, and moral arguments have been used to oppose and support the cause of homeless individuals throughout American history. Stowe viewed homelessness and slavery as sins to be eliminated. Similarly, religious and moral

arguments have been used to secure basic human rights for the needy. However, it is equally likely that the homeless individual will be blamed for committing a sin. Historically, compassion has been withheld and condemned on the grounds that "God helps those who help themselves."

[4] Hovet goes on to argue that *Uncle Tom's Cabin* represents the social and philosophical shift in America from a spiritual/agrarian society to a materialistic/industrial one. Such a shift violates the theory of correspondences because people became divorced from the divine and became "physical entities subject to natural law" (500). As a symbol of this profound shift, *Uncle Tom's Cabin* garnered interest and popularity, according to Hovet.

[5] Other critics (Hovet, Brown) have suggested that (returning to) Uncle Tom's cabin remains a positive ideal throughout the novel, but such an interpretation does not account for Tom's inability to own property or the subject position of slaves in general.

[6] William R. Taylor uses the term "antihome" to describe the Legree plantation in *Cavalier and Yankee: The Old South and American National Character* (New York: George Braziller, 1961).

[7] Whereas today's reader may see this as a failure in that integration is not possible, George and Eliza probably represent the best case scenario for Stowe. Their true home will be found in Africa, not America

[8] Appeals to readers to recognize the *rights* of slaves were common. Abolitionists used The Declaration of Independence to reveal the injustice of slavery on the obvious grounds that all men were not created equal–slaves were not granted the "inalienable" rights of "life, liberty and the pursuit of happiness." William Lloyd Garrison, Frederick Douglass, and others used The Declaration of Independence directly, while others argued for recognition of slaves' rights generally. Opponents argued that the rights guaranteed to European men did not apply to African American slaves. In *Cotton is King* (1855), David Christy asserted that The Declaration of Independence was never meant to apply to slaves: "Nothing can be further from the truth, and nothing more certain than that the rights of the negro never entered into the question then considered" (246).

Stowe was aware of this debate–George Harris declares his "declaration of independence" when confronted by a band of men seeking to capture him (298)–but she makes an emotional appeal rather than an appeal to rights. Drawing on the work of Richard Rorty, I emphasize the ability of narrative to effect social change throughout this study, particularly when the dominant culture fails to recognize the humanity of disenfranchised groups. Like Rorty, Stowe seems to realize that the debate over the rights of slaves was a dead end. Opponents simply could not see slaves as human beings, and therefore did not need to be afforded equal rights.

[9] Jane Tompkins describes *Uncle Tom's Cabin* as a "jeremiad" (139) against the moral and economic abuses perpetuated by slavery under capitalism. For Tompkins, "The home is the center of all meaningful activity" (141) and represents

an economic alternative to the male-run marketplace. This culminates in the "reformation of the human race" (143). Tompkins states, "The new matriarchy [. . .] constitutes the most politically subversive dimension of Stowe's novel, more disruptive and far-reaching in its potential consequences than even the starting of a war or the freeing of slaves" (142). Elizabeth Ammons, in "Heroines in *Uncle Tom's Cabin*," also accepts this division of economic and moral spheres. Moreover, the home and mother, representing the domestic sphere, "must not figure as sanctuaries from the world but as imperative models for its reconstitution" (160). Gillian Brown uses the kitchen as the focal point of this restructuring. Brown asserts that "In Stowe's model home, domesticity is matriarchal and antinomian, a new form of government as well as a protest against patriarchy and its manifestations in slavery, capitalism, and democracy" (25).

[10] Some critics preserve the distinction between the domestic and marketplace spheres, but resist the notion that Stowe sought to replace the latter with a "new matriarchy." Lisa Watt MacFarlane, for example, suggests that the power of *Uncle Tom's Cabin* lies in its "failure to resolve happily tensions which American culture has endured for three centuries" (144). Watt MacFarlane points to several details in the text which deny the ascendency of the domestic sphere. She concludes that it cannot replace the marketplace, nor solve the problems of sexism, racism, or capitalism. Amy Schrager Lang's essay, "Slavery and Sentimentalism: The Strange Career of Augustine St. Clare," presents a similar argument. She modifies the approach of Tompkins, Ammons, and Brown by separating the function of the home from the values it represents (the "new matriarchy"): "The function of the home is clear; the status of the domestic values it represents, however, is less so" (35). The defeat of the home and the domestic sphere is "inevitable," she posits, if it is separated from the marketplace. Finally, Myra Jehlen, in perhaps the most direct response to Tompkins, Ammons, and Brown, believes that domesticity is not the goal of *Uncle Tom's Cabin*, but rather the means to "achieve integrity in commerce" (393). She contends that Stowe did not subvert the patriarchal system or "advance the cause of women's self rule" (399). For Jehlen, Stowe's subversiveness is not the issue. According to Jehlen, "*Uncle Tom's Cabin* seeks to end slavery, not racism or sexism" (398).

[11] Unlike "real" literature, sentimentalism has often been aligned with emotion and therefore weakness. Critics such as Tompkins, Fisher, and Rorty challenge this assessment and reveal the merits of sentimentalism. Rorty notes that the "idea that reason is 'stronger' than sentiment, that only an insistence on the unconditionality of moral obligation has the power to change human beings for the better, is very persistent" ("Human Rights" 181). This idea is apparent in the distaste for sentimentalism and the historical privileging of argument/reason over emotion. Stowe made her most effective case in a narrative rather than in an essay or treatise. Although Stowe's rhetorical options were limited because women were told not to become involved in matters outside of the home, she also saw the advantages of narrative over argumentative discourse. Philip Fisher states,

> In *Uncle Tom's Cabin* Stowe had confidently reconstructed her damaged world through the universal inner life of feelings that the sentimental tradition could draw on. [. . .] Stowe's politicized sentimentality and her transcription of the stories told by the slaves themselves were the universalizing means by which the torn space of slavery could be pushed toward crisis and then reassembled on a democratic social basis. ("Democratic Social Space" 100, 105)

As Stowe and Fisher reveal, sentiment, emotion, and narrative can be more effective than logic and reason. Numerous arguments about the rights of slaves were made at the same time, but it was Stowe's novel which prompted Abraham Lincoln to remark that she was "the little lady who started the war."

[12] As mentioned in the Introduction, "testimony" has various legal connotations. First, it refers to the act of giving testimony in a court of law. Second, it represents a corrective; a crime or injustice is meant to be rectified by the presentation of testimony as to the facts of the case. As a literary form, testimony has gotten relatively little attention, but it can be recognized as a rhetorical device throughout American history. These legal connotations can even be seen in the opening of Harriet Ann Jacobs's *Incidents in the Life of a Slave Girl*: "I want to add my *testimony* to that of abler pens to convince the people of the Free states what Slavery really is" (6, italics added).

[13] Until recently, sentimentalism in literature has gotten a bad rap. Handbooks and dictionaries of literature still define sentimentalism as "excessive," as a means of "exploiting" the emotions of the reader. Some of these texts use *Uncle Tom's Cabin* to epitomize sentimentalism, noting the apparent lack of verisimilitude and the scenes which are overly emotional or dramatic. Contemporary reviews established this view and set the tone for later criticism of the novel. In *Notes of a Native Son*, for example, James Baldwin exclaims,

> *Uncle Tom's Cabin* is a very bad novel, having, in its self-righteous, virtuous sentimentality, much in common with *Little Women*. Sentimentality, the ostentatious parading of excessive and spurious emotion, is the mark of dishonesty, the inability to feel [. . .] . (14)

Although Baldwin's argument is important and informed, this passage succinctly describes all that is wrong with *Uncle Tom's Cabin* as an example of sentimentalism. In fact, the novel continues to be brushed aside for its stylistic/emotional excesses. Richard A. Posner remarks, "*Uncle Tom's Cabin* has not survived as literature–the only interest that it holds for us is historical–even though its author's opposition to slavery now commands universal assent" (313). Posner contrasts literature (art, aesthetic production) with historical documents. This binary presents a problem which I address in Chapter Five and elsewhere. I see texts of all kinds–fiction, nonfiction, photography, journalism, sociology, historical documents–circulating with one another as a discourse. This discourse has affected conceptions and beliefs about homelessness, positively and negatively, throughout American history. Just as the division between romanticism and realism excludes certain texts, the separation of fiction (literature, art, poetry) and nonfiction (history, sociology, journalism) has also restricted certain representations of homelessness.

NOTES TO CHAPTER TWO

[1] Accurate numbers are difficult to ascertain for a variety of reasons. First, publishers did not always keep accurate records. Alger estimated that sales of his own books before his death were around 800,000 copies. Second, printers sometimes produced and sold unauthorized editions of Alger's books, at times under a different name or with no author indicated, so as not to pay fees to the publisher. Third, Alger wrote under several pseudonyms, such as Arthur Hamilton, Arthur Lee Putnam, Julian Starr, and Caroline F. Starr (Roach). Finally, sales figures do not accurately represent readership, since Alger's books were published as inexpensive dime novels which were possibly passed along among several readers. In 1945, Frederick Lewis Allen estimated the sales of Alger's books at 100 million copies; in 1964, Thomas Meehan estimated 200 million copies; in 1955, Quentin Reynolds estimated 250 million copies (Roach). Marcus Klein mentions an estimate of 400 million copies, but does not indicate a source. He remarks, "Possibly no novelist anywhere has ever been more widely read" (13).

[2] Comments by several critics suggest the pervasiveness of Alger in American culture. For example, Marcus Klein states, "Horatio Alger is uniquely the measure of American imagination because no other American writer has been so surely, centrally, and continuously present in it" (14).

[3] For the most comprehensive discussion of these issues, see "Chapter 4: Guidebooks for Survival in an Industrializing Economy" in *The Fictional Republic: Horatio Alger and American Political Discourse* by Carol Nackenoff (New York: Oxford UP, 1994).

[4] I am excluding literary criticism because very little has been produced. Alger attracts critical attention because of his status as a cultural icon. Critics examine his stories in the context of his historical or cultural contributions; they rarely "do" literary criticism about his work.

[5] Biographies by Ralph D. Gardner, John Tebbel, Frank Gruber, and Edwin P. Hoyt attempted to correct the misinformation propagated by Mayes, and various critics have relied on their "corrections." However, Scharnhorst questions details in all of the biographies prior to his own. He demonstrates how the later biographers relied on earlier misinformation in several cases. Mayes admitted to the fabrications in the 1978 reissue of his own biography, but Scharnhorst has done the most to correct the errors.

[6] The revelation that Alger wrote about "rags to respectability" rather than "rags to riches" has become a mantra in Alger criticism. Nearly every critic men-

tions the distinction, which seems to indicate how pervasive the Alger myth is and how anxious Americans have been to hold onto the dream of success.

[7] Two of the most influential biographies which depended on Mayes were John Tebbel's *Rags to Riches* (New York: Macmillan, 1963) and Ralph D. Gardner's *Horatio Alger, or The American Hero Era* (New York: Arco, 1978, originally published in 1964). These books were reviewed together and contributed to the belief that Alger experienced the rags-to-riches lifestyle of his characters. Edwin P. Hoyt attempted to address some of the inaccuracies in these biographies in *Horatio's Boys: The Life and Works of Horatio Alger, Jr.* (Rador, PA: Chilton, 1974), but relied heavily on the inaccuracies in Gardner, according to Scharnhorst.

[8] Critics frequently accused Alger of being didactic and materialistic, and their comments remain influential. Patricia Bizzell and Bruce Herzberg, editors of *Negotiating Difference: Cultural Case Studies for Composition* (Boston: Bedford, 1996), assert: "[Alger's] name has become synonymous with the idea of rapid success through individual effort. His novel *Ragged Dick* was the bible from which many read the Gospel of Wealth. The successful industrialist Andrew Carnegie seemed to be a character from an Alger novel come to life" (417). This interpretation of Alger apparently relies on the earlier, inaccurate renditions of Alger and his stories. *Negotiating Difference* by Bizzell and Herzberg is an otherwise valuable and important book. The inclusion of Alger in this book reveals how intricately he has been aligned with proponents of the Gospel of Wealth, despite his serious reservations about greed, individualism, and class consciousness. The use of *Ragged Dick* as representative of Alger's work is also somewhat common.

[9] Whereas Adam Smith's notion of the "invisible hand" approximates Spenserian and Darwinian notions of charity, Alger frequently mentions the importance and necessity of a "helping hand" for those in need. Smith, Spencer, and Darwin hold that charity is not necessary because the strong and the fit will strive and survive. But Alger suggests that many individuals need assistance and help from others.

[10] Contemporary reviews noted that Alger's heroes were honest and managed their money wisely. Individualism and the quest for success were not regarded as central features of his work until later.

[11] Several critics suggest that Alger's heroes manipulated the *signs* of success. For example, Klein says, "Far from being prescriptive of the proper behaviors for ascending from Rags to Respectability, the essential action in these novels amounted to chilling parody of the American Dream as commonly understood. [. . .] Knowing well that the signs of Respectability really were not merely the signs at all but were the thing in itself, Alger's children were adepts of the signs" (64). In other words, Alger's heroes altered their clothing, behavior, and values to get ahead. Klein states that they are "subversive"; other critics emphasize their ability to manipulate others. Bruce Palmer says that "Alger's heroes prove adept at getting help from other people" (163). In *Confidence Men and Painted Women: A Study of Middle-class Culture in America, 1830–1870*, Karen Halttunen shows how one of Alger's

characters manipulates the skills of the confidence man for success in the business world. I think this line of inquiry does indicate a shift in American values but fails to recognize the importance of character for Alger. (It also blurs fictional characters and real life in some cases.) While I agree that personality and image began to replace character as barometers of success in the late nineteenth century, critics who utilize Alger as evidence of this shift rely too heavily on selected examples of his work–usually *Ragged Dick*–and on the postmodern affinity for surface over essence. In their defense, these critics are discussing a cultural shift, not Alger's work in general. At any rate, it seems that the link between Alger's popularity and his characters' subversiveness is questionable.

[12] In an oft-quoted phrase, Richard Weiss describes Alger as a "'nostalgic spokesman for a dying order'" (Weiss, qtd. in Halttunen, *Confidence Men* 202). Weiss and John Cawelti, writing in the 1960s, question Alger's role in the formation of the American myths of success and the self-made man. They argue that Alger was out-of-step, that he favored small business, moderation, and simplicity over corporations, entrepreneurial risks, and vast wealth. Similarly, Glenn Hendler states, "Alger tried to imagine a public realm distinct from overtly commercial values and linked to an older model of republican virtue" (416). Other critics–Michael Moon, Bruce Robbins–disagree. Despite the merits of both positions, Alger's anachronisms do not adequately explain his popularity.

[13] Several authors raise this question, but for a particularly thorough discussion of the flaws in Alger's writing, see Klein, Marcus, *Easterns, Westerns, and Private Eyes: American Matters, 1870–1900* (Madison: U of Wisconsin P, 1994), pages 21–28.

[14] Representations of street children in literature and popular culture and the "mysteries of the city" genre could be considered additional precursors to Alger. For a brief discussion of street children in literature in the 1840s and 1850s, see Bergmann, Hans, *God in the Street: New York Writing from the Penny Press to Melville* (Philadelphia: Temple UP, 1995), Chapter 4. Newspaper illustrations often displayed the polarization between the rich and the poor by depicting children in tattered clothes in the street, with rich adults walking by unaffected (see Fig. 1 in chapter 3). As I mentioned in the Introduction, the mysteries of the city genre, for example George Lippard's *New York: Its Upper Ten and Lower Million* (1853) and Ned Buntline's popular *The Mysteries and Miseries of New York: A Story of Real Life* (1848), reveals concern about the changes that occurred in the city at the time, as well as the division between the rich and the poor.

[15] According to Jeffrey Louis Decker, "Alger's portrait of poor boys, unlike the representation of working-class heroes in dime novels, does not remotely reflect the harsh economic realities of either the Gilded Age or the Progressive Era" (1).

[16] Whereas Halttunen says that Dick "out-cons a confidence man" (*Confidence Men* 210), I believe that Dick actually prevents a con. Ragged Dick is one of the more sneaky Alger heroes, and probably does not represent Alger's other books accurately, but the tricks he plays on others do not make them victims as the con-

fidence men and pickpockets do. His motives are earnest or humorous; he does not maliciously deceive others. Although Alger was aware of the archetype, I do not believe any of his heroes are con men.

17 Alger's use of "tramp" reflects the historical shift in definitions during his lifetime. Alger uses it as a verb to describe the act of walking or as a noun to indicate a leisurely walk (a "tramp about the streets"). In these cases, the words are neutral. These denotations began to fall away in the 1890s when "tramp" came to designate a wandering, unemployed man. Connotations could be neutral or decidedly negative, depending on the context. For example, the "tramp menace" became a catch phrase at this time.

18 Nackenoff reveals how Alger, like many others at the time, ignored the economic contributions of tramps. She shows how another author, Alan Pinkerton, writing at the same time, presents a more realistic and less destructive image of the tramp. Pinkerton's account allows tramps to be seen working in a variety of occupations, whereas Alger's characters are never seen working in factories or at similar labor. She argues, "Alger discovered the tramp, but could only recognize him with old, familiar categorizations. This framework denied the extent to which the tramp demarcated change. The tramp was merely another specter to be avoided by the virtuous" (77).

19 According to Kim Hopper and Jim Baumohl, "After about 1890, social reformers began to rapidly discard traditional arrangements based on sentiment in favor of business-like systems of 'scientific' intervention" (9).

20 Kenneth L. Kusmer states, "A common theme in the literature on tramps was that these people were not native-born Americans and thus did not understand the values that had made the United States great. [. . .] Contrary to popular myth, even in the 1870s the majority of the homeless unemployed were native-born [. . .] " (100).

NOTES TO CHAPTER THREE

1 Crane and Alger wrote for an admittedly different audience. Alger focused his attention on a much younger audience (particularly after a lack of success as a writer for adult readers), while Crane wrote for an adult audience of, in this case, magazine readers. While it would be problematic to contrast the rhetorical choices of these writers whose intentions were so radically different, it is nonetheless instructive to note the differences in approach to the same subject matter (poor street children in New York) and within the same relative time period. Crane also seems to be directly satirizing Alger, as I discuss in note #2.

2 It is not clear whether Crane *intentionally* subverts Alger's stories of "rags to riches" in "A Self-Made Man," although several details seem to suggest that this is his goal. The basic plot of a young street boy becoming successful after doing a favor for a rich benefactor is persuasive evidence. Moreover, Crane inserts a letter (dealing with a lost sum of money) in the text, as is the case in many of Alger's works. The conclusion, discussed above, also seems to parody Alger. In fact, Alger's

"luck and pluck" stories seem to elicit a direct response: "[Tom's] fame has spread through the land as a man who carved his way to fortune with no help but his undaunted pluck, his tireless energy, and his sterling integrity" (*Sketches* 204). Alger's heros invariably exhibit these traits, but Crane satirizes such perfection. Crane clearly mocks the notion that Tom was able to succeed with "no help"–a common criticism of Alger as noted in Chapter Two. Tom's self-confidence, concern with appearance, and use of tobacco also lead me to believe that Crane targeted Alger by mocking the traits of his boy-heros. For example, "[Tom] strolled along and smoked with his confidence in fortune in nowise impaired by his financial condition" (*Sketches* 200). Here, Crane seems to chide those who believe a poor boy can exude confidence through sheer willpower; Tom is able to cheerfully ignore his lower class environment, which would have been impossible from Crane's point of view.

[3] In Chapter Two I show that Alger became associated with the "Gospel of Wealth" for reasons which were not entirely fair. Here, I wish to address the general perception Crane and his contemporary audience would have had of writers associated with this tradition and their message of success through hard work, honesty, and frugality.

[4] "Down-and-outers" is Pittenger's term for writers of the late nineteenth and early twentieth century who went into the slums and tenements of New York and other cities to study, observe, and write about the poor and their living conditions. The term avoids some of the complications associated with naturalism, which I discuss later in this chapter.

[5] I also discuss the "tramp menace" in Chapter Four in the context of tramp autobiographies. The "threat" of tramps caused commentators to propose lynching, poisoning, and labor colonies to deal with the problem. In this context, Gunn's comment that Otherness poses a threat to national security seems valid.

[6] In his essay "A World of Difference: Constructing the 'Underclass' in Progressive America," Mark Pittenger discusses the fascination of "down-and-outers" like Crane with the underclass. He situates their impulse within the context of a tradition which sought out the "raw, unmediated vitality" of foreign experience. Pittenger notes how William James valued direct experience of life, including the experiences of the lower class, but warned against "speaking for" the poor. Pittenger argues,

> But down-and-outers would not always live up to James's insistence that we regard all people unlike ourselves as fully human (as James himself did not consistently do), nor would they always honor his caution that no one could finally speak authoritatively about the experience of another. (37)

I address this effect later in this chapter.

[7] Kim Hopper discusses our contemporary treatment of the homeless as odd, unusual, foreign, and mysterious in his essay "A Poor Apart: The Distancing of

Homeless Men in New York's History." He remarks, "Like 'the heath' in Shakespeare's time, 'the street' in our own has come to signify a kind of close repository of things evil and alien, and that is a badly damaging misrepresentation" (129). By contrasting the sensational or mysterious details in Crane and Riis with other, less dramatic texts later in this chapter, I demonstrate how they contributed to an understanding of the poor and homeless which is analogous to what Hopper describes.

[8] Gandal provides an excellent discussion of the contexts which influenced Riis and Crane, as well as an overview of the newspaper industry. For a thorough treatment of Crane's relationship to the newspaper industry, see also: Dooley, Patrick K., *The Pluralistic Philosophy of Stephen Crane* (Urbana: U of Illinois P, 1993), particularly Chapter one.

[9] As this chapter progresses I question the necessity and productivity of the sensational elements of naturalism, while recognizing that they may have been inseparable from the goal of social reform at the time (given the discursive expectations for sensationalism in certain dailies and magazines, for example).

[10] Donald Pizer's description of Spencer's effect on Dreiser applies to naturalism in general:

> There were, [Dreiser] believed, no discernable supernatural agencies in life, and man was not the favored creature of divine guidance but an insignificant unit in a universe of natural forces. Although these forces, whether biological or social, were the source of racial progress, they often crushed the individual within their mechanistic processes. Like many of his generation, Dreiser found that the observed realities of American society supported this theory of existence. (57)

[11] Pizer argues against such a simple definition of naturalism, opting instead to define it as a series of tensions or contrasts. He states, "The naturalistic novel is therefore not so superficial or reductive as it implicitly appears to be in its conventional definition. It involves a belief that life on its lowest levels is not so simple as it seems to be from higher levels" (87). While Pizer rightly warns against generalized definitions of naturalism, he maintains the hierarchical relationship between observer (as "higher") and observed (as "lower").

[12] Henry Golemba, in "'Distant Dinners' in Crane's *Maggie*: Representing 'The Other Half'," quotes Crane as saying, "'The photograph is false in perspective, in light and shade, in focus'" (240). Although Crane's skepticism contrasts with Riis's embrace of the medium, both writers share the desire to be scientific or objective.

[13] These effects can still be seen in the contemporary discourse of homelessness, as I explain in the Conclusion. Therefore, I feel it is valuable to trace the history and effects of this discourse back to a period when it was fairly prominent.

[14] Trachtenberg suggests that "[Riis's] technique was that of a guided tour; his aim, to convert the reader from passive ignorance to active awareness and caring. In the sensations of his disclosures lurks some residue of the city *mystery* [. . .]"

(143). Here, Trachtenberg equates the spectacle of the city with the sense of mystery I describe above.

[15] In "Stephen Crane and the Police," Christopher P. Wilson makes the same point about Crane. Referring to Crane's Tenderloin sketches, Wilson says, "[Crane] seems almost dispirited by how little there is to unveil. [. . .] Other Tenderloin pieces similarly deflate expectations of thrilling picturesqueness by citing the lamentable effects police reform have had on familiar urban scenes" (298, 300).

[16] Tracing the use and effect of the "underclass" label through American history, Herbert J. Gans, in his book *The War Against the Poor: The Underclass and Antipoverty Policy* (New York: BasicBooks, 1995), effectively assesses the cultural work of treating the poor as an object of study or entertainment.

[17] This positioning of the writer as an observer, above and separate from the members of the lower class, has been discussed in the context of "surveillance" and the "gaze" in other critical commentary. The best treatment of this issue seems to be Christopher P. Wilson's "Stephen Crane and the Police." Wilson attempts to "challenge the 'brittleness' of certain abstractions" such as the gaze in describing Crane's work (278). While warning against generalizations of this kind, Wilson shares my belief that this discourse did cultural work which was detrimental. Pittenger discusses this issue at length from a similar perspective.

[18] In Chapter One I argued that *Uncle Tom's Cabin* was productive because it minimized the separation between "us" (primarily white readers) and "them" (black slaves). I make a similar argument in Chapter Five when I say that Meridel Le Sueur portrayed the poor and homeless as purposeful and constitutive members of society, as "us" not "them."

[19] In Chapter Two I discuss the separation of the "deserving" and "undeserving" poor in the late nineteenth century and Alger's contribution to that effort. In the 1890s, this impulse was aided by the increased interest in scientific methods of classification. Moreover, the tramp was conflated with foreignness and with the slums in general. The homeless, foreigners, and the slums overall were regarded as a threat. According to Ward, "For those presently threatening the nation's cultural and eugenic character, incarceration was the preferred solution. Regulations founded on the findings of science were accepted as legitimate forms of intervention in the natural or normal workings of society" (55). Therefore, science justified divisions between "us" (ostensibly normal society) and "them" (homeless, foreign, and undeserving poor).

[20] In one version of the story, Crane writes, "'And then the youth went forth to try to eat as the tramp eats, and sleep as the *homeless* sleep'" (qtd. in Pittenger 26, italics added).

[21] Patrick K. Dooley examines Crane's relation to the newspaper and magazine industry. Dooley also shows how Crane shaped and reflected his culture. He states, "Free-lancer Crane knew the magazine market, and he knew how to deal with editors. [. . .] Besides learning what might sell, Crane's magazine reading immersed him

in the intellectual environment of the United States in the late-nineteenth century" (16).

[22] See Slotkin, Alan A., "Dialect Manipulation in 'An Experiment in Misery'," *American Literary Realism* 14.2 (1981): 273–276.

[23] Whereas romantic renditions of homelessness show the hero "*on* the road," Maggie is "a girl *of* the streets." She is a product of her environment. The title codes her as a victim. Yoshinobu Hakutani remarks that "she is not endowed with any sense of autonomy or vision" (151).

[24] In "A Dark-Brown Dog," a poor boy experiences the wrath of an abusive father and, in turn, becomes abusive to a dog. The father eventually throws the dog out the window. Crane uses the story to grimly illustrate the effect of environment in the tenements and the indifference of the universe.

[25] Gandal claims, "The slum is both a danger zone that provides opportunities for adventure and heroism, like the West and the battlefield, and a separate culture, like the Orient or medieval France, whose unrefined or more 'primitive' virtues offer a tonic for a tired middle-class society" (21).

[26] Riis was, in fact, one of the earliest users of flash photography. The technology and the method produced a new, interesting, entertaining medium for an audience experiencing the cultural changes discussed above. Leviatin argues,

> By igniting, and just barely controlling, spectacular and potentially lethal bursts of artificial light, Jacob Riis—the sentimental and stern Victorian, the realistic and pragmatic modern, the immigrant and the American— exposed and framed the Other Half while straddling a society in the throes of transition. (10)

NOTES TO CHAPTER FOUR

[1] For a list of tramp autobiographies, see Note #6 in the Introduction of this study.

[2] Historical and sociological texts frequently mention individual tramp autobiographies, but no single source addresses more than a few autobiographies. Kingsley Widmer characterizes hobos as rebels and discusses their literature at length in *The Literary Rebel* (91–107). Lynne M. Adrian's introduction to *Tales of an American Hobo* by Charles Elmer Fox briefly historicizes and categorizes the tramp autobiographies (xv-xxiii). See also: Feied, Frederick, *No Pie in the Sky: The Hobo as American Cultural Hero in the Works of Jack London, John Dos Passos, and Jack Kerouac* (New York: Citadel, 1964) and Primeau, Ronald, *Romance of the Road: The Literature of the American Highway* (Bowling Green: Bowling Green State UP, 1996).

In this chapter, I do not distinguish between tramps and hobos. I use "tramp" to indicate all of the homeless wanderers of the late nineteenth and early twentieth century—including writers and laborers—thereby subsuming "hobos" within "tramps."

[3] The intellectual emerges as a distinct "social type" during the Progressive era, according to Lasch, and the popularity of tramp autobiographies peaks at the same time. Although the figure of the "scholar-tramp" may initially appear oxymoronic, it represents a logical synthesis of the tramp and the intellectual at a time when both were relatively new developments. The interdependence of the tramp and the intellectual has been generally overlooked in discussions of the Progressive era. This gap seems to be consistent with a more general lack of commentary on the theme of homelessness in American literary history.

[4] The tramp/hobo subculture effectively blurred the distinction between tramp and intellectual. The *Hobo News*, a monthly magazine written and edited by tramps between 1900 and 1937, featured articles on social and political issues (Fox xvii). The International Brotherhood Welfare Association formed at the turn of the century to "promote a positive image of hoboes as well as help educate them" (Wormser 69). The organization was supported primarily by James Eads How, the son of a rich railroad executive. How established several hobo colleges throughout the United States in 1912, the most popular in Chicago. Although it was not an accredited university, the Chicago college provided the opportunity to study "everything from politics to law, literature to philosophy, public speaking to English composition" (Wormser 102). The college even hosted debates between the University of Chicago debating team and the Hobo College team.

"Bughouse Square" and the "Dil Pickle Club" in Chicago provided two other venues for intellectual exchange among tramps/hobos. Bughouse Square, in Washington Park, was the location of regular, well-attended debates on issues such as religion, revolution, communism, anarchy, and birth control. The Dil Pickle Club offered "debates, plays, music, and dances." It was described as a place where the "inhabitants looked like bums and talked like college professors" (Wormser 106).

[5] A few works refer to vagabonds before 1890, but the vagabond is quite distinct from the industrial tramp. The increase in the number of first person accounts in the 1890s parallels the increased attention in journalism at the time. In 1886, Harper published *A Tramp Trip: How to See Europe on Fifty Cents A Day* by Lee Meriwether, although the tramp figure is not yet clearly defined in it. Two tramp autobiographies appear in 1889. These are the earliest accounts I am aware of. The greatest number of autobiographies appeared between 1900 and 1930.

[6] Several factors contributed to the shift away from the notion of the author as an inspired, individual artist and toward the preference for descriptions of direct experience by actual participants. In *The Unvarnished Truth: Personal Narratives in Nineteenth-Century America*, Ann Fabian writes, "The growth of evangelical religion, the development of democratic politics, the rise of nationalism, the spread of print culture, and the expansion of the commercial relations of a capitalist society all fostered individual impulses toward personal narrative in printed form" (2).

[7] There are exceptions within the genre, and certain tramp autobiographies are more critical of capitalism and the values of the dominant culture than most. Other texts end ambiguously rather than optimistically. The conclusion of *Beggars of Life:*

A Hobo Autobiography by Jim Tully is not upbeat. He mentions many of the painful things he saw while tramping and remarks, "The vast crowd of [hoboes] are liars, ingrates, and thieves" (334). *The Other Half: The Autobiography of a Tramp* by John Worby describes his drug use and his unpredictable relationship with a woman. They consider settling down together but he decides to leave her. They separate on good terms, but the book ends with him on the road again: "That night I slept under the starry skies in the open country" (303).

[8] James Lundquist contends that London "never fully worked out a satisfactory reconciliation between his own rampant individualism and the egalitarianism implicit in socialist theory [. . .]" (116). Similarly, Frederick Feied argues that London embodies both a Nietschean/Darwinian individualism and a Marxist sense of class struggle (82–83). Christopher P. Wilson and Joan D. Hedrick locate London's conflict along class lines. Both maintain that London could not fit into either the upper or lower class (Wilson, *Labor* 15, 105–112; Hedrick 3).

[9] Since it is difficult to measure the direct impact of texts on beliefs and behavior (such as in the debates over the role of violent movies, music, and video games in contributing to violent behavior), I have been focusing on the ways discourse encourages or excludes particular ways of thinking about issues such as homelessness. In this case, the tramp autobiographies as a genre tend to glamorize it.

[10] An article in the *Minneapolis Tribune* in 1878 condoned farmers who sought to "'fertilize their land with their [the tramps'] dead bodies . . . as a radical and permanent cure for the evil complained of'"; in 1879, the *Railroad Gazette* reprinted an article from the *St. Louis Times-Journal* which stated, "'A wrecked freight car invariably means a dead tramp. It's an expensive but effective way of getting rid of a very undesirable class of nuisances'"; in 1888, the *Railroad Gazette* also urged people to "'exterminate these pests'" (cited in Monkkonen 15–16). Although the backlash had decreased during the Progressive era, violence was still considered a viable response to tramps.

[11] In Chapter Five I specify some of the extreme hardships faced by homeless women. Not only were they treated as sexual objects or intruders by male tramps, but they received the most caustic condemnations in the press for being immoral and unladylike.

[12] Nels Anderson, in *On Hobos and Homelessness* (1923), questions the "wanderlust" explanation for tramping. He states,

> When a young man leaves home are his reasons for migration different from those which motivated the migration of a family? Jeff Davis, who calls himself "King of the Hobos," is convinced that many young men migrate because they are moved by wanderlust. Various observers of this phenomenon have come to similar conclusions; recent students of the problem, however, give little credence to the "inner urge" reasons for migrancy. There is a trend toward explaining transiency in terms of social or economic pressures upon the individual. (153)

The tramp autobiographies clearly participate in a discourse which legitimized individual causes and minimized social or economic causes. Anderson cites two studies which indicate that "wanderlust" was rarely used as an explanation of the cause for migrancy by actual tramps. This, in turn, suggests that the tramp autobiographies over-emphasized wanderlust as an explanation and supports my contention that their cultural work was detrimental.

[13] "Why don't they just get jobs?" is a frequent response to the unemployed and homeless throughout American history. During periods of economic depressions, public attitudes become more sympathetic. However, the response of the man who offers London work is representative. The man states, "The trouble with you is that you are idle and dissolute. I can see it in your face. I have worked and been honest. I have made myself what I am. And you can do the same, if you work and are honest" (192). The tramp autobiographies did little to challenge the belief that tramps are undeserving because they did not want to work. Like Melville's Bartleby, they would "prefer not to." But such a position historically frustrates and angers the dominant culture, as Bartleby and London's interlocutor reveal.

[14] As I have attempted to show elsewhere, texts in literature, sociology, and journalism have tended to stress individual rather than structural causes of poverty and unemployment. The work ethic and the family ethic have been endorsed throughout American history. According to this tradition, honest, moral, and deserving Americans should stay at home and work in a stable occupation: searching for work on the road is not a legitimate option (despite the necessity of this course of action for many). As David Wagner states, "For at least 300 years, then, the poor person who works but who does not do so in a regular, steady, and settled way has been associated with vagrancy and deviancy" (71). The tramp autobiographies, unfortunately, did little to quell this notion.

[15] Camaraderie is also expressed in a variety of hobo poems, songs, and stories of the time.

[16] These groups had admittedly uneasy relationships with tramps and the unemployed. Individual brakemen sometimes allowed tramps to "ride the rails," but railroad companies had strict policies against this practice and often hired guards to deter, arrest, and sometimes shoot tramps. The tension was compounded by the fact that tramps frequently worked as legitimate employees for the railroad companies from time to time, so the line between "tramp" and "worker" sometimes blurred. However, these groups served several important functions for marginal workers. For example, according to Douglas Wixson,

> The Brotherhood of Railway Carmen was all-encompassing, extending its influence beyond the shops to include leisure activities. Following a solemn initiation rite, members were given a badge of fellowship and respect. The motto was "Friendship, Unity, True Brotherly Love." The fraternal function of the brotherhood was strong; for instance, members gave one another advice on problems such as alcoholism, and they offered financial assistance in time of sickness. One purpose of the brotherhood was to gain the

> respect of the employers and the community. There were reading rooms for "self-improvement" where members could read the brotherhood's journal, with its workers' correspondence. (*Worker-Writer* 54)

This sense of brotherhood, solidarity, and camaraderie is somewhat present in the tramp autobiographies, but the prevailing attitude in these texts is individualism and nonconformity. In Chapter Five I contend that the discourse of homelessness can be more receptive to texts which present homeless individuals in solidarity with the rest of society.

NOTES TO CHAPTER FIVE

[1] For a discussion of the effect of Le Sueur's membership in the Communist Party on her writing see: Pratt, Linda Ray, "Woman writer in the CP: the case of Meridel Le Sueur," *Women's Studies* 14 (1988): 47–64. Although Le Sueur was excluded from the canon as a result of being blacklisted, I suggest that her membership in the Communist Party is inseparable from her writing style and content.

[2] The issue of subject position infiltrates the entire discussion of testimony in this chapter, albeit indirectly at times. I assert that a writer of testimony occupies an entirely different subject position than the Author of a work of literature. To use Le Sueur's metaphor from "The Fetish of Being Outside," testimony is written from the "inside," literature is written from the "outside." It is clear that subject position was important to Le Sueur. She once stated, "'It makes a big difference whether you see the world from 'inside' or 'outside.' It affects how you see history, how you see time, how you see politics and how you see people'" (qtd. in Schleuning 5).

[3] In Chapter Three I argue that naturalism, while attempting to draw attention to the plight of the poor and homeless, perpetuates the division between the upper and lower classes, between "us"–the observing subjects–and "them"–the poor as the object of observation.

[4] Roberta Maierhofer argues, "Le Sueur's attempt at authenticity in portraying women's lives could be read as a struggle against the limitations of patriarchal enclosures, a creating of a-patriarchal space" (159). Although some critics question Le Sueur's success in advancing the cause of women, she addressed several issues that affected women which her contemporaries tended to ignore. Moreover, I think it is difficult to separate her concerns for gender equality from her concerns for class equality.

[5] This chapter focuses on her treatments of poor and homeless women during the Depression. However, Le Sueur wrote about a variety of issues throughout this century. Born in 1900, she produced a variety of journalism, poetry, children's book, and fiction until her death in 1996. She published her first story, "Persephone," in 1927, and continued to write into her 90s. Le Sueur covered topics such as the environment, mining conditions, trucking, Native American land rights, communism, and feminism.

[6] Le Sueur stated, "'I have always been very critical of the Naturalists. There are serious weaknesses of the Naturalist school, of American determinism defined in Dreiser, with its mechanistic psychology of ducts and glands, mechanical stimuli, the individual conceived as a mechanism driven by the equally mechanical drives of society'" (qtd. in Schleuning 124).

[7] This juxtapositioning of disparate elements occurs throughout the book and will be discussed in the context of testimony as a literary form later in the chapter.

[8] The historical tendency to blame the individual for being immoral or having personal flaws has been discussed throughout this study. Homelessness, poverty, and prostitution, for example, are often viewed as personal failings, not as economic, social, or political problems. The desire to correct this misconception seems to underlie Le Sueur's work. In this chapter and in the Conclusion, I suggest that testimony resists the "blame the victim" mentality of the dominant culture.

[9] See, for example, Gugelberger, Georg M., ed., *The Real Thing: Testimonial Discourse and Latin America* (Durham: Duke UP, 1996).

[10] This is a somewhat relative assessment, but a text such as *The Grapes of Wrath* may not be as "realistic" because of its epic scope. The style seems somewhat elevated and the struggle of the characters is noble, almost mythic:

> And the dispossessed, the migrants, flowed into California, two hundred and fifty thousand, and three hundred thousand. Behind them new tractors were going on the land and the tenants were being forced off. And new waves were on the way, new waves of the dispossessed and the homeless, hardened, intent, and dangerous. (Steinbeck 318)

Elsewhere, Steinbeck focuses on individual struggle, and the cultural work of his texts was probably productive. However, this passage tends to support Schleuning's contention that Le Sueur's orientation is more localized than some of her more famous contemporaries.

[11] The exemplar of this trait is *I, Rigoberta Menchú*. By writing this book Menchú drew international attention to the systematic murder of indigenous Guatemalans, and probably saved her own life in the process.

[12] This conflict arose over the book *I, Rigoberta Menchú*. The veracity of Menchú's account of her background and experiences has been disputed by David Stoll in his book *Rigoberta Menchú and the Story of All Poor Guatemalans* (Boulder: Westview, 1999). The extent to which Stoll's indictment undermines Menchú's accomplishment is questionable, but the debate itself reveals why and how testimony has been challenged.

[13] Tompkins's work in this area is exemplary. In *Sensational Designs: The Cultural Work of American Fiction, 1790–1860*, she traces the emergence and popularity of Nathaniel Hawthorne as an example of a writer who was politically and socially "connected" and how he experienced success as a result.

[14] Ellis objects to Le Sueur's appropriation of the experiences of poor women in a way which is analogous to my critique of Riis and Crane in Chapter Three. She asserts,

> [I]n Le Sueur's texts, working-class women subjects are silenced from two directions: their working-class status defines them as intuitive rather than intellectual, physical rather than rational, and able to express themselves best though action rather than discourse. This inarticulate, marginalized position is compounded further by Le Sueur in her depiction of gender, valorizing emotion over thought, biology over history, and nature over materiality. (178)

Ellis believes that Le Sueur, as well as other middle class intellectuals, observed and then reduced the experiences of the working-class, sometimes in order to make themselves feel better. Thus, Le Sueur's motives seem to be the same as the earlier naturalists. Whether Le Sueur's upbringing was sufficiently intolerable to consider her lower-class (and therefore able to speak for the poor) seems impossible to ascertain. Her parents were radicals, but not destitute. For additional biographical information, see Elaine Hedges's "Introduction" to *Ripening: Selected Work* by Le Sueur (New York: The Feminist P, 1982).

[15] Douglas Wixson argues that this type of knowledge can be defined as "emotional" knowledge. He states, "The fact that Le Sueur's texts reject rhetorical modes of dominance and mastery suggests that they must be apprehended emotionally, understood from within, not subjected to intellectual analysis like modernist literature" ("Question" 96).

[16] Dawahare refers here to Le Sueur's essay "The Fetish of Being Outside." He also refers more generally to Le Sueur's "cultural blindness." In other words, she fails to recognize the historical difficulty of working-class collective action. He states, "[Le Sueur's] homespun version of coming to a revolutionary political consciousness elides the historical lack of such a consciousness among the American working-class, and is, at best, a form of political wish-fulfillment" (414). Similarly, Constance Coiner critiques Le Sueur's utopianism. She asserts, "In its concluding pages, *The Girl* declares by fiat the existence of a magical, female 'island on the land' with no reference as to how to achieve such a colony [. . .]" (*Better Red* 121). Elsewhere, Le Sueur has been critiqued for essentializing the differences between men and women and for promoting women's collective action over coming together of the sexes.

[17] Neala Schleuning, Blanche H. Gelfant, Adrian Oktenberg, and Nora Ruth Roberts characterize Le Sueur as an author who had "solidarity" as a goal throughout her life and in her writing. Her affinity for communism is often cited in this context, though most of her work avoids any direct mention of the Communist Party. Some have suggested that it is more accurate and productive to conceive of Le Sueur and her writing as "commune-istic" rather than communist, since she supported the

goal of solidarity and coming-together, but questioned certain tenets of the Communist Party.

NOTES TO THE CONCLUSION

[1] Several complications arise over the use of such a broad division. Most importantly, who is included in Rorty's "us"–women? minorities? those without advanced degrees in philosophy? Critics have attacked the "liberal utopia" Rorty describes in *Contingency, Irony, and Solidarity* from a variety of angles. Many of these critiques are persuasive, significant charges. It would be ridiculous to say that everyone treats poor and homeless people as objects; therefore, the categories of "us" and "them" could become meaningless. However, I believe the division offers an adaptable, visceral means of analysis. It provides a criterion or benchmark to be applied to texts, although it is dependent on context. In this case, does the text represent homelessness as a category of difference or otherness, or as a relatively normal condition that occasionally affects average Americans?

[2] The "backlash" against homeless people since 1980 parallels the backlash against tramps in the late nineteenth century, often in remarkably disturbing ways. Anti-loitering and anti-panhandling laws, "homeless proof" architecture, violence (hate crimes) against homeless people, the arrest and dispersal of the homeless (such as in Atlanta during the Olympics), and various discussions of "compassion fatigue" indicate that some Americans see the homeless as different and inconsequential. For discussions of the "criminalization" of homelessness, see Stoner, Madeline, *The Civil Rights of Homeless People: Law, Social Policy, and Social Work Practice* (New York: Aldine, 1995) and "Cracking Down on the Homeless" by Jodie Morse et. al., *Time* 154.25 (20 Dec., 1999): 69–70.

[3] See Rorty, Richard, "Human Rights, Rationality, and Sentimentality," *Truth and Progress: Philosophical Papers, Volume 3* (Cambridge: Cambridge UP, 1998): 167–185.

[4] The current discourse of homelessness is immensely varied. I do not want to suggest that every text subscribes to the division mentioned above. Instead, I argue that discursive representations of homelessness from the past continue to cast a shadow over the current discourse. While this is not a strict Foucauldian analysis, I attempt to demonstrate how discourse produces certain normative representations of homelessness.

[5] For discussions of the causes of homelessness in contemporary America, see Jencks, Christopher, *The Homeless* (Cambridge: Harvard UP, 1994); Bingham, Richard D., Roy E. Green, and Sammis B. White, eds., *The Homeless in Contemporary Society* (Newbury Park: Sage, 1987); Rossi, Peter H., *Down and Out in America: The Origins of Homelessness* (Chicago: U of Chicago P, 1989); Baum, Alice S., and Donald W. Burnes, *A Nation in Denial: The Truth About Homelessness* (Boulder: Westview, 1993). This list is meant to be suggestive, not comprehensive. Sociologists disagree over the causes and extent of homelessness. As

was the case in the nineteenth century, commentators still dispute whether individual or structural causes are most significant.

[6] In 1983, *Books in Print* listed four titles with the subject heading "homelessness." During the 1990s, that figure held in the 100s and other subject headings related to homelessness have been added. For a comprehensive list of films about homelessness, see Fuller, Linda K., "From Tramps to Truth-Seekers: Images of the Homeless in the Motion Pictures," *Reading the Homeless: The Media's Image of Homeless Culture*, Ed. Eungjun Min (Westport: Praeger, 1999, 159–173).

[7] See *Critical Vehicles: Writings, Projects, Interviews* by Krzysztof Wodiczko (Cambridge: MIT P, 1999).

[8] See "$10 Bill Give-Away To Migrant Workers Loses a U.S. Subsidy" by Seth Mydans (*The New York Times*, 5 Sept., 1993: A1, A11).

[9] Perhaps the most comprehensive discursive analysis of homelessness is *Reading the Homeless: The Media's Image of Homeless Culture* edited by Eungjun Min (Westport: Praeger, 1999). Allen Carey-Webb's "Representing the Homeless" (*American Literary History* 4.4 [1992]: 697–708) addresses the contributions of three books and two movies to the discourse of homelessness, and specifically how they reinforce or challenge notions of charity and pity. Maurice Penner and Susan Penner analyze representations of homelessness in comic books in their essay "Publicizing, Politicizing, and Neutralizing Homelessness: Comic Books" (*Communication Research* 21.6 [Dec. 1994]: 766–781). Their essay is based on the influential "Neutralizing Homelessness" by Peter Marcuse (*Socialist Review* 18.1 [1988]: 69–96). See also, Gagnier, Regenia, "Homelessness as 'An Aesthetic Issue': Past and Present" in *Homes and Homelessness in the Victorian Imagination* edited by Murray Baumgarten and H. M. Daleski (New York: AMS, 1998, 167–186); *Youth Homelessness: The Construction of a Social Issue* by Susan Hutson and Mark Liddiard (London: Macmillian, 1994); and Wright, Susan E., "Blaming the Victim, Blaming Society or Blaming the Discipline: Fixing Responsibility for Poverty and Homelessness" (*The Sociological Quarterly* 34.1 [1993]: 1–16).

[10] Wright intimates that more study in this area is needed. Similarly, Herbert Gans states,

> The first task [to reduce homelessness] is to encourage the country's public media to use what is currently known about poverty and the poor in "debunking stories" in both news and entertainment media that correct inaccuracies and try to puncture stereotypes about the poor, deserving as well as undeserving. (119)

[11] Kingsley Widmer's quotation at the beginning of the Introduction is one of the few places in which someone has brought together the romantic sense of life "on the road" with the realist mode of being "down and out." Generally, literary criticism and sociology have accepted and perpetuated the division of texts as either

romantic/adventure or realist/abjection by focusing on one form or the other. To my knowledge, no other sources have traced the discursive effect of this separation.

The power of discourse to produce "familiar" forms can also be seen in texts such as *The Murder of a Shopping Bag Lady* by Brian Kates (San Diego: Harcourt Brace Jovanovich, 1985).

[12] See *Checkerboard Square: Culture and Resistance in a Homeless Community* by David Wagner (Boulder: Westview, 1993) and *Out of Place: Homeless Mobilizations, Subcities, and Contested Landscapes* by Talmadge Wright (New York: State U of New York P, 1997).

[13] Although I am focusing my attention on literary texts, Talmadge Wright indicates that sociologists have taken a greater interest in involving homeless people directly in studies of the issue. These efforts go beyond earlier participant-observer accounts such as those described in Chapter Three. Wright says that

> Research that involved the voices of the homeless themselves, integrated with a critical analysis of market economies and the uses and meanings of social-physical space, did not begin to fully emerge until the 1990s [. . .] . Only now is a critical perspective on homelessness beginning to develop with material from homeless members themselves. This new line of research calls into question the manner in which academics speak "with," "for," "about," or "to" the homeless. (30–31)

[14] For discussions of testimony regarding the Holocaust or Latin America, see Beverly, John, *Against Literature* (Minneapolis: U of Minnesota P, 1993); Carey-Webb, Allen, and Stephen Benz, eds., *Teaching and Testimony: Rigoberta Menchú and the North American Classroom* (New York: State U of New York P, 1996); Felman, Shoshana, and Dori Laub, M.D, *Testimony: Crises of Witnessing in Literature, Psychoanalysis, and History* (New York: Routledge, 1992); Franco, Jean, "Going Public: Reinhabiting the Private," *On Edge: The Crisis of Contemporary Latin American Culture*, Eds. George Yudice, Jean Franco, and Juan Flores (Minneapolis: U of Minnesota P, 1992, 65–83); Gugelberger, Georg M., ed., *The Real Thing: Testimonial Discourse and Latin America* (Durham: Duke UP, 1996); Langer, Lawrence L., *Holocaust Testimonies: The Ruins of Memory* (New Haven: Yale UP, 1991); and Young, James E., *Writing and Rewriting the Holocaust: Narrative and the Consequences of Interpretation* (Bloomington: Indiana UP, 1988).

[15] Critics occasionally use the term "testimony" in the context of American literature. Unlike its treatments in Holocaust studies and Latin American studies, however, it often appears as a generic term for a text which has significant meaning or impact. For example, it has been used to describe examples of Native American and African American literature and in *The Oxford Book of the American South: Testimony, Memory, and Fiction* (New York: Oxford UP, 1997) to designate texts that can be seen as forms of witnessing, but not in all of the senses of the definition in Chapter Five.

Deborah Carlin utilizes the term with the connotations of surviving the trauma of multiple personality disorder in the novel *When Rabbit Howls* by Truddi Chase in her essay "Trauma, Testimony, and Fictions of Truth: Narrative in *When Rabbit Howls*" (*Texas Studies in Literature and Language* 37.4 [Winter 1995]: 475–492). Bell Gale Chevigny uses testimonial literature as a category of comparison in "Twice-Told Tales and the Meaning of History: Testimonial Novels by Miguel Barnet and Norman Mailer" (*The Centennial Review* 30.2 [Spring 1986]: 181–195). Chevigny states, "While the true-life novel, the documentary, non-fiction or testimonial novel has been gaining prominence and exciting theoretical discussion for some years now in the United States, testimony–fictional and straight–is so important in Latin America that the prestigious Casa de las Americas in Havana has instituted a prize for the genre" (181).

[16] I have observed the ability of Angie's essay to do cultural work firsthand. In the composition courses in which I have assigned the essay, students consistently and explicitly indicate that it has affected their stereotypes of the homeless. They have said that it has changed their perception of the homeless, and admit that their views were previously based on incomplete and slanted information. (And I know they are not "telling me what I want to hear" because, in the same essays, they will often reveal that other testimonial texts did *not* change their opinions about certain groups.)

Works Cited

Alger, Horatio, Jr. *Adrift in the City*. New York: Street & Smith, 1895.

———. *Charlie Codman's Cruise: A Story for Boys*. New York: Hurst. [1866].

———. *Driven from Home or Carl Crawford's Experience*. New York: Hurst. [1890].

———. *Herbert Carter's Legacy*. Chicago: M.A. Donohue. [1875].

———. *Nothing to do: a tilt at our best society*. Boston: James French, 1857.

———. *Slow and Sure; Or, From the Street to the Shop*. New York: Hurst, 1872.

———. *Strive and Succeed:* Julius or The Street Boy Out West *and* The Store Boy or The Fortunes of Ben Barclay. Introduction by S.N. Behrman. New York: Holt, 1967.

———. *Struggling Upward and Other Works*. With an Introduction by Russel Crouse. New York: Bonanza Books, 1965.

———. *Tony, the Hero*. Chicago: M.A. Donohue. [1880].

———. *Walter Sherwood's Probation*. Chicago: M.A. Donohue. [1897].

———. *The Young Bank Messenger*. Philadelphia: Henry T. Coates, 1898.

———. *The Young Outlaw; or, Adrift in the Streets*. Philadelphia: John C. Winston, 1875.

Allsop, Kenneth. *Hard Travellin': The Hobo and His History*. New York: The New American Library, 1967.

Ammons, Elizabeth. "Heroines in *Uncle Tom's Cabin*." *Critical Essays on Harriet Beecher Stowe*. Ed. Elizabeth Ammons. Boston: Hall, 1980. 152-165.

Anderson, Beatrice A. "Uncle Tom: A Hero at Last." *American Transcendental Quarterly* 5.2 (1991): 95-108.

Anderson, Nels. *On Hobos and Homelessness*. Edited and with an Introduction by Raffaele Rauty. Chicago: U of Chicago P, 1998.

Andrews, William L. *To Tell a Free Story: The First Century of Afro-American Autobiography, 1760-1865*. Urbana: U of Illinois P, 1986.

Angie. "Creativity Has Got to Find an Expressive Channel Somehow." *I Have Arrived Before My Words: Autobiographical Writings of Homeless Women*. Eds. Deborah Pugh and Jeanie Tietjen. Alexandria, VA: Charles River, 1997. 151–166.

Baldwin, James. "Everybody's Protest Novel." *Notes of a Native Son*. Boston: Beacon, 1955. 13–22.

Baum, Alice S., and Donald W. Burnes. *A Nation in Denial: The Truth About Homelessness*. Boulder: Westview, 1993.

Berger, Peter, Brigitte Berger and Hansfried Kellner. *The Homeless Mind: Modernization and Consciousness*. New York: Vintage, 1973.

Beverly, John. *Against Literature*. Minneapolis: U of Minnesota P, 1993.

Bizzell, Patricia, and Bruce Herzberg, eds. *Negotiating Difference: Cultural Case Studies for Composition*. Boston: Bedford, 1996.

Boehnlein, James M. "Meridel Le Sueur, 'Corn Village,' and Literary Pragmatism." *Midamerica: The Yearbook of the Society for the Study of Midwestern Literature* 21 (1994): 82–97.

Bowerman, Richard. "Horatio Alger, Jr.; or, Adrift in the Myth of Rags to Riches." *Journal of American Culture* 2.1 (Spring 1979): 83–112.

Bramen, Carrie Tiardo. "The Urban Picturesque and the Spectacle of Americanization." *American Quarterly* 52.3 (2000): 444–477.

Brevda, William. "At the Crossroads of Vagabondia, Hobohemia, and Bohemia: Harry Kemp's *Tramping on Life*." *Markham Review* 11 (Spring 1982): 46–50.

———. *Harry Kemp: The Last Bohemian*. Lewisberg: Bucknell UP, 1986.

Brodzki, Bella, and Celeste Schenck, eds. *Life/Lines: Theorizing Women's Autobiography*. Ithaca: Cornell UP, 1988.

Brown, Gillian. *Domestic Individualism: Imaging Self in Nineteenth-Century America*. Berkeley: U of California P, 1990.

Carey-Webb, Allen. "Representing the Homeless." *American Literary History* 4.4 (1992): 697–708.

Chevigny, Bell Gale. "Twice-Told Tales and the Meaning of History: Testimonial Novels by Miguel Barnet and Norman Mailer." *The Centennial Review* 30.2 (Spring 1986): 181–195.

Christy, David. From *Cotton Is King*. *Negotiating Difference: Cultural Case Studies for Composition*. Eds. Patricia Bizzell and Bruce Herzberg. Boston: Bedford, 1996. 244–249.

Coiner, Constance. *Better Red: The Writing and Resistance of Tillie Olsen and Meridel Le Sueur*. New York: Oxford UP, 1995.

———. "Literature of Resistance: The Intersection of Feminism and the Communist Left in Meridel Le Sueur and Tillie Olsen." *Left Politics and the Literary Profession*. Eds. Lennard J. Davis and M. Bella Mirabella. New York: Columbia UP, 1990. 162–185.

Crane, Stephen. *Maggie: A Girl of the Streets (A Story of New York)*. Ed. Kevin J. Hayes. Boston: Bedford, 1999.

———. *The New York City Sketches of Stephen Crane and Related Pieces*. Eds. R. W. Stallman and E. R. Hagemann. New York: New York UP, 1966.

Davies, W. H. *The Autobiography of a Super-Tramp*. London: Jonathan Cape, 1942. [c. 1908].

Davis, Michael. "Forced to Tramp: The Perspective of the Labor Press, 1870–1900." *Walking to Work: Tramps in America, 1790–1935*. Ed. Eric H. Monkkonen. Lincoln: U of Nebraska P, 1984. 141–170.

Dawahare, Anthony. "Modernity and 'Village Communism' in Depression-Era America: The Utopian Literature of Meridel Le Sueur." *Criticism: A Quarterly for Literature and the Arts* 39.3 (Summer 1997): 409–31.

Decker, Jeffrey Louis. *Made in America: Self-Styled Success from Horatio Alger to Oprah Winfrey*. Minneapolis: U of Minnesota P, 1997.

Denning, Michael. *Mechanic Accents: Dime Novels and Working-Class Culture in America. Revised Edition*. London: Verso, 1998.

Dooley, Patrick K. *The Pluralistic Philosophy of Stephen Crane*. Urbana: U of Illinois P, 1993.

Douglas, Ann. "Introduction: The Art of Controversy." *Uncle Tom's Cabin or, Life Among the Lowly*. By Harriet Beecher Stowe. New York: Penguin, 1981. 7–36.

Duncan, Erica. *Unless Soul Clap Its Hands: Portraits and Passages*. New York: Schocken, 1984.

Edge, William. *The Main Stem*. New York: Vanguard, 1927.

Eighner, Lars. *Travels with Lizbeth: Three Years on the Road and on the Streets*. New York: St. Martin's, 1993.

Elam, Samuel Milton. "Lady Hoboes." *The New Republic* 61 (1 Jan. 1930): 164–169.

Ellis, Jacqueline. *Silent Witnesses: Representations of Working-Class Women in the United States*. Bowling Green: Bowling Green State U Popular P, 1998.

Elsing, William T. From "Life in the New York Tenement-Houses." *Maggie: A Girl of the Streets (A Story of New York)*. By Stephen Crane. Ed. Kevin J. Hayes. New York: Bedford, 1999. 133–144.

Etulain, Richard W., ed. *Jack London on the Road: The Tramp Diary, and other Hobo Writings*. Logan: Utah State UP, 1979.

Fabian, Ann. *The Unvarnished Truth: Personal Narratives in Nineteenth-Century America*. Berkeley: U of California P, 2000.

Feied, Frederick. *No Pie in the Sky: The Hobo as American Cultural Hero in the Works of Jack London, John Dos Passos, and Jack Kerouac*. New York: Citadel, 1964.

Felman, Shoshana, and Dori Laub, M.D. *Testimony: Crises of Witnessing in Literature, Psychoanalysis, and History*. New York: Routledge, 1992.

Fisher, Philip. "Democratic Social Space: Whitman, Melville, and the Promise of American Transparency." *The New American Studies: Essays from* Representations. Ed. Philip Fisher. Berkeley: U of California P, 1991. 70–111.

———. *Hard Facts: Setting and Form in the American Novel*. New York: Oxford UP, 1985.

Flynt, Josiah. *My Life*. New York: Outing, 1908.

Foucault, Michel. "What Is an Author?" *Critical Theory Since 1965*. Eds. Hazard Adams and Leroy Searle. Tallahassee: Florida State UP, 1986. 138–148.

Fox, Charles Elmer. *Tales of an American Hobo*. Preface by Albert E. Stone. Introduction by Lynne M. Adrian. Iowa City: U of Iowa P, 1989.

Franco, Jean. "Going Public: Reinhabiting the Private." *On Edge: the Crisis of Contemporary Latin American Culture*. Eds. George Yudice, Jean Franco, and Juan Flores. Minneapolis: U of Minnesota P, 1992. 65–83.

Gandal, Keith. *The Virtues of the Vicious: Jacob Riis, Stephen Crane, and the Spectacle of the Slum*. New York: Oxford UP, 1997.

Gans, Herbert J. *The War Against the Poor: The Underclass and Antipoverty Policy*. New York: BasicBooks, 1995.

Gelfant, Blanche H. "'Everybody Steals': Language as Theft in Meridel Le Sueur's *The Girl*." *Tradition and the Talents of Women*. Ed. Florence Howe. Urbana: U of Illinois P, 1991. 183–210.

Gilman, Sander L. *Difference and Pathology: Stereotypes of Sexuality, Race, and Madness*. Ithaca: Cornell UP, 1985.

Golemba, Henry. "'Distant Dinners' in Crane's *Maggie*: Representing 'The Other Half'." *Essays in Literature* 21.2 (Fall 1994): 235–250.

Graulich, Melody. "Violence Against Women in Literature of the Western Family." *Frontiers* 7.3 (1984): 14–20.

Gresset, Michel. "Home and Homelessness in Faulkner's Works and Life." *William Faulkner: Materials, Studies, and Criticism* 5.1 (May 1983): 26–42.

Gunn, Giles. *The Interpretation of Otherness: Literature, Religion, and the American Imagination*. New York: Oxford UP, 1979.

Hakutani, Yoshinobu. "Jennie, Maggie, and the City." *Dreiser's* Jennie Gerhardt*: New Essays*. Ed. James L. W. West. Philadelphia: U of Pennsylvania P, 1995. 147–156.

Halttunen, Karen. *Confidence Men and Painted Women: A Study of Middle-class Culture in America, 1830–1870*. New Haven: Yale UP, 1982.

———. "Gothic Imagination and Social Reform: The Haunted Houses of Lyman Beecher, Henry Ward Beecher, and Harriet Beecher Stowe." *New Essays on* Uncle Tom's Cabin. Ed. Eric J. Sundquist. Cambridge: Cambridge UP, 1986. 107–134.

Hedges, Elaine. "Meridel Le Sueur." *The Heath Anthology of American Literature. Volume Two*. Ed. Paul Lauter. Lexington: Heath, 1994. 1805–1807.

Hedrick, Joan D. *Solitary Comrade: Jack London and His Work*. Chapel Hill: U of North Carolina P, 1982.

Hendler, Glenn. "Pandering in the Public Sphere: Masculinity and the Market in Horatio Alger." *American Quarterly* 48.3 (1996): 415–438. 27 Jan. 1998. <http://muse.jhu.edu/journals/american_quarterly/v048/48.3hendler.html>

Hoch, Charles. "A Brief History of the Homeless Problem in the United States." *The Homeless in Contemporary Society*. Eds. Richard D. Bingham, Roy E. Green, and Sammis B. White. Newbury Park: Sage, 1987. 16–32.

Homeless, Joe. *My Life on the Streets: Memoirs of a Faceless Man*. Far Hills, NJ: New Horizon, 1992.

Hopper, Kim. "A Poor Apart: The Distancing of Homeless Men in New York's History." *Home: A Place in the World*. Ed. Arien Mark. New York: New York UP, 1993. 108–132.

Hopper, Kim, and Jim Baumohl. "Redefining the Cursed Word: A Historical Interpretation of American Homelessness." *Homelessness in America*. Ed. Jim Baumohl. Phoenix: Oryx, 1996. 3–14.

Hovet, Theodore R. "Modernization and the American Fall into Slavery in *Uncle Tom's Cabin*." *The New England Quarterly* 54.4 (Dec. 1981): 499-518.

Howard, June. *Form and History in American Literary Naturalism*. Chapel Hill: U of North Carolina P, 1985.

Howells, William Dean. *The Vacation of the Kelwyns: An Idyl of the Middle Eighteen- Seventies*. New York: Harper, 1920.

Jacobs, Harriet Ann. *Incidents in the Life of a Slave Girl: Written By Herself*. Ed. L. Maria Child. New York: AMS, 1973.

Jay, Gregory S. *America the Scrivener: Deconstruction and the Subject of Literary History*. Ithaca: Cornell UP, 1990.

Jefferson, Thomas. *Notes on Virginia* (1788). *Negotiating Difference: Cultural Case Studies for Composition*. Eds. Patricia Bizzell and Bruce Herzberg. Boston: Bedford, 1996. 180–187.

Jehlen, Myra. "The Family Militant: Domesticity versus Slavery in *Uncle Tom's Cabin*." *Criticism* 31.4 (1989): 393-400.

Kaplan, Caren. "Deterritorializations: The Rewriting of Home and Exile in Western Feminist Discourse." *The Nature and Context of Minority Discourse*. Eds. Abdul R. JanMohamed and David Lloyd. Oxford: Oxford UP, 1990. 357–368.

Kemp, Harry. *Tramping on Life: An Autobiographical Narrative*. New York: Boni, 1922.

Kerouac, Jack. *On the Road*. Introduction by Ann Charters. New York: Penguin, 1991. [c.1955].

Klein, Marcus. *Easterns, Westerns, and Private Eyes: American Matters, 1870–1900*. Madison: U of Wisconsin P, 1994.

Kusmer, Kenneth L. "Conceptualizing Social History: Homeless Men in America, 1865–1940, as a Case Study." *Reconstructing American Literary and Historical Studies*. Eds. Gunter H. Lenz, Harmut Keil, and Saline Brock-Sallah. New York: St. Martin's, 1990. 94–109.

Labor, Earle, Robert C. Leitz III, and I. Milo Shepard, eds. *The Letters of Jack London*. 3 vols. Stanford: Stanford UP, 1988.

Lang, Amy Schrager. "Slavery and Sentimentalism: The Strange Career of Augustine St. Clare." *Women's Studies: An Interdisciplinary Journal* 12.1 (1986): 31–54.

Lasch, Christopher. *The New Radicalism in America [1889–1963]: The Intellectual as a Social Type*. New York: Norton, 1965.

Lemeunier, Yves. "Vision of Poverty and the Poor in the Novels of Horatio Alger." *All Men Are Created Equal: Ideologies, Reves et Realities*. Groupe de Recherche et d'Etudes Nord Américaines. Université de Provence, 1983. 121–135.

Le Sueur, Meridel. *Dread Road*. Albuquerque: West End, 1991.

———. *The Girl*. Albuquerque: West End, 1978.

———. *North Star Country*. Lincoln: U of Nebraska P, 1984.

———. *Winter Prairie Woman*. Minneapolis: Midwest Villages & Voices, 1990.

———. *Women on the Breadlines*. Cambridge: West End, 1977.

Leverenz, David. *Manhood and the American Renaissance*. Ithaca: Cornell UP, 1989.

Leviatin, David. "Framing the Poor: The Irresistibility of How the Other Half Lives." *How the Other Half Lives: Studies Among the Tenements of New York*. By Jacob A. Riis. Edited with an Introduction by David Leviatin. Boston: Bedford, 1996. 1–50.

Lindsay, Vachel. *Adventures while Preaching the Gospel of Beauty*. New York: Macmillan, 1916.

Lippard, George. *The Quaker City; or The Monks of Monk Hall*. Philadelphia: Published by the Author, 1845.

London, Jack. *Novels and Social Writings*. New York: The Library of America, 1982.

Lukács, Georg. *The Theory of the Novel: A Historico-Philosophical Essay on the Forms of Great Epic Literature*. Trans. Anna Bostock. London: Merlin, 1971.

Lundquist, James. *Jack London: Adventures, Ideas, and Fiction*. New York: Ungar, 1987.

MacFarlane, Lisa Watt. "'If Ever I Get to Where I Can': The Competing Rhetorics of Social Reform in *Uncle Tom's Cabin*." *American Transcendental Quarterly* 4.2 (1990): 135-147.

Maierhofer, Roberta. "Meridel LeSueur: A Female Voice of the Thirties." *Women in Search of Literary Space*. Eds. Gudrun M. Grabher and Maureen Devine. Tubingen: Narr, 1992. 150–162.

Maxwell, Cliff. "Lady Vagabonds." *Scribner's Magazine* 85 (March 1929): 288–292.

McQuade, Donald, et al., eds. *The Harper American Literature: Volume Two*. New York: HarperCollins, 1993.

Michaels, Walter Benn. *The Gold Standard and the Logic of Naturalism: American Literature at the Turn of the Century*. Berkeley: U of California P, 1987.

Miller, Henry. *On the Fringe: The Dispossessed in America*. Lexington: Lexington, 1991.

Monkkonen, Eric H., ed. *Walking to Work: Tramps in America, 1790–1935*. Lincoln: U of Nebraska P, 1984.

Myers, David Geesham. "Between Stories." *Philosophy and Literature* 22.2 (1998): 457–467.

Nackenoff, Carol. *The Fictional Republic: Horatio Alger and American Political Discourse*. New York: Oxford UP, 1994.

Napora, Joseph. "The Story and the Living: Meridel Le Sueur's *The Girl*." *The Girl*. By Meridel Le Sueur. Albuquerque: West End, 1978. 147–158.

Oktenberg, Adrian. "From the Bottom Up: Three Radicals of the Thirties." *A Gift of Tongues: Critical Challenges in Contemporary American Poetry*. Eds. Marie Harris and Kathleen Aguero. Athens: U of Georgia P, 1987. 83–111.

Palmer, Bruce. "The Disappearance of Community and Responsibility in the Literature of the American Dream of Success: Cotton Mather to Robert Ringer, with Some Stops in Between." *Knowledge and Society: Studies in the Sociology of Culture Past and Present*. Eds.

Henrika Kuklick and Elizabeth Long. Greenwich, CN: Jai, 1986. 153–207.

Peters, Lisa. "Images of the Homeless in American Art, 1860–1910." *On Being Homeless: Historical Perspectives*. Ed. Rick Beard. New York: Museum of the City of New York, 1987. 42–67.

Pittenger, Mark. "A World of Difference: Constructing the 'Underclass' in Progressive America." *American Quarterly* 49.1 (1997): 26–65. 27 Jan. 1998. <http://muse.jhu.edu/journals/american_quarterly/v049/49.1pittenger.html>.

Pizer, Donald. *The Theory and Practice of American Literary Naturalism: Selected Essays and Reviews*. Carbondale: Southern Illinois UP, 1993.

Posner, Richard A. *Law and Literature*. Cambridge: Harvard UP, 1998.

Primeau, Ronald. *Romance of the Road: The Literature of the American Highway*. Bowling Green: Bowling Green State UP, 1996.

Raban, Jonathan. "The View From a Literary Dumpster." *The New York Times Book Review* 10 Oct., 1993: 1, 32–34.

Reckless, Walter C. "Why Women Become Hoboes." *The American Mercury* 31 (Feb. 1934): 175–180.

Reitman, Ben L. *Sister of the Road: The Autobiography of Box-Car Bertha*. New York: Sheridan, 1937.

Riis, Jacob A. *How the Other Half Lives: Studies Among the Tenements of New York*. Edited with an Introduction by David Leviatin. Boston: Bedford, 1996.

Roach, Bill. *Horatio Alger, Jr.: Frequently Asked Questions*. The Horatio Alger Resource Site. 8 March 1997. <http://www.wuacc.edu/sobu/broach/algerFAQ.html>.

Rorty, Richard. *Contingency, Irony, and Solidarity*. Cambridge: Cambridge UP, 1989.

———. "Human Rights, Rationality, and Sentimentality." *Truth and Progress: Philosophical Papers, Volume 3*. Cambridge: Cambridge UP, 1998. 167–185.

Scharnhorst, Gary, with Jack Bales. *The Lost Life of Horatio Alger, Jr.* Bloomington: Indiana UP, 1985.

Schleuning, Neala. *America: Song We Sang Without Knowing, The Life and Ideas of Meridel Le Sueur*. Mankato: Little Red Hen, 1983.

Schneider, John C. "Tramping Workers, 1890–1920: A Subcultural View." *Walking to Work: Tramps in America, 1790–1935*. Ed. Eric H. Monkkonen. Lincoln: U of Nebraska P, 1984. 212–234.

Scoblionko, Andrew. "Subjectivity and Homelessness in *Soldiers' Pay*." *The Faulkner Journal* 8.1 (Fall 1992): 61–71.

Steinbeck, John. *The Grapes of Wrath*. New York: Viking, 1939.

Stowe, Harriet Beecher. *House and Home Papers*. Boston: Ticknor and Fields, 1865.

———. *Uncle Tom's Cabin or, Life Among the Lowly*. New York: Penguin American Library, 1981

Sumner, John S. "The Censorship Forum." *The Publishers' Weekly* (May 31, 1930): 2736.

Tierney-Tello, Mary Beth. "Testimony, Ethics, and the Aesthetic in Diamela Eltit." *PMLA* 114.1 (Jan. 1999): 78–96.

Tompkins, Jane. *Sensational Designs: The Cultural Work of American Fiction 1790– 1860*. New York: Oxford UP, 1985.

Trachtenberg, Alan. "Experiments in Another Country: Stephen Crane's City Sketches." *American Realism: New Essays*. Ed. Eric J. Sundquist. Baltimore: Johns Hopkins UP, 1982. 138–154.

Tully, Jim. *Beggars of Life: A Hobo Autobiography*. New York: Albert & Charles Boni, 1924.

Wagner, David. *Checkerboard Square: Culture and Resistance in a Homeless Community*. Boulder: Westview, 1993.

Ward, David. *Poverty, Ethnicity, and the American City, 1840–1925: Changing Conceptions of the Slum and the Ghetto*. Cambridge: Cambridge UP, 1989.

Weiner, Lynn. "Sisters of the Road: Women Transients and Tramps." *Walking to Work: Tramps in America, 1790–1935*. Ed. Eric H. Monkkonen. Lincoln: U of Nebraska P, 1984. 171–188.

Whitman, Walt. *Leaves of Grass*. Oxford: Oxford UP, 1990.

Whyde, Janet M. *Encoding Imperialism: Homelessness in American Naturalism, 1890– 1918*. Diss. Louisiana State U, 1995. Ann Arbor: DAIA, 1996. 9609132.

Widmer, Kingsley. *The Literary Rebel*. Carbondale: Southern Illinois UP, 1965.

Wilson, Christopher P. *The Labor of Words: Literary Professionalism in the Progressive Era*. Athens: U of Georgia P, 1985.

———. "Stephen Crane and the Police." *American Quarterly* 48.2 (1996): 273–315.

Wixson, Douglas. "The Question of Meridel Le Sueur's Lost Patrimony." *Midamerica: The Yearbook of the Society for the Study of Midwestern Literature* 25 (1998): 96–108.

———. *Worker-Writer in America: Jack Conroy and the Tradition of Midwestern Literary Radicalism, 1898–1990*. Urbana: U of Illinois P, 1994.

Worby, John. *The Other Half: The Autobiography of a Tramp*. New York: Lee Furman, 1937.

Wormser, Richard. *Hoboes: Wandering in America, 1870–1940*. New York: Walker, 1994.

Wright, Susan E. "Blaming the Victim, Blaming Society or Blaming the Discipline: Fixing Responsibility for Poverty and Homelessness." *The Sociological Quarterly* 34.1 (Spring 1993): 1–16.

Wright, Talmadge. *Out of Place: Homeless Mobilizations, Subcities, and Contested Landscapes*. New York: State U of New York P, 1997.

Young, James E. *Writing and Rewriting the Holocaust: Narrative and the Consequences of Interpretation*. Bloomington: Indiana UP, 1988.

Zinn, Howard. *A People's History of the United States*. New York: HarperCollins, 1980.

Index